Books by Willie Snow Ethridge

Russian
Duet

the story of a journey ❦ ❦ ❦

❦

❦

❦ ❦ *by Willie Snow Ethridge*

❦

❦

simon and schuster
new york · 1959

Contents

I

The Batory

<u>1</u>   July 17

IN A FEW MINUTES Nila Magidoff and I are leaving on the first
leg of our trip to Russia—that is, if my nervous stomach will
behave long enough for me to get out of the bathroom. We
are going to Russia to try to find Nila's mother, Maria Ivan-
ovna Shevko, and her sister, Zinaida, and her niece, whom she
hasn't seen in eleven years and hasn't had a word from in ten.
They are living, she believes, in a town not far from Moscow.

Nila has been afraid to write to them in all these years, for
in 1937 she married an American, Robert Magidoff, who in
1948 was accused by the Soviet government of spying for the
United States and was given forty-eight hours to leave Russia.
Fortunately, by this time Nila was a United States citizen. She
had taken out naturalization papers after spending four years
in this country during the last war.

It was in those years I had got to know her. As Kentucky
chairman of Russian War Relief, I had appealed to the national
office to send me a speaker to spur a drive for old clothes, and
they had sent me Nila. She stayed with my husband, Mark,
and me for several weeks and by the end of the visit she had
become what she termed an "ersatz" member of the family.
She came back for many other visits until the close of the war,
when she returned to Russia to rejoin Robert, who had stayed

on his job there as head of the Moscow Bureau of the National Broadcasting Company.

Then came the awful spy accusation, and Nila, with Robert, was once more in the United States. They even lived for a few years in Louisville and I got to know Nila even better. Finally I put her life into a book, *Nila*.

And now here we are, setting out for Russia together.

I have come to Nila's and Robert's summer home, Marya, on Squam Lake in New Hampshire for the "take-off." She insisted that I see where she has put down her roots. So I arrived yesterday and saw the long, low-lying gray house she designed herself and had built in the deep woods on Squam's shore; the huge rocks that she and Robert moved and laid into terraces and steps; the firs, pines, ferns and wildflowers that she planted about the doorways and along the slope from the house to the lake.

And I met last evening, at the gayest, toastingest, dancingest party, all the neighbors whom Nila had told me about and whom I had put into the book. They brought presents (six of them brought elastic ropes and clothespins so that Nila would be sure to have a way to hang her wash on the trip) and poems. Robert had written a poem, too, and so had my mate, Mark, whom I left behind in Louisville. I'm not biased, but Mark's really was the best, and when Robert finished reading it I embarrassed my own self, which isn't easy, by shouting out, "Read it again, Robert, and with more passion."

It went this way:

Amerikanski Delegatski Shatiet:

To pretend that I am good at versifying
Would be the rankest sort of lying,
So I cannot join Squam's laureate (Robair)
In lyric songs to our departing pair;
But I can with him commiserate
While we hold our breaths and wait
The end of this damfool hegira.

Perhaps Khrushchev, in fear of our two satellites,
Will refuge our way in panicked flight
And play golf at Burning Tree
Or accept Goldfine's New England hospitality.
Sure with this pair he'll not seek a meeting at the
    summit
Or else rue the day he done it.
He wouldn't get a word in edgewise
To say *da* or even *nyet*, or tell more alcoholic lies.

So, here's a "What's the hells!" and *Vashe zdorovye!*
To our two innocent broads, Willinski and Nilova:
So whoop it up with mazurka and song,
Down the vodka and kick the gong.
Look out Moscow and Odessa!
You'll never be the same again, I betcha.

Robert also read telegrams, all of which, excepting one, he
and Nila had made up. My favorite was "You come to Russia
over my dead body. Signed, Stalin."

Now, though, the reading and the dancing are over and the
time has come to put the bags in the car. Robert is going to
drive us to Montreal to catch the Polish ship *Batory*, which
will take us, we trust, to Copenhagen, Denmark, where we hope
to catch Russia's only passenger ship in European waters, the
Baltika, for Leningrad. Nila and I chose the *Batory* because we
want to experience the behind-the-Iron-Curtain countries' state
of mind as quickly as possible, and also because a goodly number of spine-tingling incidents have happened on it—and others,
we figure, might at any moment. The captain before the present
one, remember, jumped the ship at Southampton and asked for
asylum, and the notorious Communist Gerhardt Eisler escaped
on it from the United States and was arrested when the *Batory*
anchored off the English coast. After that, our government
refused to allow it to dock at New York or at any other port
in the United States. To board it on this side of the Atlantic,
passengers must go to Montreal or Quebec or Halifax.

3

At this minute, however, it doesn't look as if I'm going to board it anywhere. I, who have always had such a strong stomach that my doctor, Morris Flexner, has said—pronounced, I believe, is the word—that I have buzzard blood, can't get out of the bathroom. Robert comes for my bags (I'm staying in the guest house) and I yell through the door that they're ready, but I'm not. "I've just got to wash my hands," I say politely.

It's foolish, I know, but I've never been so nervous about a trip before. I wasn't when Nila first proposed it; but then so many people seemed to be frightened for me that I got frightened, too. Almost everybody said, "Aren't you afraid to go to Russia with Nila? Aren't you afraid you'll never get out?" And my mother and one of my children pleaded with me not to go.

Then just yesterday, after I reached Marya, I went to a small farewell lunch and, of course, the trip came up in the conversation. Someone inquired, "If you do get out of Russia, *how* will you get out?" And I answered, "I'm flying from Moscow to Frankfurt."

"And how about you, Nila?"

"I'm flying to Zurich, Switzerland, for a physical checkup."

"Who leaves first?"

Suddenly Nila looked at me with frightened eyes and said with vehemence: "Willie, you cannot leave me in Russia. Think what might happen to me if your plane goes ahead of mine. You can't do that. I will have to go ahead of you or we will have to go together."

"Anything suits me, Nila," I answered. "But I have to go to Frankfurt to get my Pan American flight, you know. Pan American doesn't fly from Zurich."

"Then I'll go to Frankfurt with you and go from there to Zurich. You know what Mrs. Roosevelt said to me? She said, 'Nila, don't let Willie leave you alone in Russia for a minute,' and so I promised her—not even to go to the bathroom without you."

As you can imagine, this conversation instilled fear in my mind, where little or no fear had been before, and turned butterflies aloose in my stomach.

🌳 🌳   Later

FINALLY my upset stomach quieted down and I joined Nila and Robert in the main house. Nila was giving the wood floors a quick going over. She is a big-boned woman with the most expressive face I have ever seen. At times she can look excitingly alive, radiant, glamorous, even beautiful. Then, at other times, she looks homely, drab, bored, tragic. I am convinced the stage missed a combination of Lucille Ball and Helen Hayes when she didn't choose acting as a profession. Her face is broad, with a scar resembling a dimple on one of her high cheekbones; her eyes are small, alert and greenish gray; her complexion is smooth and wrapping-paper brown; and her shoulder-length hair, which is almost black, she draws tightly back from her forehead and confines in a net. She loves to be taken for an American; but her features are unmistakably Slavic.

Nila dropped the mop, put her arm around my waist and drew me to a front window. "Come, Willie, and look at the lake," she said in the same solemn voice in which a person would say, "Come and for the last time look on his dear, dead face."

It was a bright, windy morning and the sky was intensely blue, with puffy clouds like feather mattresses airing upon it. The lake was intensely blue, too, and on the far side the mountains rose gently, their dense woods a bright green except where the clouds laid shadows on them.

"Now come and let's sit down—and you, too, Robert," Nila said, and she pulled me down on an uncomfortable, too narrow bench which she herself designed. Robert took a seat across from us. "Let us sit in silence for a minute."

I used my minute to pray.

"Now, Willie," Nila said when the minute was over, "I want to promise you something." She paused and held my eyes intently with hers. "I want to promise you to be my best self as long as we are in Russia. Only afterward will I be mean and base. I promise to be inexhaustible, untirable and irresistible."

I repressed a smile, for Nila was very serious.

"And now," she exclaimed, jumping up, "I kiss you and I kiss Robert." Quickly she kissed us both. "And now, Willie, you kiss Robert."

"And now . . ." She drew in her breath on a long sigh. "And now we start our great adventure, so help us God."

✤ ✤

2 ✤ *July 18*

AFTER SPENDING the night at a motel on the outskirts of Montreal, Nila and I were in our stateroom on the *Batory* on the dot of eight o'clock.

"Well, here we are!" Nila cried exuberantly, rushing about, rubbing her palms together, admiring everything. "*Bozhe moi*, it's all so elegant and I expected it to be so simple. Can imagine a bell each for the maid and steward? And two telephones, white ivory at that! Why we need 'em? And, Willie, look at the beds. They're as Russian as they can be. Aren't they sweet?"

I was not so sure about this. The beds were spread with an envelope, as it were, of white linen and lace, holding a brown blanket, and in the top sheet of the envelope was a diamond-shaped window through which the blanket showed. I could see at once it would be impossible to sleep under one layer without sleeping under all three.

Nila swooped into the bathroom, which is as large as the stateroom, with black and white tiles on the floor, a black-enameled tub, toilet and bidet. Eying the glistening tub, she asked, "Who do they think we are—Cleopatra?" Then she spied the huge bath towels and the just-as-huge linen hand towels. Grabbing up one of the hand towels and draping it about her, she cried excitedly, "Willie, I can make you a sack dress out of one of these in no time a-tall when you run out of changes."

Robert, who had been parking the car, joined us, and after Nila had shown him everything we went in search of breakfast. Everybody was eating in the same dining room this morning, we were told; later the classes would be separated. We had grapefruit, soft-boiled eggs, Polish ham and hard rolls.

"The Polish ham is noted as being the best in the world," Nila gloated.

Other passengers had arrived by now and were drifting into the dining room. Practically all of them looked like first-generation immigrants. The young women were in light, summery, low-necked, sleeveless dresses, the old in neat ginghams that reached almost to the ankles, the men in loud sport shirts and poorly tailored suits.

"They're all Poles," said Nila with a note of condescension in her voice.

"So?" I questioned.

"Russians have never liked Poles," she answered, "and Poles have never liked Russians. There is no love lost between them. You know, I wouldn't be surprised if we were the only two Americans on board." Then, evidently recalling her own Russian birth, she added, chuckling, "I mean the only one and a half Americans."

Finished with breakfast, we wandered about the ship. It had one huge salon, furnished with innumerable heavy chairs, all upholstered in the same loud green, red and yellow print, and almost as many card tables; two bars (one, just behind our stateroom, was quite modern, with a colorful, striking mosaic); a well-furnished writing room; and a closet-sized library. Dark red velvet curtains emblazoned with the words NO ADMITTANCE hung at the foot of the stairs leading to the cabins of the first-class and de luxe passengers.

We landed on three stools in front of the bar and ordered orangeades. While sipping mine, I became conscious of a very distinguished-looking man standing in the doorway. He had white hair brushed back in a high pompadour, a ruddy complexion, a thin, aristocratic nose and bright-blue eyes.

He came over to the bar, bowed and to my surprise asked, "Are you Mrs. Mark Ethridge?"

When I said I was, he introduced himself as Robert Keyserlingk of the United Press and explained that his boss, Ed Allen, had telephoned from New York and asked him to come to the

Batory to see me off. I introduced him to Nila and Robert and offered him an orangeade.

Nila was too excited to sit still, so she left us, but almost immediately she was back. "Come quickly," she called from the doorway. "We are full of flowers. I walked in our cabin and here they were."

We rushed to the cabin. While we were admiring the flowers, the maid arrived with a large, square pasteboard box, and Nila dug into it wildly, her gray eyes glowing. She uncovered boxes of cookies, chocolate candy, fudge, nuts; but she continued to dig.

"There must be stockings somewhere," she wailed from the box's depth. "Nobody would send all these things to eat—and no stockings!"

Mr. Keyserlingk looked startled and amused.

Nearing the bottom, she unearthed two cans of maple syrup. "Maybe they send us some flour," she exclaimed, holding them up, "and a little stove, so we can make pancakes when we starve in Russia."

Then hurriedly she put the cans down and returned to her explorations; but finally, convinced there was nothing more, she cried disgustedly, "Just think of it! All this would easily buy four pairs of stockings. Maybe six. And how I need 'em! The Russians adore silk stockings."

The signal sounded for everybody to go ashore who was going ashore. Nila gave Robert several boxes of candy and Mr. Keyserlingk a can of maple syrup. Robert's face was white and strained as he kissed Nila goodbye.

The deck from which the gangplank extended to the pier was a jostling mass of people, weeping torrentially. Men, more than women, were hugging, kissing and crying on one another's shoulders. An elderly man kissed a young man—perhaps his son —buried his head on the young man's shoulder and sobbed as if his heart would break.

"I never saw such a tragic sailing," I said to Nila.

"It is because they are Slavic people and are very emotional."

To escape the crush, Nila and I climbed to the upper sun deck and pushed our way to the rail. The people on the pier were still crying pitifully. One scrawny, wrinkled, brown-faced woman with a babushka tied beneath her chin wept into a big colored handkerchief.

"Look," said Nila, disapprovingly. "She hasn't changed at all in the twenty-five years she's been in this country."

A teen-age girl in a bright-red blouse had sobbed until her nose and cheeks were as glowing as charcoal when it is at the stage for broiling steaks. While I watched her, my heart hurting, she gnawed desperately at the corner of her white straw lunch-box-shaped pocketbook topped with a gay little bunch of plastic fruit.

Robert and Mr. Keyserlingk appeared in the last line of the crowd, backed against the gray walls of the pier shed. They were still clutching the boxes of candy and maple syrup. We waved. They waved. Then for some interminable time we stood, the four of us glancing at each other, smiling slightly, then glancing away. Nila murmured, "Look at poor Robert, tears running, but he brushes them off so careless with the back of his hand."

The *Batory's* band, conscious of its Canadian berth, burst into "God Save the Queen." "Poor, poor Robert," Nila murmured again. "I know he is very, very worried about me on this trip; but he hasn't said one word against it."

The gangplank came up. Longshoremen ran along the edge of the wharf and took their places by those fat iron plugs to which the ropes are tied.

But, of course, we didn't move. No ship ever moves when it is supposed to. Nila hurried away to our stateroom and reappeared with two carnations hidden in the folds of her skirt. Surreptitiously she handed me one. Robert's face looked whiter and whiter, and somehow, though we weren't moving, it looked smaller and smaller.

The band played the Polish anthem—at least, that's what Nila and I thought they played. The ropes were tugged off and plopped into the river. Slowly we began to drift away from the pier. Nila and I threw the carnations—she, of course, to Robert and I to Mr. Keyserlingk. They caught them gracefully with

9

one hand as if they caught carnations every day, kissed them and waved them to us.

We swung out into the channel. A roguish boy on a tug chugging by us mimicked the weeping people. He buried his face again and again into a dirty rag and pumped his shoulders with heartless exaggeration.

No longer able to distinguish the dear features of Robert and Mr. Keyserlingk from the pale, blurred blobs massed against the long shed, Nila and I returned to our stateroom and started unpacking. In a dead, heavyhearted silence I was progressing slowly when Nila cried out, "Oh, God!"

Frightened, I wheeled to look at her. She was standing in the middle of the floor, her fingers pressed to her mouth, her eyes staring. "Oh, God, Willie, I forgot the hat!"

I breathed again. "What hat?"

"The hat for my mama. My mama never had a hat in her life and I decide to give her one of my speaking hats." (Nila speaks for the Lee Keedick Bureau and the clothes she wears on the platform she calls "speaking clothes.")

"Maybe Robert could airmail it to you in Copenhagen," I suggested.

"Maybe," she agreed, but without enthusiasm; then, shrugging, she proceeded with her unpacking.

Right outside our windows, which open onto the promenade deck, the loud-speakers blared out announcements continuously in three languages: Polish, Danish and English.

Our unpacking accomplished, we tended to such matters as getting our places in the dining room and depositing our cash —$44.65—in the purser's safe. The purser was very pleasant in spite of our handing over to him the responsibility of such a staggering sum.

"Your stateroom number, please," he said.

"Stateroom B," we answered.

"Oh, of course, you're traveling in Lux."

"No, in Joy," I was terribly tempted to answer, but I restrained myself. It was true Nila and I were traveling in what Intourist, the Soviet's official travel agency, labels "de luxe," for it is the only way people can travel in the Soviet Union without being members of a large party—which, because of the purpose of our trip, we don't want to be.

(Intourist has, peculiarly enough, considering the proletarian climate of the country it represents, five classes: de luxe; "Superior"; first class, which, believe it or not, is "slightly inferior to Superior"—the brochure says so; and second and third classes. If you go Superior there must be at least eight in your party; first class, fourteen; and second and third classes, twenty-five or more, or, as Nila describes them, "a demonstration.")

Our places in the dining room are a disappointment. We are put with another lone woman, who has the lovely first name of Michele, in a small room with only two other tables. One of these was reserved for the captain, or the master, as he is called on the *Batory*, but he wasn't present; and the other one for the lesser officers, but they weren't present, either. We ate in lonely grandeur, with a quick, tense waiter named Bruno giving us his undivided attention. The other Lux and first-class passengers ate in an adjoining dining room not much larger than ours. There are only thirty-one of us Luxers and first-classers. The other six hundred or so passengers ate in the dining room where we had breakfast.

Michele is small and dainty, with huge, velvety-brown eyes, and she twists her thick russet-colored hair into a loose knot on the top of her head. She speaks English with a decided accent.

I began to make friendly overtures. "Are you going to Poland?" I asked her, smiling warmly.

"Yes," she said after a moment. "Yes, I am."

"Are you Polish?"

She hesitated again. "I was born in Poland, but I haven't lived there for many years."

"Really?" My voice was as encouraging as I could make it; but it got me nowhere.

The waiter, with a courtly bow, presented very handsome menus to her, Nila and me. On the menu cover was a gay painting of girls in peasant costumes, dancing, and on the inside a long, long list of many delectable dishes. Not even on the *Liberté* had I seen such a gourmet's menu.

"It is too bad to be on a ship," Michele murmured, "and be unable to enjoy the food."

My heart was wrung. "Oh, how awful! Do you have something wrong with your stomach?"

"Well . . . not exactly. But I was quite ill before I left home and I have to be very careful."

"That's terrible," I said sympathetically. "Just terrible."

"Yes, it is." She sighed and, as Bruno bent above her, ordered a glass of apple juice.

Nila and I ordered an assortment of hors d'oeuvres.

With her big, mournful eyes, Michele stared at our plates; then, beckoning Bruno, she said, "Another glass of apple juice, please."

She sipped the second glass, then once more studied Nila's and my still heaped-up plates. "Maybe," she said tentatively, "maybe I will try just a few of the hors d'oeuvres. They do look so tempting." Again she beckoned Bruno and asked him to pass the platter of hors d'oeuvres. He presented the smoked salmon first, and she said, "Chou . . . chou," or something that very much resembled *Chou . . . chou.*

"What does that mean—'chou . . . chou'?" I inquired.

"It means 'a very little.' "

"Oh."

She allowed Bruno to help her to pickled bell peppers, sliced tomatoes, cabbage salad and celery, murmuring, "Chou . . . chou" all the time. She really sounded like the little engine, puffing up that mountain grade, that thought it could.

Next she had creamed asparagus soup ("Chou . . . chou," of course); next a broiled half chicken, Brussels sprouts, beets, string beans and two slices of black bread; next a fruit compote of stewed grapes, pears and peaches.

Chewing on the last grape, she summoned Bruno and said in a wheedling voice, "At lunch today we had such a lovely cherry compote . . ."

"Yes," spoke up Nila impatiently as if she were running the kitchen. "Yes, at lunch cherry compote, so no cherry compote for dinner. We don't repeat."

"Oh," Michele said meekly. Then, after a minute or so, a

slight frown on her pretty face, she reached out and took an orange from the dish of fruit that Bruno had put on the table. With indifferent fingers that seemed barely to touch the rind, she peeled it and slipped the quarters into her mouth.

Then Bruno appeared with a platter of fat, sugar-dusted, freshly baked cream puffs. Nila helped herself, then turned and eyed Michele with an icy, I-just-dare-you-to-take-one look. Michele whispered, "No, thank you." It cost her something, though.

To cheer her, I tried again during coffee to make conversation. "If you haven't been living in Poland, where have you been living?"

She sipped her coffee and considered this. "I lived for a while in France and then I came to the United States."

"Are you returning to Poland to visit relatives?"

"Yes."

"Close relatives?"

"Yes."

"Mother and father?"

"No, not that close, but close."

I gave up.

As Nila and I took a few fast turns around the deck before going to bed, Nila said, "That woman at our table is scared to death of us. She sees us two storms coming, one with the Anglo-Saxon name and one with the Russian name, and she smells spies and will say nothing."

"Oh, Nila, don't be foolish," I protested.

"I'm not being foolish. She, just like everybody else on this boat, is going somewhere with a mission, a secret mission. I don't expect us to have any fun. Even if there is gaiety, there will be fear behind it."

❦   ❦

3   ❦   July 19

STILL WEARY from the activities of yesterday, Nila and I didn't get up for breakfast. As befitting people in Lux, we had it in bed. Our steward, a young, thickset, quick-smiling blond by the name of Cheslov, brought us all that our hearts could desire: honeydew melon, Polish ham, rolls and coffee. Indeed, it filled our desires so completely, we told him to bring the same every morning. Nila, especially, is mad about honeydew melon.

Then, our body wants satisfied, we continued to lie in bed and talk over the struggles we'd been through since we decided to make this trip. As Nila lived in New York and I on the outskirts of Louisville, Kentucky, this was our first chance to compare notes on what had happened during the intervening months.

It was in February that Nila first asked me to go with her to Russia to find her people. She had sent them away from Moscow in the spring of 1947, a year before Robert was expelled as a spy. The hate-America campaign was in high gear and Nila was afraid that her marriage to Robert would bring disaster upon their heads. When the spy accusation struck, she had time only to rush to the post office and mail her mother a big box of clothes.

"In the one letter I got from my mother since then," Nila recalled in a calm, flat voice, "she wrote she got everything. In a peasant way she wrote exactly what she got. There was no emotional thing except the doctor had told her she had cancer on her intestinal tract, but she said that could be operated on if she had the money to make the trip to Moscow or Leningrad to a good hospital."

A cold spray of fear washed over me. How can Nila even hope to find her mother, I wondered, if she had cancer in 1948 and was then in her sixties?

I kept my grave doubts to myself, though, and Nila went on quietly. "I got this letter after I arrived in the United States and I immediately wrote to Harrison Salisbury, who was then in Moscow as the correspondent of *The New York Times,* and asked him to please try to get money to my mother. Robert and I sent two hundred fifty dollars and after some time passed he wrote me, 'What shall I do? I sent the money to the address you gave me, but I never got the confirmation it was received. I think it is no use to send more.' But I wrote him two more times to please continue to send it and enclosed

14

each time two hundred fifty dollars. Then he refused to send more."

Abruptly Nila sprang out of bed and swept across the stateroom to her closet. She opened the door, reached into the pocket of some coat or skirt, pulled out a yellowed envelope and, with a quick, dramatic swing of her long right arm, held it out to me. It is well covered with Russian stamps and is addressed to her mother in the town of Kostroma.

"I have carried this envelope with me ever since I left Russia," she said, her voice no longer quiet, but thick with emotion. "Many, many times I had the temptation to write, but I never did. As much as I wanted to hear from her and my sister, as much as I wanted them to know I hadn't dropped them and gone for a good life, I never did. 'All right!' I said to myself again and again. 'You'll put your soul at peace by writing, but you might do them harm.' You see, Willie, living under the terror of Stalin, a letter from the wife of an accused American spy can be against them. It can be the evidence that might hurt them. So I've always lived with this feeling of guilt."

Nila beat one clenched fist on top of her other clenched fist and her gray eyes burned feverishly bright.

"Do you really think your mother is still living, Nila?" I asked as gently as I knew how.

"Of course I don't know, but she was strong like me. We weigh a lot and stay strong and it's the strength that holds us. My mama and I are just the same. Our diseases are mortal, but they pass quickly. She enjoyed the life, Willie; she enjoyed all the little things of life. When Robert and I used to go to Sweden, guess what she wants us to buy her. You will never guess. Never!"

Sobbing now, Nila whirled back to the closet, reached up to a high shelf and lifted out a small green cellophane bag. "Bubble bath!" she cried. "It just shows the character. If anybody was going from Russia to Sweden I'd ask for shoes, underwear, clothes; but not my mama. She wants bubble bath. Not bath oil, Willie. Bubbles. She used to sit in the bubbles in Robert's and my apartment in Moscow and enjoy herself so,

I can't tell you. . . . And then she'd go back home and work with her hands like a peasant and feel no envy for the good life, just have pleasure in the memory." Nila sobbed until her wide shoulders shook.

I longed to say something comforting but could think of nothing.

Nila turned back to the closet again and brought out a blue crepe-de-Chine gown, pleated from head to toe. Her sobs quieted miraculously as she held it up against her. "Look what I also got for my mama."

Then she brought out pink-and-blue nylon panties and a white nylon blouse with white satin bows down the front. "These, too, are for my mama. They look, as you can see, Willie, very *zagranichny*, which means, remember, 'from abroad.' If I bought her something simple she would say, 'Ugh.' But these with stripes and lace—" Nila draped the fancy panties out on her widely spread hands—"these are *zagranichny*. Ah-h-h . . ." She purred like a cat.

"I also bought long black nylon evening gloves. Why they need 'em? I'm sure I don't know, but they will love them. When I went shopping I suddenly saw everything from the point of view of me before I came to America. I didn't buy a blue belt; I bought a *bright* blue belt. Whether my sister or mother have anything to match it I don't know; but just to have something bright . . ." Her deep, throaty laugh gurgled up.

With loving hands, she folded her purchases and laid them back on the shelf in the closet.

"And, oh yes!" she cried excitedly. "I almost forgot—I bought enough popover beads to wreck the Russian economy." Like a magician springing a rabbit from a hat, she hauled out dozens of strings of Poppit beads: loud rosy strings, lavender, blue, pink and white strings. "I just can't tell you how the Russians will love these; they are both gadgets and ornaments."

She put the beads away, too, then returned to bed.

"Nila," I asked, "when we reach Leningrad will you write your mother a letter and mail it in that already-addressed envelope?"

"I haven't decided yet. I'm going to wait until I get a feeling—I'm going to try to smell the sit-u-ation." She hesitated. "If I push too fast, they might ask me to leave."

Nila pondered her problem in silence for some minutes; then she said, sighing, "I will wait. I've waited for ten years—I can wait a few more days until I have contacted friends. Of course, none of my old friends might want to see me; but I will telephone from a . . . how you call it? a boot—" she held an imaginary telephone receiver to her ear—"and call them."

She was silent again. No doubt she had gone over this situation many, many times, and yet she had not been able to make up her mind about the best way to proceed.

"You see, Willie," she said finally, "I've already lived through the belief that I will never see my family again. When Robert was expelled I was absolutely convinced that I had had my last look at them. I never expected to see Russia again. This is goodbye forever, I told myself, and I believed it. I bid my mama and sister goodbye in my heart right then for all time."

Then Stalin died, and one day Nila saw in a paper a five-line story; it said American newspapermen had gone to the Soviet Embassy in Washington and were greeted with smiles, and immediately she decided that the party line had changed because no Russian official would dare to smile without permission and that perhaps she could return to Russia. Then she wrote me and asked would I go with her if she could get a visa.

Almost casually I said yes. Deep down I didn't believe Nila could get a visa and so I thought it would cost me nothing in pocketbook, body or mind to humor her.

We applied at once for visas through the Cosmos Travel Agency, and in due time Cosmos sent us all the travel information about the tours that Intourist offers. We could choose any one of thirty-seven tours, lasting from five days to twenty-three. We asked for the twenty-three-day tour and for eight extra days in Moscow so that Nila would have more time to locate her family and visit with them.

Having chosen the de luxe class, we had to pay in advance thirty dollars apiece for every day we planned to stay in Russia.

For this thirty dollars, each of us would receive transportation everywhere we went in Russia, whether by plane, train or ship; the use of a private car for three hours a day if it was a big, fine touring car, or five hours a day if it was a small one; rooms with baths in "de luxe" hotels; four meals a day, including tea; and a guide-interpreter whenever we wanted one.

We then sat back to wait for the visas. In a few weeks mine arrived, but not Nila's. Nevertheless, a Mrs. Burroughs, who was handling our trip for Cosmos, assured Nila that hers would come; it just took time.

When almost four months had passed and Nila had still heard nothing, she went back once more to the travel agency.

"Mrs. Burroughs was kind like a doctor is kind to relatives when he has to break the bad news," Nila told me now, her eyes staring at the stateroom's beamed ceiling. "As soon as I was seated, she bent close to me and said, 'I feel I must advise you to give up the idea of going to Russia, for I don't believe you'll get a visa.'

" 'Was I refused?' I asked.

" 'No, they were just silent,' she said.

"I argued, 'But you told me when I first applied that Russia now gives visas to everybody.'

" 'Yes, that's right,' she said. 'They give visas to everybody except rabbis.'

"Involuntarily, Willie, I hold up my hand and said, 'I assure you I'm no rabbi.' She laughed, but not me. It was no laughing matter.

"Then I came back to my hotel and I thought to myself, I've got to do something; this is my last chance. So I telephoned to the secretary of Mrs. Roosevelt, Maureen Corr. She's my ardent fan and I say to her, 'Maureen, I'd like very much to see Mrs. R.' Maureen says she's in North Dakota, or maybe it was South Dakota—anyway, she was in a Dakota. Then Maureen asked me when I was leaving New York. I said the next day. She says Mrs. R. will arrive by plane at four-thirty the next morning and cheerfully reads me what appointments she has for her. Then she asks, 'Can you come at eight-thirty?'

" 'Certainly,' I say, and at eight-thirty I was there, sitting downstairs. In a few minutes Mrs. Roosevelt came with a ribbon tied around her hair and the first thing she asked, 'Did you get your visa, Nila?' I said, 'No,' and she said, 'I never thought you would.' Then I said, 'You remember, Mrs. Roosevelt, how Khrushchev told you he'd give a visa to anybody who wanted to come to Russia? Well, I want you to do a favor for me. I've known you for sixteen years and I never ask a favor, but this is above personal matters.'

" 'What can I do?' she asked.

" 'Write a letter.'

" 'They will not listen to me.'

" 'The name F.D.R. will always be F.D.R. to the Russians,' I told her. 'They will listen to you.'

" 'To whom do you want me to write?'

" 'Let's go as high as can be,' I said. 'Gromyko will do. He's more than an important man; but if he refuses we still have Khrushchev left.'

"You know, Willie, Mrs. Roosevelt has this beautiful, soft face; but suddenly her face got hard. 'I'll do it!' she said. 'I'll do it this very minute.' Then she made a little pause and added like an afterthought, 'He came for lunch here twice.'

"I decided I will not keep her from the letter, so I got up quickly and left. Robert was waiting for me behind the corner. We were already on the way to New Hampshire. I told Robert the conversation and we started to count the days. It was then Tuesday, May twentieth. We know Mrs. Roosevelt is going to send the letter by airmail, so we allowed four days for it to get to Moscow. But then it will be the weekend, and Gromyko not even for Mrs. Roosevelt will attend to my visa on the weekend. But on Monday morning he will come, read the letter and send the telegram to Washington. We figure the very earliest I can get the visa will be nine days away—on May twenty-ninth. And at four-thirty on May twenty-ninth the telegram came. Robert and I were shopping in Center Harbor—that's our village near Squam—and Mrs. Nichols run and say, 'Telegram is come for you.' And it was the telegram from Cosmos, saying the visa is granted.

"Mrs. Roosevelt doesn't believe it was her letter. She says,

'I don't believe the Russians could have moved so fast.' But Robert says, 'When the Russians want, they can move very fast.'"

Nila swung her legs off the bed, stood up and stretched herself. "So here I am going back to Russia for the second time. When I went back in 1945 after the war, it was absolutely essential for me to go. I knew if I didn't go back I wouldn't survive. I had to hear the Russian language, smell the Russian countryside and see the Russian people. Then I had no roots. I wasn't tied deeply to America like I am now.

"This time I'm going back for entirely different reasons." Her voice was coolly matter-of-fact. "Besides wanting to find my family, I'm going out of a full, healthy curiosity about Russia and to get material for a new speech."

She spread one of the huge towels on the floor and began to take exercises for her back. She needs no exercises for her spirits, I mused to myself. She can snap back faster than any human I've ever known.

4   July 20

AFTER A LAZY MORNING of circling the deck; of leaning heavily on the rail, staring as if hypnotized across the wide, silvery, gently undulating sea without seeing anything except one small object which brought from Nila "The *Kon-Tiki*, no doubt"; of lolling in our deck chairs on the sun deck, reading a little, but mostly watching the other passengers drift by ("How she keeps the food and all her utensils in that thin body?" Nila remarked bitterly about one) Nila and I started for our stateroom to wash up for lunch; but on our way through the bar a lively, twinkling, blue-eyed man invited us to join him and his wife for a drink.

He is Chris Burnadowski, formerly of Poland but now a solid—well, not too solid, thank goodness—citizen of Montreal, and his wife is a tiny, pretty, laughing creature named Helena.

Chris talks with his hands, his arms, his eyes and even with his barely sprouted, carefully clipped, finger-wide, twitching mustache. He and Helena are returning to Poland for a month's visit. "I have seventy relatives in one village," he said, chuckling, "and now everybody there cleans the house."

He plans to arrive in the village around noon on a Saturday so that he can greet all the population at one time. He expects to kiss and kiss and kiss. (His eyes gleamed wickedly in anticipation.) And he will hire an orchestra, buy champagne and have a dance in the village square. There is only one problem troubling him. He is not sure whether his car, which he has on board with him, will get over the rickety wooden bridge that spans the little stream just before the road enters the village. Maybe his friends will have to build a new bridge to get it across.

He and Helena aren't returning alone. Traveling tourist class are three others in their party: a niece from Poland who has been visiting them for a year, the mother-in-law of Helena's brother and a man whose relationship is even more distant. The visit of the niece has been a terrible disillusionment to them.

"She appreciates nothing," Chris exclaimed bitterly, both widely spread hands flying outward. "I spent fifteen hundred dollars to bring her all the way from Poland and she appreciates nothing. She came with two dresses and now she is going back with four trunks, but she appreciates nothing."

His mustached upper lip shoved out his lower lip and he rocked to and fro. "Now take last night. Last night I was dancing with her, and I don't want to brag, but I'm the best dancer on the boat—I've seen 'em all and I'm the best—but guess what she says to me? She say, 'Dance natural.' I tell you, she appreciates nothing!"

"But she will cut quite a figure in the village, won't she, with those four trunks of clothes?" I asked, hoping to divert him from these corroding thoughts.

"Yes. But the Poles won't be surprised," he answered readily. "They think America is from out of space. The only thing that would shock 'em is if she didn't have four trunks of clothes. I knew once a guy who returned from Montreal to my village in Poland. He had the name of a girl there and he had her picture and they had been writing to each other and so he decided to go back and marry her.

"Well, this girl met him at the station and immediately she disliked him completely." Both Chris's arms swept out. "I can't tell you how immensely she disliked him, and all because he came from America and was dressed in a leather windbreaker with no tie." He shrugged, threw back his head and whooped. "He was the greatest disappointment imaginable—especially with that leather jacket.

"And she was just as great a disappointment to him. You see, the girls in the Polish village dress very rough all week when working, but they have one good dress which they save for Sunday and she had hers on to meet him and looked just like a queen. And this upset him. He expected her to be beautiful but poor and here she was dressed so nice he couldn't be sure of her. So he came back alone to America."

Chris slapped the table so hard with the flat of his hand that the glasses rattled, and he shouted with laughter.

This gay creature left Poland with his mother and younger brother twenty-two years ago, when he was only twelve years old, to join his father, who was already in Montreal and had sent them the money for the trip.

"I was flat as a fish all the way over," he related dramatically, holding his closed-fingered hand level in front of him and rolling his eyes heavenward. "But my brother went everywhere." His nose wrinkled up as if he smelled something bad. "He missed nothing. Absolutely nothing."

Just two weeks after they reached Montreal the father became paralyzed and Chris went to work for ten cents an hour as a carpenter's helper in a factory. He had no schooling; but he got ahead.

"I was smart," he told us frankly, "and the man liked me."

And today he owns his own factory, a furniture factory, and employs sixty-five people. Every Friday afternoon, when the factory closes, he invites everybody to a tavern for drinks.

"It's not that I care for the drinks," he explained, shrugging one shoulder and waving a hand airily, "but it's there that the guys tell me what's troubling them. It costs me twenty dollars every Friday, but I'm happy to pay it.

"It's a Polish tavern and no woman is allowed. The wife has to stand in the door and call to her husband. 'Come here, please.'" His blue eyes bright with teasing, he crooked his finger at Helena and chuckled elatedly.

"Oh, darlink," she protested, but she chuckled elatedly, too.

"For a Pole to have a factory is exceptional," he continued, still laughing a little. "Practically all Polish and Ukrainian people in America have either taverns or funeral parlors. Funeral parlors and taverns are ways of making a living that other nationalities don't care for, but they're the quickest way to make a fortune. Especially funeral parlors. Just that box costs five hundred dollars."

But a furniture factory isn't a bad way to get ahead, either, Chris admitted in the next breath. Who would have believed when he left his village in Poland that he would be returning with trunks and suitcases full of presents? And traveling first class, too.

And what a farewell party his employees gave him!

"Every one of the sixty-five people came to tell us goodbye," he boasted. "And to drink champagne. At first I hold myself good, but when the bookkeeper, who never in my life I saw cry before, cried, I couldn't hold no longer. I bawled like a baby. I—"

"During the party," Helena broke in, "a bottle of Chanel Number Five, which somebody brought me as a farewell present, disappeared."

"Somebody brought," Chris remarked philosophically, tilting back his chair, "and somebody took away."

🌱 🌱   Later

IN A HAPPY MOOD we descended to the dining room for lunch. Michele was already there, staring at a platter of cold pork, tongue and salami that Bruno held out to her. "Maybe," she said undecisively, "a small piece of pork. Chou . . . chou . . ."

"I'll have herring," announced Nila, rubbing her hands together.

"Yes, madame," Bruno murmured.

"I'll have herring, too," I said.

Michele looked with her big, troubled eyes at Bruno. "I believe I'll also have a little herring. It might settle my stomach. But not on this plate with the pork, please—I'll have it on a separate plate."

Then on this separate plate she piled cucumbers, green onions, tomatoes, celery and haddock *à la grecque*.

Having finished the herring, Nila studied the menu and found beef *paupiettes à la varsovienne*, which she highly recommended. Michele and I agreed to try some.

It looked, when Bruno passed it, like a deep, covered pottery baking dish, shading from light to dark brown, filled—as we saw when the lid was removed—with slices of thin beef rolled around small cucumber pickles, in a thick sauce; but it turned out that the baking dish was also edible. It was made of the lightest, flakiest dough. Can imagine, as Nila would say.

Following this mouth-watering entree Nila and Michele ordered chocolate pie, and as they consumed it Bruno brought a cut-glass dish of fruit and put it in the center of the table.

The last bite of pie disappearing, Michele, with an I-must-force-myself-to-do-it air, ate two dozen cherries and a huge red plum, then rooted about in the dish for more cherries.

"I believe I could live on fruit," she said, sighing wearily.

"Yes," shot back Nila in a flash, "with pie on the side, and pork and haddock *à la grecque* and beef and herring and tomatoes and celery and onions . . ."

"Yes, that's right," Michele agreed, and she laughed as merrily as Nila and I.

✤   ✤

5   ✤   July 22

ABOUT ELEVEN O'CLOCK this morning, while I was in the middle of writing a letter to Mark, the engines of the ship stopped. One second before there was this steady, shuddering, throbbing beat; then suddenly silence. Absolute silence.

Fear gripped me. I have been on a good many ships in my life, but I have never known one to stop absolutely dead in the middle of the ocean. We had hit a submerged iceberg, I was sure. I had been too engrossed in my letter to hear the collision. Just yesterday, Cheslov, the steward, was telling Nila and me about this huge iceberg seven and a half miles in circumference that the *Batory* had picked up on its radar on the last trip to Montreal. "The captain never left the bridge for two days and nights," Cheslov said.

But this trip he had evidently left the bridge and we had hit the iceberg.

"The engines have stopped," I cried to Nila, who was in her bed reading.

"No," said Nila with her usual positiveness.

"But they have," I insisted.

Nila listened for a moment, then quickly said, "Yes, Willie, you're right. There is no pulse."

Instantly we sprang out of our beds and dashed to the window. "But we're still moving," Nila said.

"Only rolling," I corrected her. "We roll whether the engines run or not—even worse, maybe."

It was a terrible day: cold, bleak and faintly foggy.

Nila tried the lights. They went on. Then she hurried into the bathroom and turned the water taps. "The electricity is still working," she called encouragingly. She returned to my side at the window just as two officers tore by, headed toward the bow.

"They go to their posts," said Nila.

"I suppose so, but I've never seen officers run before, not even to their posts. We really must be sinking."

"Let us dress quickly," Nila ordered, her voice steady, but her face putty-white. "Put on all your warmest clothes, Willie, just in case . . ."

My heart hammering, I pulled on my longest girdle and my warmest pants. Oh, dear God, why didn't I bring some woolen snuggies, I wondered; these flimsy nylon numbers will be nothing in a lifeboat. I decided to put on two more pairs.

"Why don't they announce something on the loud-speaker?" I asked Nila angrily. "They can announce everything else imaginable, but now when we're about to sink they're as silent as the grave."

"Willie, call the purser on the telephone and ask him why the engines stop."

I dialed the purser's number. But nobody answered. I dialed the chief steward's number. Still nobody answered. I poked the bells of our stateroom steward and maid—but nobody came.

"You'd better finish dressing," Nila advised curtly.

I put on my slip, my black sweater, my red sweater and my red suit. My knees were shaking terribly.

Nila was already dressed, and to the teeth, or to be absolutely correct, to the chin. Besides her underclothes, she had on a blouse and skirt, two sweaters, a fluffy white muffler wrapped several times around her neck and heavy white cotton gloves. The awful thought that she was dressed to meet her God crossed my mind.

"Let us take our passports," Nila directed, still outwardly calm, and she dived into the closet and retrieved the passports from their secret hiding place.

"Nila, I'm scared to death," I confessed, unable to keep my feelings to myself any longer.

"Yes, Willie, I see you are. Your teeth are just tittering. But maybe—" she threw out her hand—"maybe only the captain jumps." She chuckled hollowly and I tried to chuckle, too, but couldn't.

There I was writing to Mark, my mind raced, and the ship hits an iceberg. My last thoughts were of him, but he'll never know it.

"Listen, Willie, I think I'll take the popover beads so in case we come to Russia we will not be empty-handed," Nila said, and she grabbed up three strings and stuffed them into a deep pocket of her skirt.

When she was sure they were secure, she took down our life belts and laid them on a chair. "Now, Willie," she ordered, "give me your raincoat, your stole—everything warm—and put on your beret."

I clawed through all the shelves in the closet, but couldn't find the beret.

"You must find it," said Nila, like Stalin.

"Maybe it's in my raincoat pocket."

Nila, who had laid all the coats with the life belts on the chair, snatched up the raincoat and pulled out the beret. "Here, hurry, put it on. We have no time to lose."

Without combing my hair or even putting on my lipstick, I staggered with Nila out into the hallway. I was so laden down with clothes I could scarcely wobble.

The hallway was deserted. We struggled toward the opening to the sun deck, but to reach it we had to pass through the bar and there we saw the barman standing behind his counter, rag in hand. Evidently he, just like the boy eating peanuts on the burning deck, cannot desert his post even if he has to go down with the ship.

"What's happening?" Nila and I cried out together.

"A holiday," he answered casually.

"A holiday and the engines stop," I said accusingly. I really thought he was joking to allay our terror.

"Yes, a holiday."

A strike, he must mean, I then decided. A strike against the ship. A mutiny.

"It's the twenty-second of July, Poland's Independence Day," he then explained, "the day Stalin established the Lublin government in Warsaw as the legal government of the country, and so we're celebrating. There has already been a band concert and now they're getting ready to throw a wreath overboard." He waved his rag toward the stern.

Looking through the doorway, we saw hundreds of people on the far side of the deck, pressing against the rail, peering downward. White and blue balloons floated above them.

Hurriedly we joined them. "There is no danger written on any face except ours," Nila commented sagely.

On the deck below, two sailors were balancing a huge wreath of red and white gladioli between them and two lines of officers were standing at attention. (No wonder there was no one to run the ship and answer the telephone.) An officer snapped an order, hands saluted, heels clicked, a bugler bugled and the two sailors with the aid of a rope, slowly lowered the wreath down to the sea.

The engines turned, the ship moved forward and shortly we glimpsed the wreath in the lovely wake—a wake of aquamarine pools edged with wide, flowerlike borders, fresh and full-blooming for brief seconds, then shattered and scattered on the wind.

No one cheered; no one even spoke or smiled.

How many of these people, I wondered, really consider the twenty-second of July Poland's Independence Day?

Nila and I drifted away with the crowd and in our drifting we ran into Cheslov. "Why didn't you tell us this morning that today is Poland's Independence Day?" I asked him.

He grinned his very young, quick smile. "I had no memory to tell you," he answered.

"Well, your no memory almost cost you two passengers from heart failure."

"Now, Willie, don't say that," Nila reprimanded me. "I think it is good it happened. We see how we face danger and not panic."

6   Afternoon

THIS MORNING, BEFORE Nila and I decided the ship was sinking, a steward appeared with two handsomely engraved invitations from "the Master of the *M.V. Batory*," inviting us to a cocktail party in the Lido Bar at 5 P.M.

So, a little after five, dressed in our very best, we showed up at the entrance to the bar. Here a tall, handsome officer with two stripes and a small grayish-blond mustache swayed stiffly toward us, smiled and asked, "May I present you to the master?"

"Please do," we murmured.

He led us across the room to the captain, who was sitting at a card table with a man and a woman. The captain got up and, slightly stooped, like a shy, too tall man, shook our hands. He is good-looking in a lean-faced, rugged fashion. His hair and eyebrows are black and thick, his complexion ruddy and deeply lined and his nose extremely large.

The Batory

Before either Nila or I could start a conversation—and that doesn't take either of us long—the two-striper whisked us away to sit at the last table on the right in a semicircle of tables that lined the room. All except the master's were very little, low tables covered with white cloths polka-dotted in blue. The officer introduced us to the three people sitting at the table next to us: Mr. Jan Wetek, who was the Polish consul in Washington but is now on his way to a new post in London, Mrs. Wetek and the ship's doctor. Mr. Wetek is a medium-sized, dapper, brownish man. His eyes, which are gentle and intelligent, his hair and his neat mustache are a dark brown and his complexion is deeply sun-tanned.

We sat down, Nila on the outside, I next to Mr. Wetek.

A waiter passed a tray of cocktails known simply as Polish cocktails. They couldn't have looked more innocent. They were a clear pink, with one red cherry and a curving green stem in the bottom of each glass. But innocent as they looked, they were a concoction of vodka and cherry brandy. Whew! Another waiter passed a tray of sandwiches such as I have never seen before. In the center stood a tree the size of a Christmas table decoration, the limbs made from very thick slices of toasted bread and laden with every kind of open-faced sandwich. A bouquet of radishes, spring onions and celery sprouted from the top.

Right away Mr. Wetek and I began to talk about life in Washington; but Nila, after staring about at the other guests, only twelve in number—ten men, two of whom were Catholic priests, and two women—slumped in her chair, her head back and one arm dangling toward the floor, a red chiffon handkerchief drooping from her listless fingers. Every line of her body and face testified to her utter boredom, and I was uneasy; nevertheless, I suffered shock when she blurted out in loud, disgusted tones, "My God, we look like we're at a wake!"

I struggled to ignore her and to listen more attentively and respond more animatedly to Mr. Wetek, but it was terribly difficult. Nila continued to look as if she might slide out of her chair onto the floor from sheer lassitude, and if she did she would lie there, I felt certain, inert and to all appearances dead.

Then, to my immense relief, she momentarily came alive.

She saw Michele, wearing a loud print scarf about her russet head, a pink sweater, black velvet slacks, pink socks and pink sandals, appear in the doorway to the sun deck and march resolutely across the bar, darting quick, bright looks to the right and left, and disappear into the companionway on the far side, then reappear after a couple of minutes and march back to the sun-deck opening.

Nila, who told Michele at lunch about our invitation to the party, leaned languidly toward me and muttered, "She checks to see if our un-graved invitations are real." Then she lapsed back into boredom.

I beat my troubled brains for a fresh subject of conversation —Mr. Wetek and I had worn life in Washington to shreds— and I thought of Captain Jan Cwiklinski, who jumped the ship, but naturally he didn't seem to be a suitable subject to discuss with a Polish consul at the present captain's cocktail party, and I determinedly shoved him back—away back; however, suddenly in my extremity I heard myself asking, "Did the former master who jumped the ship at Southampton have a girl friend in England?"

"Oh, no," Mr. Wetek answered promptly without batting an eyelash. "He had a wife and three children in Poland."

"Really?" I murmured. Then, trying to sound completely ignorant, which isn't hard, I asked, "Why in the world, then, did he do such a thing?"

The answer came as a jolt. "He chose freedom, as you say in the United States."

I looked at him sharply, but his face was passive. "Where is he now?" I inquired.

He hesitated. "I'm not sure."

"Were his wife and children permitted to join him?"

Again he hesitated. "I can't say. I really have no interest in the fellow."

Well, that was that. I'd had my comeuppance.

I glanced at Nila. She was smiling slightly at a rotund, bald-headed, middle-aged man at a table catty-cornered from her; evidently she had grown bored with her role of being bored. The man got up—defying all the laws of gravity, for not a single other guest had moved, except to lift his glass to his mouth—and came over and sat down beside her. I heard him ask, "Haven't we met somewhere before?" Rejoicing, I turned back to Mr. Wetek. I detected a decided coolness in his manner. I took a gulp of my cocktail. I really must make amends.

I plunged. "In Georgia, where I was born, the Polish hero Pulaski is muchly revered. We have a fort named for him, as you no doubt know."

Mr. Wetek's gentle brown eyes brightened and a smile touched the lips beneath the trim mustache. I had hit pay dirt, thank God. He began to talk about the part the Poles have played in the history of the United States and mentioned that his embassy in Washington is planning a big celebration of the first settlement of Poles in America in 1608.

"Where was that?" I asked casually, sensing no bombshell.

"In Jamestown."

"Jamestown where?"

"Jamestown, Virginia."

"No!" I exclaimed emphatically—much too emphatically, but I was flabbergasted. Not that I have anything against Poles, you understand. After this trip some of my best friends are. But while living in Richmond once upon a time I listened so frequently to Virginians, especially the great historian Dr. Douglas Southall Freeman himself, tell of the pure Anglo-Saxon blood of their heroic forefathers that I never suspected that other nationalities might have touched the Old Dominion's sacred soil.

The guests began to leave. I looked at Nila and she nodded her head, so we got up, did our manners and departed.

Reaching our stateroom, Nila fell back against the wall, her spread hand to the base of her throat, and shouted with laughter. "It was the funniest cocktail party I ever went to in my life," she gasped between peals. "And did you see my pickup? He heard me speak once and so he decided he knows me." For a minute she was too overcome with merriment to go on. "He asked me is my man here and when I say no, he is as pleased as can be.

"Then I feel I must ponder the sit-u-ation and so I ask him is his wife on the boat and, with happy eyes, he says no, she is back home sick. Then I ask him is he a capitalist. You know, Willie, he has a little importance in his face and so I thought he must be rich. He shrugs the way it means he's too modest to say he is and says he is a sausage manufacturer. 'How many is working for you in your factory?' I ask and he says, 'Thirty-five.' Can imagine—thirty-five?" Nila's voice dropped with disdain. "Huh! Thirty-five. Then he reached in his pocket and gave me this." She fished about in her small red leather bag and brought out a pen on which was inscribed: "Don't give me that baloney, give me V——sky's."

Again Nila was convulsed, but finally she quieted and said, "And, my God, all the time he is talking to me he is pinching my arm and calling me 'zee.' "

"Is that good?" I asked.

"Of course. It is very familiar, like *tu* in French."

I got excited. "Nila, how do you spell this 'zee'?"

"You know, 'zee' like in the Bible—t-h-e-e."

7   July 24

THIS MORNING BEFORE Nila was awake, I heard over the loud-speaker, "China has declared war on America."

Naturally I was horribly upset, but not too surprised. I read yesterday in the ship's news bulletin that the members of the Chinese ballet, appearing in London, had broken their six-week engagement after just two weeks of performances, and so I thought to myself, "Huh, their government warned them in time for them to skip out. How clever and sneaky are these Chinese."

I got up immediately, dressed and tried to run the announcement down to ground—and that's not easy at sea, as you can understand. At last, however, I met an officer and after much questioning, for he didn't have an idea what I was talking about, it turned out what the loud-speaker said was that the

S.S. America was passing the *Batory* on her starboard side. (Of course, by this time the *S.S. America* no doubt was just before docking in Le Havre.)

It was still raining and cold, and besides eating and sleeping Nila and I didn't do much except open a gigantic present that had been lost in the hold these many days.

Cheslov panted in with the box, which was about the size of a big doghouse, and deposited it in the middle of the floor. Nila and I were in bed and we stared rather helplessly at the pasteboard cubicle.

"Shall I open it for you, madame?" Cheslov asked Nila, since, darn it, it was addressed to her.

"Please," said Nila in a small voice.

Cheslov cut, tore and pulled, and finally he was on the inside. He plucked out a big envelope with "Bonwit Teller" scrawled on the outside and handed it to Nila.

"It's from Kick," Nila announced.

"Wonderful," I said, for Kick is Mrs. Milton Erlanger, Nila's good and very generous friend.

Cheslov threw out storms of white paper and produced box after box of face tissues, "hand lotion pillows," Mary Chess toilet water, "a perfect wash for intimate apparel," concentrated mouthwash . . .

Nila reached out eagerly for each package, exclaimed over it and piled it on top of her in the bed. "Look," she cried, "I'm covered with boxes over my brim. Kick has overdone everybody."

Cheslov came up with two packages of washcloths, the kind that is pressed into the shape of roses; a box packed with "The Miracle Moist Toilette"; bath oils—White Lilac, Carnation, Strategy, Musk . . .

"Oh, I love bath oils," Nila proclaimed, sniffing loudly at the little round bottles. "When I'm in a bath with oils I'm always sorry I don't speak Roman."

Cheslov was as transported as Nila. He evidently had never seen such luxurious gifts. (But who has?) He grinned constantly from ear to ear and frequently burst over into laughter. I had a Christmasy feeling.

33

He then discovered many rolls of the softest baby-pink toilet paper. He presented them importantly, one by one. Then a hundred toilet-seat covers, a can of spray that comes out a liquid and turns to powder when it hits the body, and a bottle of hand lotion.

At last he scratched the bottom of the barrel, gathered up all the papers and strings and prepared to leave.

"Cheslov, have you a wife?" Nila asked.

"No, madame, my wife died in childbirth three years ago."

"Oh, I'm so sorry. But maybe, then, you live with your mother?"

"Yes, madame, and I have some girl friends, too."

Nila heaped his arms with presents. He had been so enthusiastic she felt he must share in Kick's lavishness.

And I shared, too. Exhausted from so much excitement, I was just sinking into a heavy sleep when Nila stood at the foot of my bed and ordered, "Get up and take a bath."

"But I've had a bath today," I protested.

"It makes no difference. The revolution has come and you will have a bath now."

I stirred myself. The cabin was filled with the heady odor of lilac. Nila had dumped a whole bottle into the tub she had drawn for me. The least I could do, I decided, was wallow in it.

<u>8</u>   July 25

IT WAS ANOTHER awful day. The sea was choppy, the sky a muddy monotonous gray, and the rain poured steadily down. Nila and I stayed in our stateroom and wrote letters. It had been announced the ship would arrive off Southampton at five o'clock in the afternoon and letters posted before nine o'clock in the evening would be taken ashore by the pilot and sent on their way.

We had already had breakfast and gone through a spine-tingling experience. Shortly after we pushed Cheslov's bell for breakfast one of our two ivory telephones rang. Startled, Nila and I looked at each other. For eight days we had been on this ship and this was the first time that either of the phones had even tinkled. Many times I had thought of Nila's remark when she first saw them, "Why we need 'em?"

"You answer it," said Nila.

"No," I said, "you answer it."

We were both terribly excited. I especially. I thought maybe it was the captain—I mean master—asking us to join him for dancing. Of course he never had asked us, but I'm an optimistic soul.

"No," said Nila, "you answer it."

So I did, and, of all people, it was Cheslov, somewhere in the bowels of the ship, saying apologetically, "Madame, what am I to do? There is no honeydew melon this morning. They have only enough left for one evening's dinner."

Naturally, Nila and I were disappointed; but by now we were recovered and, as I said, were busily writing letters. Then, suddenly, the ship's horn began to blow and continued to blow and the engines slowed down.

"My God, what has happened *now?*" Nila asked, and she beat me to the window by a hairsbreadth.

We saw one of the bedroom stewards and the waiter from the bar at the rail, staring down into the sea.

"The captain, without a doubt, has finally jumped," I said, "and is swimming to Southampton."

"That's right, Willie," Nila agreed enthusiastically, and we both began to dress.

Our clothes on, we reached the deck just in time to see one of the lifeboats, packed with sailors, rowing away from the side of the ship.

"They go to the rescue," the bedroom steward told us as we joined him and the waiter at the rail.

"Ah, it's true, then—someone has jumped overboard," cried both Nila and I, absolutely beside ourselves with excitement.

"No, madame," he corrected us. "They only practice now in case someone does jump."

This, of course, was not what we had hoped for, but it was better than nothing. Not every ship practices rescuing a man overboard as it approaches Southampton.

Standing in the sweeping-down rain, Nila and I made out,

about a quarter of a mile behind us, a white marker with a staff atop it, flying the Polish flag, and a life preserver that had been thrown overboard as soon as the imaginary person jumped. Slowly the *Batory* began to move in wide circles.

The sailors in the lifeboat were having a hard time. Not only was the rain slashing furiously at them, but the sea was quite rough. The boat floundered into troughs between the waves, all but disappearing, then reared up and vaulted over the next crests. The sailors were wearing life jackets, and above them hovered the first sea gulls we'd seen since leaving the St. Lawrence River—no doubt praying for the worst.

The lifeboat neared the drowning man—at least, he should be drowning by now.

"They've just a hundred feet or so to go now," a woman, sounding most relieved, remarked at my elbow.

Finally the sailors reached the spot and hauled in the marker and the life preserver.

"He's rescued!" the woman at my elbow rejoiced.

"Or caught," muttered Nila out of the corner of her mouth.

She went inside to finish her letters, but I hung around, watching the end of the maneuvers, and fell to talking with one of the crew who had been on the *Batory* when the former captain jumped ship, though "jumped," as I discovered for the first time, doesn't mean he dived into the sea and swam for it. The crewman, who evidently learned to speak English the hard way, said the master "threw out the ship."

"Did what?" I questioned.

"Threw out."

"What?" I was completely in the dark.

"You know to throw out food, don't you?" he asked patiently. "To discard it?"

"Oh!"

"Well, he discarded the ship. When it was docked at Southampton, he and the doctor walked off."

I somehow had forgotten about the doctor, but I didn't mention it. Instead, I asked, "Did the ship wait for the captain to come back?"

"No, madame. An immigration officer came on board and

said the master wants to stay in England and for the first mate to be master."

"I always thought he literally jumped off," I said, hating to relinquish this picture of daring action.

"No. It was the music steward who actually jumped off."

I brightened. "Oh!"

"Yes, madame. The political officer told the music steward that he was going to be arrested just as soon as the ship reached Poland, and so when we were anchored off Southampton he jumped through the porthole and swam ashore."

Well, this was more like it. "Did somebody go after him?"

"No. None of the crew were allowed ashore at that time."

"Why did he jump through the porthole? Wouldn't it have been easier for him to jump from the rail?"

"Yes, but this political officer was following him everywhere he went. You see, madame, this political officer was a most nosy, suspicious person. He made constant trouble for everybody on the ship, for all the crew and all the passengers, too. Everybody was afraid of him. Now, of course, we don't have a political officer on board and everybody breathes much more free." He smeared the rain off his face with the palm of his hand. "The whole political situation in Poland is much easier now. But when the music steward jumped it was very tight."

"Did he have far to swim?"

"Yes, madame, a pretty long ways, but he'd been training himself for it in the swimming pool. Every day, after all the passengers swim, he practices for one hour. So, that day we was anchored off Southampton, he watched for his chance and jumped."

The sailor eyed me to see if I appreciated the seriousness of the situation. I did.

"Finally, he's going to his cabin and he's conscious that he's followed not only by the political officer, but by three men, and he understands he's very much wanted. So what to do?"

Again he looked at me inquiringly; but I had no suggestions.

"So, he undresses himself, puts on his swim suit and jumps through the porthole."

As there seemed nothing to be added to this, we were quiet

for some seconds, and then I said in casual, conversational tones, "A great deal has befallen the *Batory*, hasn't it, in and around Southampton? Were you on it when the Communist Gerhardt Eisler stowed away and was arrested at Southampton?"

"Yes, madame, and we aren't far from where we were anchored that day. You see, the master had to stay offshore, for if he went into Southampton he had to report any blind passenger."

"Blind?"

"That's a passenger who comes on board without a ticket. The master is supposed to report such a passenger at the next port of call, so, not to do that, he anchored out. And whilst he was anchored out, a tender comes with detectives from Scotland Yards in civilian clothes. Eisler, though, knowed who they were and he went into his cabin and locked the door."

He paused for dramatic effect and I asked, "What happened?"

He shrugged. "They broke the door down and took him off."

"Didn't the master protest?"

"Yes, madame. He wouldn't let them have him until our Polish consul came on board and gave the permission."

"Did the consul come on the tender with the detectives?"

"That I can't say. I wasn't on deck at the time."

"Was it the same master we have now?"

"No, madame, it was the master who threw out."

I realized I was back where I came in, so I excused myself and returned to my letter writing.

9   July 26

WE ARE ANCHORED some distance off Southampton in what is known as Southampton Waters. We can't see the city, but Cheslov told us that a large stack that is barely visible on the far side of an arm of land marks the spot. Unless one were a Channel swimmer, he couldn't possibly make it.

On the shore just opposite us, grayish-yellow walls stand up solidly on a bright-green hillside. A castle, I decided without asking anybody. Several miles farther down the shore, or up (I'm a stranger here, remember), are the weathered red and yellow buildings of some town.

It is still cold, but the sea gulls apparently don't mind. Hundreds of them sway so close above the ship's decks I can see through the gauzy fringes of their almost motionless wings, and other hundreds bob like dirty rubber balls on the heaving water.

Nor do the sailboats mind. All morning they round our stern, their gold, blue, red and white sails skimming the frothy tops of the stirred-up waves. Evidently a regatta is going on nearby.

We reached this anchorage, as was predicted, at five o'clock yesterday afternoon and have been sitting here ever since with no activity—nautically speaking, that is—other than the pilot leaving the ship, bent low, with Nila's and my letters.

In fact, Nila and I caused quite a flurry when we bought our stamps. After standing for fifteen minutes or more in a long line, we reached the purser's counter and Nila said, "We'd like stamps for twenty letters, please."

At which a young officer who had been typing away at a desk a goodly number of feet behind the counter stood up, bowed deeply and said in heavily accented English, "It's nice to meet a poet."

"That's right," said Nila, and she bowed deeply in return.

And now we wait for the tender to bring the new passengers for Copenhagen and Gdynia, Poland, and to take off our passengers for England. The tender is many hours late and we hear that the master is in a rage and that the Polish agent stationed at Southampton is due for a terrific tongue-lashing.

Finally, however, just before lunchtime, the tender drew alongside and Nila and I rushed to the rail to see the people come aboard; but, abruptly, at the sound of a foreign word spat out by a short, moonfaced man, Nila whirled and stopped. Innocently I stopped, too; then Nila deliberately turned her back on me as if she had never known me. After a hesitant moment I took the hint and moved farther down the rail.

Until the lunch bell sounded I watched the people come

aboard; then I walked along the deck to pick up Nila. However, as I approached she made an impatient, go-away-from-me
gesture behind her back and so I slunk away to the dining
room.

Michele was already at the table and we chatted and ate
through several courses before Nila rushed in. She was terribly
wrought up. Her cheeks were flushed and her eyes feverish.
Ignoring Michele as if her chair were empty, she leaned over to
me and whispered, "Oh, Willie, I feel as I already smell Russia.
This Russian man I talked to on deck tells me everything;
then another man comes up, gestures like this—" Nila jerked
her head back and narrowed her eyes—"and he dropped me
dead. God, it was interesting! After lunch I will try to make
the contact again."

She settled back in her chair, piled her plate with whatever
Bruno passed to her and, in a preoccupied silence, wolfed it
down. Then, without having dessert or coffee, she muttered,
"If you will excuse me," and departed.

I went to our stateroom and waited. More than two hours
passed and then she whirled in like a cyclone. "Willie, I got
everything!" She slapped her hand to her forehead and swayed
to one side. "Everything! It is fantastic. Just fantastic. Look,
I'm all wet." She grabbed off her coat and held her soaked
blouse out from her body. "Even after dancing I'm not so wet."

Hurriedly she peeled off her clothes, put on her gown and
bathrobe and got into bed. "Now, Willie, I will tell you everything!"

"You think you'd better shut the window?" I whispered,
caught up in her excitement.

"It's shut; I already looked." She sat up in the bed and
eyed me for a long, dramatic moment, then began. "I was
walking with you there on the deck and I heard this man use
a very rough Russian word—Willie, if you put it in a book, it is
so dirty it will not be permitted. It means—how can I say it in
polite English?—it means, as best as I can translate it in polite
English, 'My God, what a junk!' He was talking about the
luggage of the passengers on the tender. You know, the cheap
suitcases tied with rope, the cardboard boxes, the cloth bags.

"So quick as that I stopped dead and we began the conversation. In Russian, of course. I said, 'I heard you speak in a language that I hope soon to hear every day.' And he asks, 'Are you going to Russia?' and I say, 'Yes, are you?' and he says, 'Yes,' and I say, 'For a visit?' and he says, 'No, I'm going back to live.'

"Then for the first time I ever heard of it he uses this word, vozvrashchenetz. It means a person who voluntarily left Russia and is voluntarily returning. Never, Willie, have I been so shocked. 'How you go?' I ask. 'How they accept you?' He says in 1955 Khrushchev declared an amnesty for all Russians who left Russia, willingly or unwillingly. Some are people who the Germans took to Germany to work, some people who deserted to the German Army. You remember General Vlasov? He—"

"Who, Nila?"

"General Vlasov. He—"

"No, I don't remember him."

"It makes no difference," she answered impatiently. "During the war, he with his whole division joined the German side and fought against Russia. Many others did, too. They were considered traitors to Russia. And now Khrushchev makes the amnesty. All can come back—traitors and nontraitors alike.

"I ask this man what makes him return and he said he didn't make his place abroad. He said he didn't believe any one Russian could do it. Any other nationalities could—Poles, Latvians, Italians, French, but not Russians. Of course, Willie, I don't agree; I'm just repeating you his words. His homesickness, he said, becomes so acute it stays right here—" Nila beat rapidly with both fists against her chest. "He said, 'I can't fight it no longer.'"

"You won't believe it, Willie, but there are twenty-five of these Russians on this boat. They go to Gdynia, where everything is arranged for them with Polish officials. Train cars will come right to the boat and carry them straightway to Brest, the frontier city between Poland and Russia, you know, where they will be met with music and flowers. This would frighten me terribly, especially knowing what I know.

"This man I talked to lived in Canada and he, like the

Russian writer Gorky, said America—and by America he meant
Canada and the United States—was the country of the yellow
devil. How you respect a country, he asked me, where a student
in college, who already comes to the third year, will drop his
studies to become a professional baseball player because it pays
more money? How you respect a country that sells its intellect
for money? Then he said, 'What America needs is a revolution,' and he went just like that—" Nila's jaws hardened, her
eyes glared, she pummeled the air with her clenched hand.
"He said the banks, the factories, the farms, the railroads,
everything must be nationalized. He said he can't understand
how America can permit seventy or so people to own everything.

"Then I asked him nicely, 'What kind of an apartment you
have?' and he answered, 'I had my own house.' Then I said,
'You must be one of the seventy or so who own everything,'
and quickly he said, 'I had a small house.'

"Then he said, 'You take the Negro,' and he went on and
on and on. He was boiling, and finally an old man who came
up and joined us tried to calm him down. 'You must always
remember what Nikita said,' he murmured with such rever-
ence you would have thought he was quoting Jesus and Moses
rolled into one instead of Khrushchev. 'You must always remember Nikita said the revolution in America is inevitable; it
is only a matter of time.'

"Willie, I want you to remember I looked at him with such
a hardness in my eyes. These people left Russia with hatred for
Stalin and Russia in their hearts. They were considered traitors
to Soviet Russia you understand. And now because they didn't
become rich in America, they are traitors to her, too, and everything is pink—rosy, as you say—in Russia." Nila was also boiling. "Life will show them," she added vehemently, "and it will
serve them right."

"What kind of work did the man do in Canada?" I asked.

"He worked in a gold mine and made four hundred dollars
a month and now he goes back to Russia with two thousand
pounds of goods."

"Not two thousand pounds, Nila," I protested.

"Yes, two thousand pounds. Just think of it. Can you understand that or not? One whole ton from this hard life in America."

"Is he allowed to take that much?"

"Yes, he said there's no limit. The Soviet Embassy told him he could take as much as he wants. Everything except seeds. They encourage the people to bring all they can. He has an electric sewing machine—he says he leaves the refrigerator and deep-freeze behind—a transformer, a motorcycle, and clothes, underwear, shoes and boots to last for four years, and hundreds of yards of material. With great excitement he asked me, 'You know how much I can get in Russia for all these yards of wool?' and so I asked him, 'Have you spent all your money for these two thousand pounds of goods?' and he answered, 'Oh, no, I've not spent all my money. Russia encourages you to bring back money even more than goods. At the border I will exchange all my money for rubles. Also, the government will give me one thousand rubles to help me get settled.' "

(To a Russian 1,000 rubles equal $250. The Soviet Union official rate is four rubles to the dollar; but to encourage tourism, it gives American visitors ten rubles to the dollar.)

"I asked him," Nila went on, " 'Why you need it? You already have plenty.' He shrugs his shoulders and says the government gives it to everybody who comes back whether he needs it or not. Then I asked him, 'How will it feel to live like a capitalist among the Russians?' and he said, 'My baggage is just peanuts compared to what others are bringing.' He said there is one Russian on the ship who has four thousand pounds. Two tons, Willie! He has a refrigerator, a deep-freeze, mattresses, clothes, shoes, everything. He is going back to a wife and four children he hasn't seen in sixteen years—not since he left Russia for Germany. Can imagine what a shock it will be to find a wife he has remembered all these years as young, pretty and slim, now sixteen years older. And think of the children! They were babies when he left—and now? He will not know them.

"Also, this man told me that last month on the *Batory* he had a friend who took twenty-five trunks, a refrigerator, deep-freeze and two hundred thousand dollars to exchange. 'What do you mean, two hundred thousand dollars?' I asked him. 'Yes, two hundred thousand dollars,' he repeated. 'He had a very good business in America. And at Brest they will take his two hundred thousand dollars and they will exchange it at the tourist rate for two million rubles.'

"Naturally I said then, 'He will be a millionaire, and that's against Marx, Lenin, Stalin, the line and everything. Have you thought why the Soviet government would permit a person who left Russia to return and live as a capitalist?'

" 'The Soviet government needs dollars,' he says. 'Then,' I say, 'just give them the dollars and forget about the rubles.' He doesn't answer, so I say, 'Okay, I understand the deep-freeze, if he will have anything to freeze, and the refrigerator, if he will have anything to put in the refrigerator, but what will he do with two million rubles? Do you know,' I ask him, 'this old story of Ilf and Petrov about the Russian who suddenly got a lot of money? So what to do? How to spend the money? What to buy? There are no goods, no houses, no nothing. So finally he bought a ticket from Moscow to Vladivostok by first-class traveling—each trip takes at least nine days—and went four times. It was the only way he could spend his money.'

"He said everything is changed now and there are things to buy. He said he has read it in the Russian papers and Khrushchev has said it in his speeches."

Nila leaned back on her pillows and stared at the ceiling. "God, what a conversation! You read about such people and they sound so unreal, but this is a firsthand story. You can touch the people; they are flesh and blood right here."

10   Evening

HELENA AND CHRIS BURNADOWSKI invited Nila and me to their cabin for champagne. They had met the chief of the *Batory's* fire department and wanted to share the pleasure of his company with us. He's a nice-looking young man, but since he speaks only Polish and I speak only English, we were lost to each other.

Nila was still highly excited over the going-home-again Russians and she told Chris about them; but he was not as surprised as she expected him to be. He knew a Pole from Winnipeg who, after thirty-five years, was returning on the *Batory* to live in the Old Country.

"And he has fourteen trunks of stuff and a stove," Chris said.

"An electric stove or a gas stove?" I asked.

Chris whooped with delight and two-stepped about the small cabin. "What you think? He returns to America to live? It's a coal stove, of course."

Chris filled everybody's glass. Besides the chief of the fire department, Nila and me, there was only one other guest, the mother-in-law of Helena's brother. She was in a blue cotton print with long sleeves and ankle-length skirt.

"He's fairly handsome guy, too," Chris continued about the returning Pole, "and he's a bachelor. He says there are twenty-four women waiting to marry him and he's going to have a hard time making up his mind. It made me laugh like hell."

Chris laughed like hell now. His bright-blue eyes flashed, his lips with the crayon line of mustache spread wide and his pink cheeks puffed up.

In spite of Chris's gaiety, Nila had to know the reason for the Pole's return.

"He didn't create anything in America," Chris answered, sobering.

"But he had freedom," Nila reminded him.

"There are some guys if they have food, they don't worry about freedom." Chris stood in the middle of the cabin, his filled glass at a perilous angle. "This guy was free, but he didn't do anything with the freedom. He works all day, he comes home at night dead tired and goes to bed, then gets up and works hard all the next day." Chris shrugged. "And so he goes back to Poland."

Chris drained his glass and returned to the bottle to pour himself another one, but the bottle was empty. "It's all right," he announced cheerfully. "We have a bottle of cherry brandy and it's even better than champagne."

He circled the room with the brandy and in no time at all the Poles and Nila were singing Ukrainian songs. They sounded sad—the songs, that is—and plaintive. Helena's brother's mother-in-law crossed her arms beneath her full breasts and held them up as if to keep them from being a drag on her voice.

"She sings from the top of her head to her feet," Nila whispered to me, cocking her head toward the mother-in-law. "Like all peasants, she lives through what she's singing; she forgets all else."

"What are they singing?" I whispered back.

"It's a song about a girl who committed suicide for love—a workers' song. When I used to sing it in prison, all the prisoners would cry. You see, two doctors and a nurse are trying to save the girl's life, but she says, 'I do not care whether you save it or not. My life is not expensive to me.' Then she dies and they bring her to this place where you bring the body before you bury it and she is so beautiful it is unbelievable. Then the lover comes and says, 'Why did you do this to me?' and he goes out and stabs himself. It is the silliest, unprettiest song, but everybody falls into the line."

And so did Nila. She added her high, thin, eerie, sweet voice to the swelling, swaying, mournful voices of the other four. She, too, sang from the top of her head to her feet; she, too, lived through what she was singing and forgot all else. She was suddenly as foreign as any of the Poles. I felt completely alien and alone. What am I doing here, I wondered, traveling so far from home with this stranger?

At last, after a half-dozen more songs, Chris seemed to sense my aloneness and, as host, tried to make amends. He replenished everybody's drink; then, stepping in front of me, he bent slowly from the waist, clinked his glass against mine and toasted, "Down with you!"

I no longer felt alone. I felt convulsed.

<u>11</u>   July 27

IT WAS OUR LAST DINNER on the *Batory* and, as on every other night except one—the master's dinner, which was nothing to write about, for the minute the dinner was over the master and his fellow officers stood up, clicked their heels, mentally if not physically, and marched from the room—Michele, Nila and I were alone in our corner.

Michele started off the meal with a thin slice of rare roast beef. "Just one slice . . . chou . . . chou . . ." she murmured to Bruno, her little finger flying out helplessly like a flower petal opening. "Well," she added bravely, "maybe one more slice." Then she took the usual cold vegetable hors d'oeuvres. I started with the same.

Nila started with honeydew melon, the last honeydew on the ship, as we well knew. There was a platter of six slices on the serving table. Rapidly she finished with the first slice and began on the second, then even more rapidly finished the second and began on the third. Bruno swung back and forth like a pantry door from the serving table to Nila's side.

Nila was stacking the three rinds together like dirty plates when Michele looked up with her big, pleading eyes, gestured languidly to Bruno and said, "Perhaps, a piece of melon like Madame."

Nila stiffened as if a lump of ice had been slipped down her back, turned upon Michele and said in outraged tones, "Not melon after hors d'oeuvres!"

"Yes, I thought I'd try it."

How Michele swallowed it with Nila glaring at her I don't know, but she managed it; also afterward a piece of steak ("chou, chou . . . and very done, please, Bruno—I'm not able to eat it rare"), a baked potato ("Just one, please, chou, chou"), fresh asparagus and a mixture of peas, celery and carrots.

Nila and I had practically the same but for the first time in nine days, even though Nila is a terrifically fast eater, Michele finished before her, signaled to Bruno and said, "The melon was so refreshing, I think I'll have another piece."

Nila turned and shot beams of hate at Michele, and I realized that she had counted on having those two remaining slices for dessert and was furious at being thwarted in this fashion. However, when Michele took only one of the slices, she relaxed somewhat and went on eating her main course. At least she'd get one piece.

Then Michele called out gently to Bruno, "This piece wasn't the same as the first piece I had. It must have come from a different melon. Maybe . . . the other piece is better."

Instantly Nila smelled danger. She dropped her knife and fork into her plate with a clatter, anchored the backs of her hands on her hips and drew herself up until she seemed to tower above Michele.

Yet, queerly enough, Michele didn't seem to notice. Bruno, though, most certainly did. He stood like a slightly tilted statue where Michele's words caught him and said in a conversational tone, as if discussing the weather, "Maybe so, madame."

For a second Michele hesitated and I breathed more easily; but then she, too, drew herself up and spoke with resolution: "Bruno, I'd like to try the other piece, please!"

I didn't look at Nila. I couldn't. I got very busy balling up my napkin in my lap. Then murmuring, as if I were on the verge of being seasick, "This room is so stuffy—I need air," I escaped.

🌳   Later

As NILA AND I were sitting with a small group of people around the dance floor, a rather handsome, middle-aged blond Russian sauntered up, bent above Nila and chucked her familiarly under the chin.

Though Nila jerked her head away and angry color rose in her cheeks, she didn't say anything.

The man was wearing a loud plaid flannel shirt, open at the neck, with no coat.

Continuing to bend over Nila, he talked in Russian very urgently until the man on her left, sensing her discomfiture, invited her to dance.

Naturally I was consumed with curiosity; but I had no chance to ask her what the Russian had said, for she was either dancing with Poles or preoccupied with other Russians all evening.

There were ten or twelve Russians sitting around a big table across the floor from us, drinking first beer and then champagne. They laughed and talked loudly and once even burst into song. Nila, recognizing the tune, swayed her head and shoulders and, after a moment or two, hummed it along with them.

When it was finished, she said to the group about our table, "It was very interesting what they sang. It was a famous Soviet song. It began, 'My country is wide; there is no other country where man breathes so freely.'"

A Pole on the right of Nila murmured, "I want to see how freely they breathe after they have been back for a while."

"And so would I," said Nila as she turned her eyes and attention to the Russians. They got louder and louder and threw their hands about in sweeping gestures.

"The Russians on a party always behave with this abundance," Nila said to me, leaning over. "You'll have to get used to it, Willie. Just the smell of alcohol makes them very gay."

Finally, coming up to me after a dance, she announced in a low, thrilled voice, "The Russians have asked me to join them. What shall I do?"

"Join them, by all means," I said.

When the music stopped for the evening, she was still with them, bending far across the table, talking earnestly, her arms flung out and her face flushed.

I came back to our stateroom without her, but I was still awake when she came in, very much excited.

"Begin at the beginning," I said to her, "and tell me what the blond man in the plaid shirt said to you when he chucked you under the chin."

She looked grim for a moment, then said, "He asked me a question. He asked, 'Did you tell them—' and he stared, Willie, at you and the other de luxe and first-class passengers with such a hardness—'did you tell them who gave you the education to make it possible for you to be where you are? You sit there—' and, Willie, he spread both his hands out angrily; he wants to show how elegant I sit with my beautiful red linen dress and popovers—'you sit there, but did you tell them Soviet Russia made it possible, that Soviet Russia educated you?'"

"Then what happened when you went to the Russians' table?"

"I spoke mostly with a man and his young wife, who with their three children also go back to Russia to live. The man is very tense, very high-strung and nervous. He said they had no choice but to go back. He said the depression is coming, it is inevitable, and as he is a foreigner he will be the first to be thrown out of a job. I asked what makes him think the depression will come and he says after war—and there is certain to be war—always will come a depression. Then he begins to develop the Marxist theory—you know, Willie, the upsy-dopsy to the capitalist system—but I stopped him dead. I said, 'You forget I lived almost forty years in Russia, so don't develop the Marxist theory to me. From the time you start to school until your grave, you are developed this.'

"Then the young wife came into the picture. She said they were *toska po rodine*—it means homesick for the motherland. She said, 'We kept asking ourselves what will happen to our children if we die in America. At least we know what will happen to them if we die in Russia.' Quickly I ask, 'What?' and she said, 'They will at least be in their mother country.'

"She also told me that when the Germans came and occupied her village in Russia they appointed a starosta who agreed to co-operate with them. The Germans did this every time they occupied a town, and the word "starosta" came into all languages, all books, for this man played such a part in the occupation. The starosta didn't like this girl's family and he said they must send one member to Germany to work, and so they got together and, instead of the mother or the father going, they gave her, though she was only fourteen years old at the time. So, with the other girls and boys of the village capable to work she was taken to work in the factory."

"Nila, did she say what kind of factory?" I asked.

"No, she was so hard crying, I didn't ask her. It was really very dramatic. Here she was crying over this table all wet with champagne. To tell the truth, the whole tablecloth was spilled with champagne. This is the Russian way. When they drink, they wet everything! That's their temperament. It gives them a feeling of abundance.

"So, she was crying. She had on these little white net gloves that just come to the wrist. Maybe you saw her. She was one of the two people who danced with gloves on all evening. Well, she kept wiping away the tears with the gloves and all her make-up comes off on them, but it makes no difference. She's so happy crying.

"She tells me she met her husband at the factory and they got married and lived some years in Germany and then, not wanting to go back to Russia, they went to Canada."

"Why didn't they want to go back to Russia?"

"I asked her that and she said they couldn't prove they were taken by force by the Germans and they know if they went back there they will be sent to the 'far places.' You remember, Willie, the first train of Russians that came back from Germany after the war went straight to the concentration camp, without even stopping at the border.

"So, they went to Canada and for fifteen years, counting the years in Germany, they had no connection with her family. Then two years ago when they heard what Khrushchev done for Russia, she wrote to her family and got letters back through the Russian consulate. It is a big family—mother and father and three or four sisters and, I believe, one brother. Her family said everything was just fine and they must come back.

"Now one more story, Willie, and I'll let you go to sleep. "This young wife had on a beautiful light-blue dress with consequences."

"With what?"

"What you call it—these shiny things?"

"Sequins."

"That's right. Well, all these sequins just shine nicely and around her neck is a chain with stones and she has earrings to match and white shoes—quite nice shoes. And an evening-looking watch. I told her the Russians will love her dress and she looked at me as if I had slapped her to the face and said, 'I will never wear this dress in Russia.'

" 'But why?' I asked her. 'The Russian women will just love it and try to copy it.'

" 'The first thing I do when I step on the Russian soil,' she said, 'will be to wear just the same things they do. I just want to be one of them.'

"I told her, 'Of course, it's your business what you wear, but I think you will make a terrible mistake. The Russians will expect you, returning from America, to be well dressed.' "

Nila was quiet and I thought she had dropped off to sleep; but suddenly she sat up and said with doleful shakes of her head, "Ah, Willie, the return of these people is the smartest propaganda Russia ever did. This is the most beautiful, looking-forward propaganda. Every one of them who is returning will try to beat their heads to say how horrible is Canada and the United States. Of course, it will be hard for them to explain to the Russians how horrible the life is with four thousand pounds of luggage, but nevertheless they will drink vodka and remember every black thing."

Again she was quiet; then, sighing deeply, she added, "What fools these returning Russians are. Still, I wish them luck. They will need it."

II

The Baltika

<u>1</u>   August 4

AFTER AN UNEASY WEEK in Copenhagen, we are once more moving toward our goal, Russia.

The week was uneasy because we didn't know whether we could sail, as we had hoped, on the Soviet ship, the *Baltika*, that plies between Southampton and Leningrad. When planning this trip we had set our hearts on entering the U.S.S.R. at Leningrad because Nila in her early twenties had been a sailor in the Russian merchant marine and had taken off from that port to see the world; but the Cosmos Travel Agency had been unable to get our reservations confirmed.

However, just thirty-six hours before the *Baltika* was scheduled to sail from Copenhagen we were notified we had space, but not together and not de luxe. We were in second class and each of us would share a stateroom with three other people.

"We most likely will be put in cabins with men," Nila informed me calmly. "The Russians think nothing of putting women and men in the same cabins on ships and in the same compartments on trains."

"Oh, no!" I protested.

"Oh, yes. And you, Willie, will no doubt draw a Russian general and his two aides, and I three privates."

But the prospects didn't dampen Nila's enthusiasm for the

trip. In fact, she was in such a state of anticipation last night that she said, about six o'clock, "Let's go to bed early, so tomorrow will come fast." She sounded exactly like a child the night before Christmas.

And so we did go to bed early and now we're on board but without a general or an aide or a private. I'm in a cabin no larger than my bathroom at home with an old, old cushiony fat woman who speaks, so far as Nila and I are concerned, an unknown tongue, and a chubby blond Russian girl with long, thick plaits, and a woman who I presume is the girl's mother, though I haven't seen her yet.

I'm in the upper berth above the old woman, and my clothes closet, about the size of a florist's box for chrysanthemums, is wedged behind a stationary square table. To reach it I have to take off my clothes, draw in my stomach, lower my derrière and inch along between the table and a built-in windowseat. How I wish for some lard to grease myself! The table cover and the curtains at the windows are of drab red plush. There is no toilet nor bath, just a washbasin against one wall with a small mirror above it.

Nila doesn't fare any better; but she is in a very happy mood. She has undoubtedly been terribly homesick for Russian sights, Russian sounds and Russian people. While I was still unpacking, she burst into my cabin, cried, "We're in, baby!" threw her arms around me and kissed me. Then she hurried me out to tour the ship.

It is large. Of course it isn't one of the Queens, but it is large. It accomodates four hundred passengers. However, the steps climbing from deck to deck aren't wide enough for our feet, pointing forward, and so we have to turn them sideways.

"Aren't they absurd?" Nila asked in the tones of an indulgent mother commenting on the behavior of a wayward child.

We must go first to the music room, she said. "My maid tells me it is beautiful." She chuckled softly to herself. "Willie, you know what my maid asked me? She asked, 'Have you a group to conduct?' and when I said, 'No, I'm with just one person,' she was as impressed as could be and said, 'You mean they sent you for just one person? She must be very important.' I didn't even answer. I just made the face." Nila illustrated the face. Her head went up, her eyebrows rose to the middle of her forehead and her lips pursed. Judging from her airs, she could have been conducting Mamie Eisenhower.

The music salon is a big, glaring room in the stern of the ship, with innumerable chairs and tables of too brightly stained honey-colored wood and an upright piano on the edge of a loud green flowered rug cut out in the middle to bare the floor for dancing.

We next went out on deck and a man and a woman swept by us. "They are very important Russians," Nila whispered. "I can tell by his walk and her bosom. You, Willie, will get so you can recognize the walk. Notice it close. He walks like nothing—not nature, not God, not man—exists."

Soon we realized the ship is full of important Russians— easily a hundred and fifty, if not more. They were lolling in deck chairs, sitting on benches, standing in groups in the lounges, pacing the decks. They had to be from the Soviet Union's embassies returning home for their summer vacations, we decided, for only diplomats and members of delegations could be traveling outside their country in this fashion.

Also on board are a goodly number of English men and women, some Swedes and Finns and two or three Americans. Practically all the English are planning brief visits to Russia. They will have three days in Leningrad and three in Moscow and then return to Leningrad to board the *Baltika* for its return trip to Southampton.

Also, right slap in the middle of the deck chairs and the promenading "lanes" are several automobiles belonging, from the looks of their licenses, to the diplomats. Nila stopped and peered excitedly at each one. "This is a Buick," she informed me. "This is a Pontiac. . . . This is a Ford. . . . This is a Chrysler. Hah! How the Russians love automobiles! It is really too amusing."

I kept my face straight.

On the bow is a new pale-green Austin, the hood swathed in cellophane. Nila was simply enchanted. Walking about, studying every foot of it, with narrowed eyes, she discovered it is addressed to the Russian musician Lev Oborin and explained to me that she supposed he is permitted to own a foreign car because he is such a distinguished artist.

"As you know, Willie," she said, "no cars are allowed to be imported into Russia except from the satellite nations. You'll see no American cars unless they belong to diplomats or tourists."

Having admired the Austin sufficiently, we headed for the dining room to have lunch. The dining room is in the bow of the ship, with all its curving outside wall made of windows, so that you sit and look out over the sea.

"Isn't it lovely?" Nila asked. "I've never seen a ship's dining room like it and I think it is a splendid idea."

By the side of each plate was a linen napkin rolled in an old-fashioned silver ring with a number engraved on it. My number was 147. Also at each place was a plate with a piece of cold fish, a slice of cucumber cut the long way and one slice of tomato, and a compote of two stewed quinces in syrup.

"Look at the china," said Nila. "Isn't it nice?" Then, in the very next breath, "Ah, a very chic fish."

I was not sure of its chicness, but I did know I wanted vinegar for my cucumber and said so.

Nila's face clouded up. "You mean you'd have the waitress go all the way to the kitchen for vinegar for that one slice of cucumber?"

"Why not?" I asked, but timidly. I'd already begun to sense that Nila considered herself one of the hostesses, if not The hostess, of the *Baltika*. "Even if it's just one slice, I'd like it right."

"Okay," she said resignedly, her face still glum, and she called the waitress. They talked for some time in Russian, making me feel quite uncomfortable. No doubt Nila was telling her I'm a crochety, spoiled American. At last, though, the colloquy was over and the waitress moved off. "She speaks so lovely I can't tell you," Nila said, beaming.

The next course consisted of a small helping of beef Stroganov and a generous helping of beautifully cooked rice.

As I was finishing this, I saw a waitress going by with plates of thin pancakes and sour cream. "Look at those wonderful pancakes," I said to Nila.

"You mean you could actually eat pancakes after all you've eaten?"

"Why, I haven't eaten nearly as much as I usually ate for lunch on the *Batory*."

"It makes no difference." She shut me off in her most Stalinish manner. "You are not allowed them. You could have had either the first course or the pancakes."

"I didn't know that. Nobody told me."

"How could they when we just got on the boat?" Haughtily she studied a typewritten sheet of paper with three menus printed on it. "These are the menus for tomorrow. You have to choose today what you will eat tomorrow."

"Like in a hospital," I said gaily, but Nila was not amused.

"That's right," she said, most matter-of-fact.

I ate my two quinces, then asked gently, "Do we have coffee?"

"No, there is nothing more."

As I rolled my napkin to pull it through the ring, Nila spied streaks of lipstick on it and was horrified.

"You must bring some tissues to the table," she lectured me, "and wipe your mouth before you begin to eat."

"I'll think I'm in a dentist's office," I demurred. "My dentist's assistant always hands me a Kleenex the first thing when I sit down."

"I wouldn't know about that." She sounded superior. "Of course, I never use lipstick except when I make a speech."

After lunch we decided to sit on deck, so Nila asked the steward where was the deck reserved for second-class passengers.

"Madame, you and your friend can sit anywhere you like," he answered sternly. "I'd like you to understand this is a Soviet ship and all classes can sit anywhere they please. We make no differences between classes in the Soviet Union and you and your friend had just as well get accustomed to it. Everybody in our country is equal. It's a real democracy."

So rebuked, we crept about until we found two chairs, lugged them to a spot out of the wind and settled down. Then, for the first time, I noticed the brilliant yellow-red Soviet flag with the gold-colored hammer and sickle upon it flying from the staff on the stern. It was a colorful sight against the curving, satiny-blue sky; nevertheless, I went into shock every time I looked up from my book and saw it there.

Walking about the deck later, we saw a Russian woman keeping an eye on two well-dressed children, a girl and a boy, and we stopped and leaned against the rail within speaking distance. The girl had her hair plaited, like the girl in my stateroom, and tied with two electric-blue chiffon handkerchiefs.

I waited for Nila to start a conversation; but she stared out to sea indifferently, as if she were deaf and dumb. So finally I spoke to the mother—a heavy-set, black-haired, handsome woman—and she answered in heavily accented English. She is the wife of a member of the Russian Embassy staff in Washington, she said, and she and her husband and children are on their way to Moscow on home leave.

"And how do you like Washington?" I asked.

"I find it a very dull city," she answered, taking my breath away. "There is absolutely nowhere to go, except the movies. By eight or nine o'clock the streets are empty and everybody is in bed."

"Really?"

"Yes, but still I prefer it to New York. New York is such a dirty city."

A man, evidently her husband, who I hope is more of a diplomat than she, came up and stared coldly at her, Nila and me. Hurriedly Nila took me by the arm and propelled me away.

"Nila, why didn't you talk to the woman?" I asked.

"I didn't want to."

"But why?"

"It would have embarrassed her."

"How would it have embarrassed her?"

"She wouldn't know how to place me."

Baffled, I started to ask another question, but Nila shut me off. "I'm going to my stateroom and rest before dinner," she said coldly, and departed.

The Baltika

NILA AND I WENT to the bar before dinner to celebrate with a glass of vodka the fact that we were actually on the *Baltika* and only three nights and two days from Russia. As there are no waiters in the bar, we approached the barman and Nila made known our wants.

"Fifty grams or a hundred grams?" he asked.

Nila and I, frowning, looked at each other. Whoever heard of buying vodka by the gram? "Fifty?" I questioned Nila.

"Yes, fifty. I don't know how much that is, but I'm sure it is enough. You go on, Willie, and find a table and I'll bring the vodka when it's ready."

I found a round oak table surrounded by four deep brown leather armchairs. Shortly Nila joined me, carefully placed the little glasses on the table and sank into one of the chairs. "Hah!" she said. "Such nice leather." Then she rapped on the table with her knuckles. "And the height of the table is perfect, too. I'm so tired of those down tables."

The vodka was warm and I found it hard to take. "Maybe it would be better with a piece of ice in it," I suggested.

Nila went to the bar for ice, but returned with the word that there is no such item on the ship. "Can imagine," she remarked, "the barman looks so international, yet he has no ice. He says he has the machinery to keep things cold, but no machinery to make ice."

In front of the bar were two cardrooms filled with many men and two or three women, playing chess and dominoes.

Sipping her vodka, Nila eyed the domino players in silence for some minutes, then confided, "Willie, I used to be an absolute ass at dominoes. When I was a sailor I used to play like mad, and also before and after I was a sailor. It might take me a few minutes now to catch onto the game, but I mean it—I was an absolute ass."

"Not ass, Nila," I protested. "Surely you don't mean ass."

She looked at me sharply. "What does ass mean?"

Well, what *does* ass mean? Suddenly, face to face with the question, I realized I was very vague myself about asses. "I believe it means a little mule or donkey."

Nila grinned. "No, I certainly didn't mean that. But I was absolutely something that sounds like ass."

The light dawned. "Ace, Nila—A-c-e."

"That's right. I was an absolute ace. I used to play day and night with sailors and I continued even in prison though the political prisoners had no passion for dominoes; in fact, they had no passion after politics for anything. Once when I was working in the factory in Leningrad, building windows and doors, I became notorious because of dominoes. You see, in the old days practically every factory would be a patron for some school or some regiment in the Army or some branch of the Navy, and my section was patron for a small military boat which guarded the shores. And from time to time the boat had some celebration. So once some boys and I were sent to the boat to represent our section at one of these celebrations. We brought some present—a picture or something—to give.

"Well, when we came there, a man took us around to see the boat, and in a small room I saw some sailors playing dominoes and instantly they saw this hungry look in my eyes and just to be polite they invited me to play. I played steadily until twelve o'clock that night. Several times this man who was showing us about pulled my dress to stop me, but I paid no attention to him.

"We just shifted all the ceremonies. I gave the present without speeches or anything. And you know what the sailors did to me? They throwed me in the air. Z-z-zhip!—here I went. They just cheered me up and shouted, 'The best patron we ever had!'

"But the secretary of the Communist Party in the door-and-window plant didn't think so. He reprimanded me severely; then he said the reprimand in his office was not enough. He said he would put this question about my behavior to the whole meeting. And so he did. It was on—how you say?—the agenda 'The Disgraceful Behavior of Our Representative,' and then he made a speech that I went to help put on this celebration and instead I played dominoes with the sailors for six hours. 'Shame on you, Comrade Shevko!' he shouted, and they made the resolution to publish the story with a drawing of me, wild with dominoes and sailors.

"Nevertheless, I saw that everybody just loved me. All day the next day I was standing at my bench—my job, you see, was putting with the machine these little holes in windows—and the people came up and asked, 'Did you win?' and of course I answered, 'Sure I did.' And in a way I became quite a celebrity."

We finished our vodkas and went in to dinner. To Nila's joy there was a pink glass vase, holding small, square paper napkins, in the middle of the table. "Now wipe your lips with one of those paper napkins, Willie," she ordered. "Lucky bum, you don't even have to bring your own tissues."

The main dish for dinner was a cutlet with Russian mushrooms. Nila's shining eyes rested upon me with happy expectancy, her lips rounded to expel like bubbles a chain of oh's.

"They're delicious," I said.

"Yes, they're absolute Russian mushrooms," she said exultantly. "They haven't change the taste since childhood."

Then for dessert we had a compote of canned cherries. Again Nila went into raptures. "The Russian fruit," she declared, "is so much better than the American fruit. The Russian cherries are so much more tasteful. They grow by the strength of nature rather than by commercial fertilizers."

After dinner, a half-hundred or so people sat about in the brightly lighted music room, staring blankly at each other. A loud-speaker was wailing out a plaintive American number, "Mama, Teach Me to Dance," but nobody taught anybody, so finally Nila and I got up, put on our coats and walked on the deck. There was still one huge golden banner of light in the black-blue sky, and all the shining, cracked mirror of the sea between the horizon and us held it waveringly. We pulled our coats close about us, for the wind was high and cold.

Passing the windows of the cardroom, we saw what was evidently a championship game of dominoes in progress, for a half-dozen people were standing about watching it. The players —three men and a woman—smacked the dominoes on the table with force, and when they passed they banged their fists down and cried out loudly in disgust.

"The more noise one makes, the better," Nila commented nostalgically.

"Come, let's go inside and watch."

"What do you mean?" Nila exclaimed in the most shocked, horrified voice, as if I'd suggested murder. "You can't do that!"

"Why not?" My cheeks suddenly felt hot. "A lot of other people are watching."

"Can't you understand? They're all Russians. That's the difference. You're an American and they'd freeze right up and think you're nye *kulturnye.*"

"Nye what?"

"Nye *kulturnye*—not cultured. You'd better learn that expression, Willie. You'll hear it over and over in Russia. For instance, if you spit on the sidewalk somebody will step up to you and say, 'Citizen, nye *kulturnye.*'"

"Well, I'll do my best not to spit on the sidewalk."

"I know you don't do it, but I just give you the example."

"Still, I can't see why it's not cultured to watch a game of dominoes," I argued. "If I were on some other ship and saw a game going on I'd join the crowd watching it."

"Well, I assure you no Russian, especially not a Russian diplomat would join an American group and no American should join a Russian group without being invited."

Nila was so vehement I gave up and a few minutes later confessed I was tired and wanted to go to bed. She came with me to my cabin to explain to the maid, who speaks only Russian, that I'd like a window opened a little.

The old woman was already asleep; but the little girl, though in bed, was wide-awake, her eyes shining brightly.

"I see your Mom-ee hasn't come to bed yet?" I said, smiling at her and gesturing toward the lower berth.

She stared at me, her brows creased. Evidently she didn't comprehend my brand of English. Turning to Nila, I said, "Why don't you speak to her in Russian?"

Nila scowled and muttered, "No, I don't want to." Then, without even a good night, she hurried out.

Why didn't she want to? I wondered, troubled. She had acted peculiarly several times today. I had thought I knew her exceedingly well, but now I had grave doubts. I piled my clothes on top of my suitcases, located the stepladder on the floor under the window and crawled into my berth. The old woman was snoring very gently; nevertheless, it was a long time before I could sleep.

<u>3</u>   August 5

WHEN I WOKE UP this morning and peeped through a crack in the curtains, I saw the girl's mother, fully dressed, washing her face with quick, vigorous strokes. She is big-bosomed, with broad cheekbones and black curly hair cut very short. The girl sat on the windowseat, watching her.

"Good morning," I said pleasantly, poking my head out.

"Good morning," the woman answered.

"I see you speak English?"

"Very little. My husband is stationed in Washington."

"I suppose he's with the Soviet Embassy there?"

"Yes."

"What position does he hold—or shouldn't I ask?"

She shook her head as if she didn't understand me, abruptly grabbed the girl by the hand, announced, "We go for breakfast," and left.

I washed, dressed and also went to breakfast. Round bowls of caviar, platters of sliced cheese and sliced bologna (called "tea sausage" because it's so light, Nila told me) and plates of black bread punctuated the long length of the table. I was delighted, but the Englishwomen sitting with Nila and me couldn't stomach such a menu so early in the morning and called for cereal.

The waitress—the one who "talks so lovely"—brought hot bowls of something that resembles Deep South grits and so, naturally, I decided to have some, too. Indeed, I was carried away with the idea of caviar and grits together. Could anything be more the height of?

When the cereal arrived, I mixed a generous helping of caviar into it with my fork and began to eat. Once again Nila was horrified. "You never use a fork for cereal," she declared. "You use a spoon."

"Oh, is it *nye kulturnye* to use a fork?"

"No," she answered, as serious as could be, "but the Russians will just laugh their heads off at you."

Quickly I switched to a spoon.

The minute breakfast was over, Nila said, "Come, Willie, I have a surprise for you." Hurrying ahead, she led me to a section of the deck we somehow missed yesterday and pointed to a car that even to my uneducated eyes looked different. "Look, Willie, I save it for you!" she caroled like a four-year-old." It is a Mercedes Benz, the very best German car there is. And look inside! Isn't it something?"

I looked and agreed it is something. The upholstery was a plush material patterned like leopard skin.

When I had feasted my eyes sufficiently to satisfy Nila, she led me to the bow where Lev Oborin's Austin is parked. "Look," she ordered again, pointing this time to the Austin's shining body. "Before you were even up this morning I cleaned off all the spots the gulls made. I felt it was as little as I could do to show my appreciation for Mr. Oborin's beautiful music."

Next to the Austin was a small car packed with people. All the windows were rolled up and they sat huddled inside, one studying the dashboard, one polishing the windshield, and three, in the back seat, reading newspapers and books. Though the windows were clouded and we couldn't see their faces too well, Nila assured me that they're Russians and that they were sitting there just for the pleasure of being in an automobile.

They did look silly, but it was really not such a bad idea. The sun of yesterday was gone and, instead, a fine, gauzy rain swished across the deck and the slightly shifting gray sea. We were steaming at a snail's pace between innumerable islands and the precipitous coast of Sweden, blackish-green with heavy woods. Small summerhouses, roofed with red tiles, perch among the trees, high above the shore.

Nila and I rested ourselves against the rail in the inverted V of the bow and let the soft spray wash our faces. Sailors were busy loosening the hatch and setting the winches in place to unload the cargo for Stockholm, where we are scheduled to spend four hours. I was astounded at the small stature of the Russian crew. They are all the same size, as if they were picked for a ballet line, and are scarcely taller than five feet. However, they look very natty in white middies with light-blue collars, navy-blue bell-bottomed trousers and wide black leather belts.

Two Englishmen were standing near us and I, in my endearing, friendly way, said, "This is real English weather, isn't it?"

"Oh, no," one of them answered. "This is what we call a Scotch mist."

"Is that right? In the United States we call Scotch whisky on the rocks—on the ice, that is—a Scotch Mist."

"Huh," he grunted disapprovingly, then added, "I'd think that would be more mist than Scotch."

A little before two o'clock, the *Baltika* sidled toward a long wharf along Stockholm's waterfront, and in some inexplicable fashion its stern rammed the bow of a German freighter already tied up next door to the space toward which it was maneuvering. Several Germans sprang to the rails and peered over the side to assess the damage, but two *Baltika* officers who were standing on the deck near Nila and me were not disturbed. "It serves 'em right," one of them said, according to Nila's translation. "They have no business being tied up there in our way."

We didn't wait for the outcome of the row, for as soon as the *Baltika* backed off from the freighter and managed to dock, two Swedish immigration officers came aboard and set up shop in the music salon to examine the passport of everybody who is going ashore. It made no difference whether you are going for a three-hour tour or are arriving to take up residence, you must wait on them with passport in hand.

For one hour and forty minutes by my watch, Nila and I stood in line. (This outdoes the lines at wedding receptions at the Louisville Country Club.) Most of the time we were in outer darkness, as it were—'way back in the cardroom and then 'way back in the bar—and couldn't see or hear anything that was going on, but finally we reached the door of the salon and discovered that the Swedes were putting all the Russian passengers through a thorough grilling. They scrutinized their passports, compared their passport pictures with their anxious faces and asked them many questions. It was very evident they had no intention of allowing this Soviet ship to smuggle some undesirable person or persons into Sweden.

When Nila and I finally presented our American passports, the examination was perfunctory. One of the officers checked our names off a list, stamped the passports and handed them back to us. We put them into our bags, rushed down the gangplank and hopped into a bus reserved for a group of tourists who weren't us—or rather we. We didn't have the required tickets, nor, to make matters worse, did we have any Swedish money. However, to get the tour under way without any further delay, the conductor of the tour offered to let us pay her when we returned to the ship.

So, on our return—after seeing the fabulous City Hall where the Nobel prizes are presented, and where one hall, about the size of two tennis courts, is done in gold mosaics, and the handsome residence of our American ambassador and the extensive offices of our embassy ("Why we need 'em?" Nila asked) and beautiful parks spilling over with fountains and flowers, and other fine sights—Nila and I, separated by several yards, sprinted up the gangplank to find somebody who would lend us enough Swedish money to pay off the conductor.

At the head of the gangplank stood the Swedish immigration officers, and as I started to dash by them one reached a hand out and demanded my passport. "But I'm going right back off just as soon as I get some money," I said.

"That's all right, I'll give it back to you when you go back off," he answered, and he plucked it from me.

Almost immediately I found an acquaintance who lent me the necessary Swedish money and I darted back down the gangplank, stopping only long enough to collect the passport.

Then, having paid off the conductor, I hurried up the gang-plank again, deposited my passport with the immigration officer and scurried around until I found Nila.

Fairly well tuckered out after all this excitement, Nila and I leaned our weights against the rail and watched the other passengers come aboard. Everybody was supposed to be back by five-thirty, according to the *Baltika's* bulletin board; but when six o'clock rolled around, somebody was still missing. And at six-thirty, he or she was still missing.

The captain, looking dour, got off and paced up and down the wharf. The first officer got off and joined him.

"It must be a Russian who hasn't returned," I suggested to Nila. "I don't imagine they'd hold the ship for anybody else."

"That's right," Nila agreed.

More time passed—a half hour, at least. The rail was lined solidly with passengers staring along the misty, darkening high-way that leads to Stockholm.

"Maybe the Swedish immigration officers refuse to allow the ship to go without everybody being accounted for," I suggested to Nila.

"That's right," Nila agreed again.

We waited some more.

At last the Swedish immigration officers left the ship and joined the *Baltika* officers on the wharf. They clustered close in conference.

"I hope those immigration officers remembered to leave my passport with the purser," I said lightly just to make conversation.

But I all but electrified Nila. She whipped around, her eyes wild. "What do you mean? Haven't you your passport?"

"No, of course not," I said, but my voice quivered, for her alarm was catching. "Those immigration officers took mine away from me when I came on board."

"Are you sure?" Nila clutched my arm with a vise grip.

"Of course I'm sure. They took everybody's away."

"And you didn't get it back from them?"

"No, I understood that when they finished checking them they would leave them with the purser . . ."

"I never heard anything like that." She stared at me accusingly. "They didn't take mine."

"They had to, Nila," I argued desperately. "They took everybody's to check up to see if everybody who got off got back on."

Nila plunged her hand into her bag and, after a few moments of scratching about, brought out her passport. "I told you nobody took it away," she said impatiently. "Now where's yours? You've got to have it somewhere."

I was positive I had given it up, but Nila was so positive I hadn't that, with my heart lurching from side to side dangerously, I opened my bag and searched it from back to back. The passport was not there.

"Come quick," Nila ordered. "We must find it before the boat sails."

Pushing our way through people and stepping on little children, we reached the purser's desk. "Have you Mrs. Ethridge's passport?" Nila demanded of a big blond Russian behind the counter.

"I believe so." He turned to a little blond man who was checking and rechecking furiously through sprawling stacks of passports. "Have you Mrs. Ethridge's passport?"

The little blond man, with nervous, shaking fingers, riffled through the stacks once more. I watched him, scarcely breathing. Reaching the E's, he slowed down, then stopped altogether. "Mrs. Willie Snow Ethridge?" he read.

"Thank God," I said fervently.

"Well, if you've got Mrs. Ethridge's, why haven't you got mine?" Nila demanded, waving hers in front of the men's noses.

For a moment I feared their eyes were going to pop from their heads. Then the big blond croaked, "Didn't the immigration officer take it from you when you came on board?"

"No," said Nila. "I came in a hurry and . . ."

The big blond spoke to the little blond. The little blond whipped about and spoke into the ship's telephone. Bells rang, horns blew, the captain and the first officer rushed aboard, the gangplank swung up and the *Baltika* edged out into the channel.

The "lost Russian" had been found.

4

As THIS WAS OUR last day at sea, an atmosphere of expectancy, bustle and urgency pervaded the ship. Except during the few hours we were tied up at Helsinki, most of us spent our time studying, with the help of the *Baltika*'s maids and stewards, the Russian language, making out declarations for the customs officers, and asking questions that nobody knew the answers to.

The old, old woman in my stateroom packed and unpacked a half-dozen cheap, small suitcases and pasteboard boxes and tied them with string and rope. From the very few English words she has spoken, I have learned she is a Lithuanian but has been living in Chicago for some years. Now, though, she expects to make her home in a village near Leningrad with her daughter and her son-in-law, who is Russian.

When she wasn't packing, she sat on the side of her bunk peering into a mirror pasted on the back of her light-brown pocketbook and plucked stiff white hairs out of her softly rolling chins. Her tiny blue eyes, peering from beneath heavy, white-lashed lids, watered from the strain.

Nila, of course, was highly excited all day. When I first saw her she asked, "You know who I write to now? Schenk." (Elizabeth Schenk is the very efficient woman who runs, so far as Nila and I are concerned, the Lee Keedick Lecture Bureau.) "I'm writing her not to write me to Russia on Keedick stationery. I don't want the Russians to know I make speeches. And that reminds me, Willie, please don't ever, ever mention Robert's name where anybody can hear you. I write M. Magidoff. Some of his old friends used to call him 'Magi.'"

She also asked me to lend her my many-colored hand-woven Greek bag with the long twisted-yarn handle, which I brought on the trip to bring back whatever presents I may buy that can't get into my suitcases. The handle goes over a shoulder and the bag hangs hip height.

"I want the Russians to get used to seeing me with it," she

explained. "It will be just the thing for me to carry out of the hotel with clothes and presents for my friends."

She also instructed me on many matters. As we were finishing breakfast and I opened my bag to get out my lipstick, she said solemnly, her eyes intent upon mine, "Willie, you must promise me something."

My heart skipped a beat. I had a premonition she was going to ask me to promise to accompany her body home in case she "meets with an accident" in Russia.

"Of course, anything," I said, reaching out my hand and laying it on hers by the side of her plate.

"Promise me you'll never put on lipstick in Russia where people can see you. I don't want the Russians to think you are nye *kulturnye*."

I smiled with relief, but Nila's face grew even more solemn. "I mean it, Willie. The Russians will consider it more polite if you undress in public."

"All right," I said, but without enthusiasm; then I added, "Is there anything else that I'm accustomed to doing that I shouldn't do in Russia?"

"Yes, several things. If you decide sometime you must put on make-up, please, please do it so that it's not noticeable. Russian women rarely use make-up."

"I'll try not to look like a clown."

"I don't mean that you ever use too much, but please in Russia be extra careful. Of course, it would be better if you didn't use any—"

I interrupted her. "What else?"

"Well, when you go into a restaurant with just one person, don't sit opposite that person. Sit next to him—catty-cornered, you know."

"Really?"

"Yes. If you sit opposite the person, somebody is likely to come up to you and say, 'Citizen, nye *kulturnye*.' You see," Nila went on, seriously, "if you sit opposite the person, you make it hard for anybody else to sit with you. If somebody wants to sit with you—and, in Russia, people almost always sit at tables with other people—you and the person you are with have to talk across him. And if two people sit with you, then you have to talk across both of them and they have to talk across you."

I was somewhat confused; but I was in the groove. "What else?"

"Don't ever clean your plate of all the food."

"Uncouth, eh? I mean, *nye kulturnye?*"

"Yes." Nila's face was sober. "It's considered very uncultured. Of course, I always do clean my plate, but then I'm a peasant. You, an American, should never do it. The Russians will be shocked. And, Willie, please don't ever wear a dress that is cut too low in front. No Russian man will understand it. You must always be very sure that not even so much as a quarter of an inch of your breast shows. Russian men are most particular about women being properly covered."

I started to say that American men are, too, but I thought better of it and said "husbands."

This concluded the *nye kulturnye* session for the morning and Nila and I went about our business of packing and writing letters to be mailed in Helsinki; but when the boat docked and we met for our safari into Finland, Nila was even more excited than before. She had been talking to a man on deck, she told me, when a Russian general approached them. "I did not say one word to him," she said breathlessly. "I just turned quickly and left him."

"But why, Nila? He might have been very interesting to talk to."

She shook her head at me as if I was absolutely hopeless. "God, Willie, can't you understand? I didn't want him to know I was Russian and get curious about me. Everybody in Russia is so suspicious—me, too." She looked hurriedly around and, finding no one within earshot, continued in a hushed voice. "You see, before I left the United States Robert and I decided that if there were any officials or diplomats on the boat, I should steer clear of them. It is their nature to report everybody and everything. They can't help it. They've been trained to suspect everybody and report."

So now I understand why she refused to talk to the young

girl in my stateroom and to the wife of the diplomat on the deck. And, no doubt, that's why she wouldn't allow me to join the Russians around the domino game; she felt if I did she'd have to go in with me and become involved with them.

"I've tried not to speak Russian to anybody," she went on, still in low, secretive tones, "but when it has been absolutely necessary I have spoke it with an accent, like a foreigner who has learned it late in life. Sometimes I speak it with a French accent, sometimes with an Italian accent and sometimes I even speak it with a Chinese accent."

She chuckled and I, relieved at the sound, grabbed her arm and we tripped down the gangplank to see what we could of Helsinki. And we saw a great deal, too, but still we were back on the ship in time to watch the other passengers come on.

For a goodly while we watched them indifferently; then suddenly Nila clutched my arm and whispered, "Look, Willie, here comes the General now—he's right there on the wharf. He doesn't look like two kopeks, but that's him all right." And without another word she hurried inside.

I continued on deck, and after an hour or so had passed and we were once more at sea, I strolled by the General, who was talking to an Englishman, and dropped like a handkerchief two of the five Russian words I've mastered up to now, "*Dobroye outro.*" They were not at all appropriate; they mean "Good morning" and now it was late afternoon; but they worked.

The General grinned all over his broad, brown face, bowed and said genially in perfect English, "Good evening. Won't you join us?"

I introduced myself, and the Englishman and the General introduced themselves. I didn't get the Englishman's name—after all he isn't a general, in fact not even a colonel—but the General's name is Rogov. He presented his card to me. He is the military attaché at the Russian Embassy in London.

Immediately, laughing all over his stocky self, he said he had a conundrum to ask me: Why is a wife like a sputnik with a dog?

I had to confess I had no idea. He couldn't have been happier at my ignorance. He locked his arm in mine and, with exuberant chuckles, explained that a wife when she is in a bad mood makes noises just like a sputnik with a dog—"Ruff-ruff-ruff."

And speaking of a wife, he remembered suddenly he had one in the stateroom and, still chuckling, excused himself to go and find out how she was doing. But in a few minutes he was back and, winking conspiratorially at the Englishman and me, whispered, "She's asleep."

Unfortunately, the Englishman was as solemn as the General was jovial. He talked fast and furiously about the new age that the sputnik has introduced and the horrible effects of the hydrogen bomb. "Every time an H-bomb goes off," he declared in summing up, "the Western world loses friends."

"Let that be a lesson to you," General Rogov said, grinning wickedly at me and poking my side with his elbow.

"And when Russia tests bombs she loses friends, too," I retorted quickly in defense of the Western world.

"Russia has finished testing bombs," the General said.

"Maybe for the present," I said, "but not for all time."

"Yes—" and now he was quite serious—"she's absolutely finished."

Then he began to talk enthusiastically about "Nikita Sergeyevich's desire for peace." But just as he was well launched a big blond woman appeared on the deck and beckoned to him.

"Pardon me, please," he said. "My sputnik calls me." And with a quick, wide smile over his shoulder, he was gone.

I looked for Nila to assure her the General was nobody to worry about; but I couldn't find her and I went to my cabin and there, as things so often happen in this world, she was. She had been waiting to give me my customs declaration.

When I told how friendly I found the General, she stared at me pityingly, glanced toward the berth where the old lady was to see if she was sleeping, and, satisfied that she was, questioned urgently, "Did he ask you anything about me?"

"No, he didn't mention you."

"Did you tell him anything about me?"

"No, of course not."

She seemed relieved; but the evening wasn't a happy one. After dinner we went to the music salon and there a huge woman (Nila commented, "She's hefty from every side"), a former opera singer from Kiev who is married to a Russian diplomat stationed in New Zealand, was leading a group in Ukrainian and Russian songs that Nila knew well; but when I suggested that she join in, she refused almost impatiently and a few minutes later announced that we must go to bed to be ready for whatever tomorrow may bring.

III

Leningrad

<u>1</u>   August 7

THE RUSSIAN CUSTOMS and immigration officers didn't wait for
the *Baltika* to dock at Leningrad, but came aboard when we
were three hours out and went methodically from one end of
the ship to the other.

By seven o'clock three of them were in our stateroom. They,
with the four of us, made quite a crowd. They were elegantly
dressed in pale-gray uniforms with blue collars studded with
gold stars, blue shirts and black ties. One was a translator and
took no interest in the proceedings unless the other two got
bogged down in a language strange to them.

They looked at my declaration. As I had put zeros where I
should have put nos, I was ordered to sit down and correct it.
These nos answer the questions Have I opium or hashish?
Have I presents for anyone in the Soviet Union? Have I anything to sell? Have I any Russian money? Writing my nos,
I wondered uneasily how Nila was answering the question about
presents.

The declaration also required that I put down how much
foreign money I have (it's humiliatingly little), what jewelry
containing gold, pearls and diamonds, and how many bags I
have.

The corrections made, the customs man glanced fleetingly

at my two bags, signed his name to the declaration and re-turned it to me with the admonition that I mustn't lose it, for I will be required to show it when I leave Russia. Then, bowing jerkily, he dismissed me.

I didn't leave the stateroom, however. I was interested to see how my cabin mates fared. The wife of the diplomat and her daughter had comparatively little trouble; but the old woman who was coming to Russia to live was given the works. They made her untie the ropes and strings about every paste-board box and every pasteboard suitcase and they rifled them with experienced fingers. A few threadbare blankets, a crocheted throw, a ball of knitted underwear, a yellowed corset, a shape-less pink nylon chemise. . . .

My mind flew to those Russians on the *Batory* returning with hundreds of pounds and even tons of goods. Oh, dear Lord, what must have happened to them when they reached the border city of Brest!

The officers were very polite; they even helped the old woman retie the boxes and suitcases; nevertheless, they left her a weeping, trembling hulk on the edge of the berth.

I had a hard time swallowing breakfast. The caviar, the smoked salmon, the hard-boiled eggs, the sliced tomatoes, the cold black bread went down slowly and lodged just below the base of my throat. Nila didn't have much appetite, either. The customs officers had opened her bags, but they didn't search through them and she answered no to the questions about presents for anyone in the Soviet Union, for she didn't want them to know she even knew anyone in the Soviet Union.

But it was before the officers appeared in her cabin that she had had the real jitters. She hadn't slept a wink all night, she told me. She'd tossed from one side of her berth to the other until she wanted to jump off the boat.

It was the thought that at last Russia was so close at hand, that in just a few hours the real test would come—the real test whether she was to be admitted into the Soviet Union or turned back—that had kept her wide-awake and almost wild. She didn't tell me this, though, and I am so insensitive a soul I didn't realize it until later.

Leningrad

As we slowly approached Leningrad through a narrow canal that bypassed the Neva River, on which this port is located, Nila paced the deck like a panther, looking neither to the right nor to the left; she spoke to no one, and as the *Baltika* eased to the wharf and I started down to my stateroom to see about my luggage, she called after me not to get off without her under any circumstances. "Don't leave me," she called urgently. "Don't get separated from me."

I heard her, but I didn't pay as much attention to her as I should have, for the old woman distracted me. When I reached the stateroom I found her collapsed in our one chair. Her loose, fleshy face was mottled from weeping and her hands lay crossed lifelessly in her lap over her customs declaration. Quickly I knelt beside her and tried to find out what was her trouble; but for many minutes I could make no sense of anything she said. Her lips trembling terribly, she mumbled something over and over, but what was it? Finally, however, I understood her to say she can't land, and I felt sick. How awful! How tragic! Here, old and weak as she is, she had traveled all the way from Chicago, first by train or plane to New York, then by boat to London, and then from London here to Leningrad, to be told she can't land. What will she do? Will they take her back to London on the *Baltika*?

I forgot Nila completely. I rushed about the boat, searching for an immigration or customs official to learn if anything could be done. I found no one and rushed back. The poor old soul was still sitting, weeping. The wife of the diplomat came in with a porter to collect her baggage. I struggled to explain the situation to her. She was sympathetic and tried to question the old woman further, but then her luggage disappeared through the door and she shrugged her shoulders helplessly and departed.

I dashed out again, up and down stairs, around decks, but, still unable to find an immigration or customs official, I returned to the stateroom and there, glory be, was a Russian man propelling the old woman out the door, and a porter following with all her baggage. She could land, after all! In fact, she could no doubt have landed all the time and was weeping only because she had to leave the ship. Who am I to understand Lithuanian?

"Are you her son-in-law?" I yelled at the man, but he didn't appear to hear me and I didn't really care.

"Goodbye! Good luck! Good trip!" I shouted. "Happy landing! Happy days!" I was really drunk with relief.

Now I must get my own baggage out and join Nila. I finally snared a porter (and this wasn't easy), followed him to the head of the gangplank and stood there as he plunged down it. Most likely it would be the last time I ever saw my bags, but I must wait for Nila. I recalled now her urgent words.

Practically all the passengers were already on the wharf, being hugged and kissed and wept over by relatives and friends carrying huge bunches of gladioli, zinnias, golden glow, roses, physostegia and just about all the flowers that grow.

I looked for the old woman and the Russian man. And, lo and behold, they were there! And now there was a middle-aged woman, too, on the other side of the old woman, holding her arm with one hand and a bouquet of flowers with the other.

Then suddenly there was Nila. Down on the wharf, of all places! She saw me and gestured wildly for me to come on. I could tell even from the deck that she was in a rage with me. And I didn't blame her. I had let her down when she needed me. And for an old woman who was practically a stranger. She will never understand it, I thought. I won't even try to make her. I won't even mention the old woman. I will mention only the milling crowds, the struggle to get a porter . . .

Yes, she was just as angry as I feared, but shortly she was swept up in locating the representatives of Intourist, collecting our bags and settling us in the car that Intourist had sent to meet us.

It was only after we had left the *Baltika* and the wharf with its innumerable Russian officials behind us that I understood the tension that had kept Nila wide-eyed the long night. Slumping into the corner of the seat like a bag of potatoes, her feverish eyes on the back of the driver and the representative of Intourist, she whispered to me, "We're in, baby!"

She didn't say another word until we drew up to the unimposing door of the Hotel Europe and made our way through several dingy marble lobbies to the woman clerk who assigned the rooms. Then she announced in English, "I'm Mrs. Ethridge's secretary and cannot be separated from her."

We were given two huge, hideous, but spotlessly clean rooms on the first floor. They have everything in them except a band. The sitting room is crowded with a heavy, blindingly bright, pale-colored desk, a cabinet, two chairs and, in the middle of the floor, a big round table with an orange cloth anchored with a cut-glass compote holding a large key.

"The covered table, dish and key are very Russian," commented Nila, sounding like her old self again.

There is also in one corner (I almost overlooked it, but how could I?) a round pedestal on which stands a marble figure. To add to the stuffiness, the sofa and the chairs are upholstered in thick red plush, slightly relieved by a small yellow design, and the two windows, opening onto the street, are hung with heavy gold plush draperies and lace curtains.

The bedroom is of the same elegance and, sure enough, as Nila predicted on the *Batory*, the beds are spread with those white envelopes, displaying colored blankets through their diamond-shaped windows.

When the porter brought our bags we thanked him but didn't tip him. Nila and I had heard and read that there was no tipping in the Soviet Union. However, he waited just where he deposited the bags and eyed us expectantly.

"If you're waiting for a tip," Nila told him, "we have no money. We're just off the boat and haven't had time to get any changed."

"I can take American money," he said quickly.

"No, I can't give you American money, but I can give you a package of cigarettes if you'd like one."

He accepted the cigarettes but still wasn't satisfied. He wanted two packs. Nila explained she hadn't another pack; the rest of the carton was somewhere in her luggage.

"Then I'll come back later for the other pack," he said, disgruntled, and he shuffled out.

So one illusion about the Soviet's proud, independent working class went down the drain.

While we unpacked, Nila mentioned casually that she might

accidentally see her "bottle" sister in Leningrad. She said the last time she had heard from her she was living in Leningrad, but as that was in the late nineteen forties, she could have moved, remarried or even died.

I had forgotten about this "bottle" sister, whom Nila had not mentioned in discussing her reasons for the trip; but now I recalled her clearly. Nila had described her very frankly for the book *Nila*: "She was so uninteresting I don't know how Mother begat her. She had no imagination, no creation, no nothing. . . . But she did have a very interesting shape. All her figure was just like a bottle . . . Whenever I was mad with her, which was almost all the time, I called her 'Bottles.' "

"If you see her, can't she tell you about your mother, sister and niece?" I asked excitedly.

Nila shrugged. "Maybe, but how can I locate her?"

In silence I hung up several dresses, then asked, "Have you decided, Nila, whether to send the letter to your mother from here or whether to wait until you get to Moscow?"

"I think I'll wait until I get to Moscow."

The unpacking completed, we hurried to the Intourist Bureau to meet the guide who was to show us about Leningrad. She was introduced only by her first name, Rheta. Her face is pale, with no trace of make-up or lipstick, her eyes somber brown, and her hair, which she wears in a large, tight bun on the back of her head, is auburn. She had on a dark, fairly well-tailored suit and short black string gloves. She speaks good English.

Standing in front of the hotel, waiting for our car, I was fascinated by an elderly woman in rusty black sweeping the wide sidewalk with an old-fashioned broom of switches, and by a young woman straddling the front part of a tractor that connects with the one forward wheel, and by all-age women hurrying past with black string bags called, so Nila told me, *avoska* bags, meaning "perhaps" or "maybe."

"Whenever Russian women leave home," Nila explained, "they put those bags in their pocketbooks just in case they see something to buy."

Today practically all of them were half filled with tomatoes, cabbages, cucumbers and loaves of bread.

None of the women was nearly so well turned out as Rheta. Their dresses were mostly of thin, sleazy materials resembling cheap voiles and rayons, and on their feet they wore socks and open-toed sandals with heavy, medium-height heels. The men looked terrible, too. They were coatless, hatless and tie-less, and their shiny, bell-bottomed trousers had enough cloth for two pairs of pants.

I hoped these people weren't indicative of the whole popula-tion of Leningrad, but when the car arrived and we swung into Leningrad's Fifth Avenue, Nevsky Prospekt, which is two and a half miles long and an impressive 108 feet wide, I saw hundreds of others just like them.

"They are dressed as they were ten years ago," Nila said sadly. "Maybe worse."

But Leningrad itself, if you can forget the shabbiness of the people, is romantic and magnificent. I kept wishing for Mark, who dearly loves history. An amazing number of buildings date back to the days of the first czars and they are extremely beautiful. There are long blocks of perfectly proportioned structures of brick covered with plaster, painted a warm, weathered shade of yellow, with a few soft-green and faded-rose ones interspersed among them; there are two hundred miles of tributaries of the Neva curving through the downtown streets beneath graceful bridges; and there are innumerable squares and parks of tuberous begonias in full bloom, of pink and red geraniums, of little carnations so much like our back-home pinks. There are also far-flung stretches of red salvia, which I'm not too fond of, but you have to admit they are *très gaies*.

Why hadn't somebody told me that the Communists plant flowers in all open spaces before palaces, museums, cathedrals, department stores, monuments and what have you? And why hadn't somebody told me there are runners of green grass and trees along the banks of the Neva?

Slowly we drove along one of these banks. On our left was the wide, gently winding, grayish-green Neva; on our right, the long, enchanting façade of the Winter Palace, a pale mayapple color, except for the white plaster moldings and countless slender pillars.

The driver stopped the car and we got out and crossed the street and, standing on the embankment, saw on the far side of the river the famous Peter and Paul Fortress, enclosing with its high granite walls the Sts. Peter and Paul Cathedral, which has the most incredibly tall, lovely, mast-thin spire. Inside the cathedral is the mausoleum of the Romanovs and the tombs of many of the other czars of Russia, including the greatest of them all, Peter the Great.

The fortress itself was the very beginning of Leningrad. Following the Russians' victory over the Swedes at Poltava in 1709, Peter decided to move his capital to the banks of the Neva and he first built the fortress to protect it.

"Peter the Great was a huge man and he stood right here on the Neva," Nila declared, holding up her long arm and shaking her fist, "and cut the 'window to Europe.' Ivan the Terrible had dreamed of it, but Peter accomplished it and it gave Russia terrific power. He built the whole city on swamps. Nobody believed it could be done, but he was the most determined, energetic man. He himself was working. He was carrying the material with his own hands and in his own shirt. Also thousands of serfs were working, mostly up to their thighs in water. Thousands and thousands died here. But as they died, new thousands were brought in.

"As you see already, Willie, Leningrad didn't grow like most Russian cities from a tiny group of houses inside a wall, spreading in widening circles; but it was built all at once on a big, magnificent plan. It is more like a modern European city. When it was finished, Peter the Great moved the capital here from Moscow. First, you remember, it was called Petrograd, then St. Petersburg, then when the Bolsheviks took over it was changed to Leningrad in honor, of course, of Lenin."

Rheta then got in a few facts about modern Leningrad. During World War II Leningrad was besieged by the Germans for 900 days, just a little less than three years, and during all that time her handsome buildings were camouflaged with streaks of black and white paint to make them look as if they had already been destroyed by bombings and her many huge monuments were either covered completely with sandbags or taken down from their pedestals and buried.

Before the war Leningrad had a population of approximately three and a half million; but during the siege 600,000 died of starvation and many thousands of others were evacuated and killed in action. However, today the population hovers at the prewar figure.

Suddenly, as Rheta talked, a gun boomed and both Nila and I almost jumped into the Neva; but it was just a peaceful announcement from the Peter and Paul Fortress that it was twelve o'clock.

Back in the car, we drove on and glimpsed the University of Leningrad with its forty institutes and fifteen thousand students, one of whom is Rheta. She goes there now absolutely free, she told us. The first year she paid forty rubles, roughly about ten dollars in the Russian exchange; but for the past three years she has paid nothing. In fact, the tuition in all the institutes and universities in the Soviet Union is free. Because of her high marks Rheta even receives extra scholarship money —260 rubles a month. Many students, she said modestly, receive much bigger scholarships because their grades are better.

"What do you want to be when you finish school?" I asked her.

"Either an interpreter or a teacher," she answered. "I'd prefer to be an interpreter, but I believe I'll be a teacher, because they need teachers more."

I didn't ask who "they" are, but I did ask does everyone have to take up the type of work that "they" say, and she answered, "Not everybody, but most do."

We got out of the car again beside the Neva and saw large groups of Russian tourists taking pictures beneath a giant bronze lion. Two of the young men were so delighted with the occasion they jumped up as soon as the camera clicked and kissed each other on the cheek and Nila commented, "I want you to notice, Willie, they aren't basic black. Russian men are just very demonstrative toward each other; much more so than women."

(These words, "basic black," are Nila's favorite expression for effeminate, "queer" men. She lifted them from the joke about the man dressed in black slacks, turtle-neck black sweater and a string of pearls who is sitting at a bar when another man comes in, notices the attire and asks the barman, "Why the pearls?" and the barman answers, "What else would one wear with basic black?")

Between beds of flowers and plots of green grass, we walked to the foot of the huge, handsome monument to Peter the Great. The statue is called the Bronze Horseman and Peter is shown with one arm outflung toward the sea, riding a rearing horse atop a granite rock weighing 1,600 tons and carved to resemble a breaking wave.

Here were many more Russian tourists, taking pictures and also listening to long lectures by their guides. Their clothes were so completely without style, so unmatched and dun-colored, I decided they must be on their first visit to a big city from faraway collective farms. However, there was nothing drab about their faces. They looked alert, eager and happy.

We drove on and saw beautiful St. Isaac's Cathedral, which is now a museum. It has a golden dome to end all golden domes; it soars higher than any other dome, spire or building in Leningrad and is as bright as new gilt, which is just as it should be, as the government has recently spent thousands of rubles to regild it.

Colorful, symmetrical flower beds are in front of it—and, incongruously, as we passed by there was also a grubby individual pulling a two-wheel cart loaded with a bed and a mattress.

"The transportation as when I was a girl," remarked Nila. "No doubt the man himself owns the bed and runs with it."

We stopped to see another palace, which is now the Lenin Museum (I was beginning to get the idea that all the former palaces are now museums) and to eye briefly the tank in which Lenin rode into Leningrad at the beginning of the Revolution. Nearby is a park dedicated to the victims of those bloody, stirring days. Beds of red salvia backed by masses of tall white day lilies fill the four corners, and a constantly burning flame centers it.

Nila was distracted from the names of the heroes chiseled into small stones by the sight of a blond girl in her teens, wearing a red sweater. "Look at her, Willie," she said, grabbing my arm. "Isn't she lovely? Such a beautiful face and no lipstick."

Returning in thoughtful silence to the car, Nila glimpsed a framed announcement outside a government building and pulled me over hurriedly to see it. "This is very, very interesting. This says people can enroll in a club here and learn to paint, to make artificial flowers, to do art embroidery, to knit and to cut and sew dresses. Can imagine the Soviet society caring about these things? I never heard of anything like it in my lifetime in Russia. It means now the people begin to care about how they live and how they dress. It is very interesting psychologically."

We spied in the distance another huge cathedral, this one with many colorful mosaic domes. Rheta told us it is the Cathedral of Blood and one of the czars was murdered there.

"Was it Alexander the Second?" I asked excitedly, having just finished reading that excellent book, *Marie Fedorovna, Empress of Russia,* in which this czar's murder is described in detail.

Rheta was not sure; so I mentioned the name of another czar who met with a tragic end.

"Why you care?" Nila broke in brusquely. "They were all killed at one point or another and that's what's important."

Rising above this, I asked Rheta could we visit the Cathedral of Blood.

"No," she said, "it's under repair."

Continuing to drive, we passed another cathedral and I asked could I visit it, and again the answer, "No, it's under repair."

"Are all the cathedrals under repair?" I asked sarcastically, but Rheta replied calmly, "Yes, practically all of them are."

"Will they reopen some day?"

"Of course. The majority, however, will no longer be cathedrals, but museums."

"There are some churches open now, aren't there?" I persisted.

"Certainly. Right now there are ten churches in Leningrad holding regular services—eight Russian Orthodox, one Roman Catholic and one Baptist—and one Jewish synagogue and one Moslem mosque.

"Where are all the statues of Stalin?" I asked just to see what she would say, for I hadn't expected to see any.

After only a moment, she answered, "They were taken away after Khrushchev's speech."

We passed more palaces, most of them that rich, weathered yellow, and arrived at the dignified, handsome Smolny Institute, which was originally built by Catherine the Great as a boarding school for the girls of the nobility but is now the City Communist Party Committee building. Over the doorway, a large gold-colored hammer and sickle stand out boldly against a sheaf of wheat. It was from here in 1917 that Lenin and his staff directed the Revolution. Two of the rooms—Lenin's and his wife's are now a museum, but Nila vetoed our visiting them. She was much more interested in the days of the "noble girls."

"Even if you were poor, but noble, you can go here in the czars' time," she told Rheta and me. "I don't understand it, but even noble families got poor sometimes and when they did, their girls can go here just like the girls of noble rich families. To be noble was the thing. Catherine the Great wanted to keep them separated so they wouldn't ever have to mix with the peasants.

"Many of these noble girls are in New York right now and every year they have a ball and come with velvet ribbons around their scrawny necks. My God, they're old; one is already ninety."

She was enthusiastically launched on a pet subject; but the appearance of a large group of Chinese tourists in the courtyard succeeded in diverting her. She crept up to the back of the circle, hoping, no doubt, to improve her Russian-with-the-Chinese-accent; but not at all—the guide was speaking Chinese.

We weren't finished yet. We must walk in Ostrovsky Square, right in the heart of the city, and look at the flowers and shrubbery and hundreds of people sitting on benches, some of them even lapping down ice-cream cones. They looked so carefree, so relaxed, so without tension and fears, I was amazed.

"I have read Russia has no unemployment," I said to Rheta. "Is that correct?"

"Absolutely. We have no unemployment at all. In fact we have more work to do than we have people to do it."

"How does it happen that so many people are sitting idly here in the daytime?"

"These people may be through for the day—they may work at night or on early-morning shifts—or this may be their day off. You may rest assured they all have jobs."

"Look, Willie," said Nila, "none of the women have on lipstick or make-up."

And nothing else either to improve their appearance, I was tempted to say, but I held my tongue.

Rheta waved her hand toward a large building and said, "The Leningrad Library, the second largest in the Soviet Union. It has thirteen thousand million books and pamphlets."

At least, that was what it sounded like, but it does sound like an unreasonable number of books, doesn't it?

Nila and I by now were both exhausted and starved, and we suggested to Rheta that we go back to the hotel and have dinner. (The Russians have dinner in the middle of the day and supper at night, just like most people in Georgia—Georgia in the United States, that is.) "I have seen all I can take in," I mumbled, and I staggered toward the car.

2   Afternoon

SAYING "LET'S HAVE DINNER" and having it in Russia are two completely different things. First we must visit the office of Intourist and get our books of meal coupons to cover our stay in the Soviet Union. There is a page of coupons for each day—breakfast, dinner, tea and supper. Each coupon is worth so many rubles, depending, of course, on the importance of the meal, and they are interchangeable. That is, if at dinner you don't eat a dinner's worth, you can give a breakfast coupon, plus, perhaps, a tea coupon. Or maybe a supper coupon fits the

87

bill. It's really better than a parlor game. If your coupons exceed the required amount, you can order candies or bottles of Narzan mineral water or even caviar to take to your room. There is no such thing as change.

Waiting for our books, we saw dozens of our acquaintances from the *Baltika*. As it had taken a considerable time to gather them and their luggage together and pile them in buses, they had only recently arrived at the hotel. Now they were being assigned to rooms in groups of eight. There is at the moment a scarcity of hotel space in Leningrad (in fact, only two hotels, the Astoria and the Europe, are considered suitable for Intourist tourists) and so, instead of spending the night, as they had understood they would do, they were being shipped out to Moscow at midnight. However, they were assured they can make up for the brevity of this visit when they return to Leningrad to catch the boat. The rooms for eight were just for washing up and resting their feet.

Coupon books finally in hand, Nila and I took an elevator to the dining room on the top floor. Luckily there are only five floors, for a sign that hit us between the eyes when we got off announced that the elevator only lifts guests up; it doesn't take them down.

Nila studied the menu, which was in four languages—Russian, Chinese, French and English—and ordered herring with sour cream, small filets of beef and tomato salad. Then we waited.

The dining room was full and everybody waited. In front of the windows overlooking the street was a long table of stocky, "no-neck" Russians—Nila was sure they were commissars of the party—and they waited. In an alcove was a big delegation of Chinese men, one attired in white robes and white shoes, and a delegation of Hungarians, and they waited. And in a corner next to Nila and me there were a group of American college boys and their tour conductor and they waited. In fact, they waited longer than anybody. One of the boys, in getting around the table to his place, unfortunately knocked off a water glass with the tail of his coat, and the tour conductor, trying to be helpful, gathered the broken glass into a plate and set it on a nearby unoccupied table. I don't know which of these simple acts insulted the waitress, but she retreated into a black, black mood. She ignored the boys and the conductor as if they weren't there.

After a half hour Nila remarked, "Willie, there is an old Russian saying, 'Take your patience in your hands,' and this is the time to do it."

After another half hour, she remarked, "My God, I'm getting a headache from starvation."

Then our first course arrived.

But the college boys still had nothing. The conductor had complained to the maître d'hôtel and the maître d'hôtel had tried to reason with the waitress, but she had turned a sullen ear and flounced away. Finally, in a sputtering and stomping rage, the conductor left the dining room for the office of Intourist.

The maître d'hôtel realized then the time had come for action. He relieved the waitress of further duties for the day and substituted a new waitress, and exactly two hours after the boys had sat down their food was put before them.

They were lucky at that, for as soon as dinner was over there was another round of sight-seeing. At least there was for Nila and me—and I'm sure for them.

"God, the life of the tourist is hard!" Nila moaned, and I couldn't agree with her more.

I tried to get more comfortable. I took off my hat, which is really a Hat, and my girdle and put on flat-heeled shoes. Nila eyed me disapprovingly, but she didn't say anything; evidently she understood this was not the moment.

We went first to see the Anichkov Bridge across one of those many arms of the Neva, the Fontanka, with its four gigantic statues full of movement and grace. Each of them depicts a huge, straining, muscular man struggling with a huge, straining, muscular horse, but each is different. They represent, so Rheta told us, the stages of man conquering nature.

Close by is the former Anichkov Palace, a favorite residence of the former czars and czarinas. It is now the Palace of the Pioneers, that organization of young people under sixteen of the U.S.S.R. and of the other "social democracies." Here Leningrad's future Communists, if they develop as planned by the Soviet fathers, gather daily in afterschool hours to study crafts, rope tying, camping procedures and such and, also, the tenets of Communism. We didn't go inside, for all the Pioneers are away at summer camps. We just stood at the handsome iron gates that used to swing open for the droshkies of the czars and czarinas and peered into the cobblestone courtyard.

Then we took a long ride to view Leningrad's biggest stadium, which holds 100,000 people—and it's only one of a half dozen. By the time we swept up the wide, circling road to the entrance, it was raining hard; nevertheless, Nila and I jumped out and gave the bowl a quick, watery glance. Across one side, above the top row of seats, is a bigger-than-life picture of Lenin and under it a banner proclaiming PEACE TO THE WORLD. Happily for the Soviet presses, the word for "peace" and "world" is the same, so the sign reads in Russian MIR MIRU.

"The plan is to put a glass roof over the stadium," Rheta informed us when we were back in the car.

"Over that whole business?" I asked doubtingly.

"Yes," she answered; then she added with pride, "And they will do it, too."

Grown boys, clad only in tiny dark-red trunks, were playing football (we call it soccer) in the street adjoining the stadium. "Look at them, Willie!" cried Nila, "Here we are almost in our woolen underwear and they jumping practically naked like a beast."

Well, I wasn't almost in my woolen underwear; but the rain was cold and so heavy we couldn't see out the car windows, and, so, secretly delighted, we suggested to Rheta to let us return to the hotel.

3   Evening

RETURNING TO OUR ROOMS, Nila and I both fell into bed and, though I constantly boast at home I can't possibly sleep in the daytime, the world was an absolute blank for me until Nila shook me awake and urged me to get up for supper.

"I don't want any supper," I moaned. "All I want to do is stay in bed."

"Cheer up! Maybe an orchestra is playing."

I couldn't have cared less at this point, but I did struggle to a sitting position.

"We'll have supper and then we'll walk about an hour," Nila said.

"Oh, lawd!" I had thought she was going to say "about a block" and was girding my loins for it—but an hour!

Trudging toward the elevator, we passed one of the English tourists who was leaving at midnight for Moscow. She barely moved and I had to speak to her twice before she heard me. "I'm beat," she said hoarsely. "Jolly well beat. But the person I really feel sorry for is the young American in our party who has to go to Paris before he can go home."

The table Nila and I were shown to was swept by a chilly draft, so, as soon as we had ordered, I went back downstairs for our sweaters. Though I was gone only a few minutes, when I returned there sat Nila as gay as you please with two fairly nice-looking youngish men.

"The waiter asked do we mind if they sit with us," Nila explained, "and of course I said no, and then the conversation started. I asked them what language they speak and they said Estonian, but naturally they speak Russian, too. All Estonians do."

I smiled and bowed at them and for a while that was as far as our friendship progressed. Nila and I were happily occupied with the lively and colorful activities around us. The dining room is big and rectangular, with a dance floor extending all the way down the middle and a large orchestra at the far end. Practically every table was filled with party-mood people, but only Nila and I seemed to have ordered supper. Waiters were rushing about, balancing trays laden with bottles of champagne and crystal compotes heaped with pale, green-skinned apples. I saw no vodka and, of course, no bourbon or Scotch.

The women, mostly in their teens and twenties, were evidently dressed in their best, but, except for two, you'd never give them a second glance. These two Nila called "wamps."

One was tall and thin and she was wearing a tight white knitted dress, the skirt split up a few inches on each side, with nothing noticeable under it, and long, loose-knitted black gloves. She was so *nye kulturnye* she didn't take the gloves off even to drink champagne and eat apples. Her shoes were black suède with squat, medium-height heels. ("Very walking shoes," commented Nila.) Yet, in spite of her clothes, from the shoulders up she resembled a Renoir portrait. Her blond hair was twisted into a huge bun atop her head and her neck was slim and graceful.

The other "wamp" was of a different school. She was a brunette with a very long black bob with bangs and she had on a skin-tight red dress, no girdle for sure, and cheap patent-leather shoes. It was her walk, though, that held the eyes of all the men, not to mention Nila's. "Look at her wiggle her hips with the slowest possible movement," Nila urged me. "She steps on one side, then makes a pause to give the people the time to admire, then steps on the other."

The men didn't look nearly so good as the women. Their two-pants-wide pants were not pressed; the shoulders of their coats had enormous padding as if they were ready to play football; and very few had on ties, though the majority wore shirts that required ties. However, there were some colored sports shirts, open at the neck, and one man even had on a sweat shirt and no coat.

"I wonder why they dress so bad?" Nila worried aloud. "Is it because they don't have or they don't care?"

The best-dressed people in the room were Finns, sitting at a table close by. One lovely, slim blonde among them was wearing a white piqué sack.

Nila was astonished to see the Finns. "Just a few years ago they were spitting on the Russians' backs and here they are! I'm so surprised I can't tell you."

As the time passed without our supper appearing, one of the Estonians grew indignant. He is a waiter back in Estonia, he told Nila, and it makes him furious to see the service in the Hotel Europe, especially with an American present. "The table hasn't even been set—no silver, no plates, no napkins. And look at the waiters in such dirty jackets. Don't they want to make a good impression on an American visitor?"

Evidently to help me pass the time until the food came, he got up, bowed in front of Nila and made a brief speech.

"The young man asks," said Nila, turning to me, "will the American lady give him the pleasure to dance with him and, my God, knowing you, I tell him yes."

The music was good; it was mostly American jazz of the twenties and thirties, and the Estonian was almost as beautiful a dancer as Ray Bolger.

I was wearing my best black crepe cocktail dress with a deep double fold down the back, caught near the hem with a bow, and black satin evening shoes. As the Estonian led me around the floor on the outskirts of the crowd where there was more space, I was conscious of the women who were dancing and sitting at the tables, twisting about and staring at me. Just what it was about me that attracted them I was not sure until I got back to Nila. "Ha-a-a!" she cried exultantly, rubbing her hands together. "How everybody turned and glued the eyes to your tail!"

The party waxed gayer. I forgot completely I had ever been weary. The dancing Estonian began to sing Estonian songs just loudly enough for Nila, the other Estonian, who sat quietly smiling like the Sphinx, and me to hear him. He looked and sounded amazingly like Danny Kaye. His bright, twinkling blue eyes rolled up into his head and down again like window shades; his thick blond eyebrows shuttled rapidly to the middle of his forehead and back; his body, his shoulders, his arms, held stiffly out from his sides, swung a fraction of an arc to and fro. He really couldn't have been more amusing.

"He should be in the movies," I kept saying to Nila, and I meant it. If I had the money and he had the permission of his Soviet-dominated government to travel I'd take him home as my gift to Hollywood.

When Nila and I finally finished supper, he invited us to join him and his friend in a glass of champagne. We said, "Thank you so much," and he called the waiter and told him, so Nila explained to me, to clean the table completely; champagne can't be served among dirty dishes and glasses. He also wanted the tablecloth changed. The waiter was stunned. He shook and shook his head. "It is impossible to change the tablecloth," he said. "The linen closet has already been locked up for the night."

"Then take off everything else," the Estonian commanded. The waiter dazedly followed instructions. He even crumbed the table with a filthy napkin.

The champagne arrived. The Estonian poured four glasses; then, standing, bowing deeply and elevating his eyebrows, he proposed a toast to America. We stood and drank. Then Nila said, "To Estonia." Then the Estonian, turning to Nila and lifting his glass, said, "To Russia."

And then, unworthy as I am, I was made an honorary citizen of Estonia. Taking a small black-and-silver pin from his coat lapel, the Estonian pinned it to the collar of my dress, lowered his head, kissed my hand and proclaimed that from this evening on I'm his fellow countryman.

The orchestra put away their instruments; the lights blinked; the waiters sprang to life, clearing tables, and most of the Russians departed; but a few Russians, all of the Finns, the Estonians, the Americans and a sprinkling of other nationalities lingered on and, suddenly, spontaneously, a conga line swept down the full length of the dining-room floor. My arms circled the waist of a Finn.

When I collapsed, Nila and the Sphinx-Estonian had their ears bent to a terrific row between a Russian man and his date at the next table. "Somebody came and asked her to dance," Nila whispered to me excitedly, "and she did and when she came back, oh my God, her man was in a rage. 'Whore' is a very polite word in Russian. He calls her a much, much worse word than whore. It is as dirty as can be."

So is whore, I wanted to argue, but the lights now not only blinked, they went out. With the Estonian singing an Estonian version of what Nila calls "rolling on the rocks," the four of us, arms locked, stepped in time down the five long flights of marble stairs. I had one comforting thought—I'm in the middle and the middle is carpeted.

94

Leningrad

<u>4</u>   August 8

As I STRUGGLED UP and began to put on my most comfortable clothes for another full day of sight-seeing, Nila, who was dressing, too, stared at me for some minutes with a dark scowl on her face, then blurted out, "I suppose I shouldn't ask you to do so much for America, but I do wish you'd wear your dressy shoes and your good hat. I hate for the Russians to think Americans don't know how to dress. There you were yesterday afternoon in that old beret and those flat, rubber-heeled shoes, looking as beaten by the life as anybody in Leningrad, maybe worse, and I was embarrassed for you and America."

Well, I must say I resented this a bit; I didn't know I had looked that bad. Nevertheless, I agreed to wear my best shoes and hat until we arrived at Peterhof, the famous palace and gardens built by Peter the Great about eighteen miles from the city, which was our goal for the morning, and then change to the beret and the flat, rubber-heeled numbers.

Beyond the outskirts of Leningrad, the highway to Peterhof passes through flat, unkept, uncultivated land overgrown with grasses and small trees, and the little houses scattered over it are built rather picturesquely of wood and painted either chocolate brown or pea green. Pansies—the Russian word for which, Nila informed me, means "eyes of Ann"—bloomed in the little fenced-in front gardens.

We were not permitted inside the magnificent palace itself, for it, too, is under repair. During the 900-day siege of Leningrad it was occupied by the Germans—not only by troops but by their horses as well. By the time they left, only the outside walls were intact.

But no matter how fabulous the palace may be behind its extensive, elaborately decorated yellow façade, it can't possibly equal the gardens that stretch below it to the Gulf of Finland. Here are 170 fountains, 127 of which have been repaired since the war and send millions of gallons of water spurting skyward, splashing downward and spilling out of make-believe rain trees.

The most terrific cascade begins at the base of the palace, which is on a ridge; from there it falls between giant bronze statues to the flat, filled-in marsh below and then flows into a canal, wide enough for pleasure boats, that runs to the Gulf. All these huge statues are new (the Nazis shipped the old ones back to Germany) and they are gilded a blinding shiny gold that upset Nila terribly.

"The damned Germans!" she muttered, clenching her fists. "The damned, damned Germans!"

We strolled along broad clay paths through heavenly forests and green stretches of open lawns. Women were cutting the grass with garden shears. There wasn't a lawn mower in sight, though there were acres and acres of grass to be cut. The muscles stood out like ropes along the big legs of one stooped-over woman.

I heard people laughing abandonedly in a clump of woods and was thunderstruck. It's only my second day in Russia, remember, and I wasn't expecting to hear Soviet citizens laugh out loud, especially in broad daylight.

We followed the sound and came to a cleared space full of children and mamas and papas, their faces amused and expectant. Hugging themselves ecstatically, they dashed under a "magic" oak tree that rains when the "spirit" moves it and dashed out again. Not to get wet was the aim, so of course the laughter was loudest when the tree rained and caught somebody. This is the Oakling Jester Fountain: it was built in 1872, but, naturally, only since the Revolution have the masses played and shouted around it.

Near it is another trick fountain, the Parasol Fountain, and still another is in the corner of the formal garden of Mon Plaisir, the exquisite little palace where Peter lived while Peterhof was under construction. This fountain is in the form of a bed of innocent-looking small pebbles, some of which send up jets of water when accidentally trod upon. Many giggling boys and girls and their elders, including me, tried to make it across the bed without stepping on the water-spouting rocks, and some managed it, but not I. I was soaked in the most unattractive and uncomfortable place, and oh! how the Russians doubled over with glee.

Close by on a bench sits an old man, his head buried in a book. Rarely does he glance up and then only fleetingly, as if the hilarity disturbs him. Yet he is the culprit who turns the water off and on. He has two confederates, of course, hidden in the bushes by the Oakling Jester Tree and the Trick Parasol. And these three are paid regular wages by the government of the Soviet Republic! I must admit they presented a brand-new side of the Communist fathers and I began to understand that there is nothing too good for the Russian Public as long as it remains public.

It is when the public breaks down into individuals that the rub comes. Driving back to Leningrad, I saw women carrying buckets of water hanging from yokes across their shoulders, and Rheta explained that very few homes and apartments in the suburbs have running water and that these women had been to a well in the neighborhood. And even those who have running water frequently don't have bathrooms. For instance, she and the other three members of her family live in one room without a bath, though there are a toilet and a kitchen which they share with four other families.

"But Khrushchev has promised," she told me, "that every family will have an apartment—not just one room—in ten or fifteen years."

"I'm sure you must be looking forward to that time," I said.

"No," was her surprising answer. "I've got used to living the way we do. I have an aunt who lives in an apartment with eleven families."

Nila spoke up. "I know how that is. I once lived in an apartment with eleven families."

"Rheta, what do you do when you need a bath?" I inquired.

"I go to a public bath."

"How public?"

"Well, usually about forty women bathe together in one room."

"Do people still have perfect strangers to scrub their backs?" Nila asked.

"Yes."

Nila and Rheta laughed gaily as if this was a delightful memory. Then Nila said, "My God, I remember like yesterday the way everybody scrubbed everybody else's back. And with such a strength! Wanting to please, the scrubber would ask the stranger, 'How you like your back—rare, medium or well done?'"

These and other happy reminiscences ended only when we arrived at the hotel and saw, across the street, a large crowd gathered around a new blue-and-white Ford station wagon, and a truck without a driver, the engine still running, standing in the middle of the street. I jumped to the natural conclusion there had been an accident and suggested to Nila that we rush right over; but she vetoed it. "It is nothing to see," she said, shrugging. "The Russians are just admiring that station wagon. When Robert and I lived in Moscow and had a Studebaker, I had to call the militia to clear the way to the car every time I went shopping."

When we finished dinner and came out of the hotel for another sight-seeing jaunt, the crowd was still there, only larger. One Russian was flat on his back on the pavement under the chassis, another was wiping the dust off the windshield, and another was lovingly stroking the hood.

I shouldn't admit it, maybe; but I would have preferred watching these station-wagon watchers to going to a museum. However, Nila and I had told Rheta we wanted to visit the Hermitage Museum, which now occupies most of what was the Winter Palace, and so go there we must.

The Hermitage has 1,058 glorious, gem-studded rooms, and though we didn't see quite all of them, my feet feel as if we did. We gazed at hundreds of El Grecos, Titians, Rubenses, Van Dycks, Rembrandts (there are forty Rembrandts alone), Picassos, Renoirs, Matisses—you name them and the Russians have them. Also sculptures by Michelangelo, Bernini, Houdon, Canova and many, many others. Also magnificent tapestries, carved ivories, porcelains, and thousands of objects made of jasper, agate, malachite, silver, gold, crystal. The collection was started by Peter the Great and it was continued zealously by all the czars that followed him.

I was surprised that these amazingly beautiful and priceless things survived the Revolution. I would have thought that during those long, bloody days of fighting all the palaces and estates of the nobility would have been looted. But Rheta explained that the Bolsheviks set up committees to take over these buildings and preserve them intact for the education and pleasure of all the people.

And all the people were here. Reminding me of cotton mill hands swarming out of the mill gates when the evening whistle blows, they surged through the spacious hallways and the huge galleries and up and down the wide, wide marble stairs.

Yet there were people outside. Many of them were still around the Ford station wagon when we got back to the hotel, and this time Nila and I joined them. They were ringed tightly about a young American, the driver of the station wagon, and were firing questions at him, mostly in Russian but some in halting English. One Russian boy was translating.

The American was a gentle-faced, clean-cut, aristocratic-looking youth and he was perfectly turned out. His suit was a neat tweed, well tailored and pressed, his shirt white with the collar immaculate, and his tie a small-figured navy-blue silk.

One man near Nila and me was curious about the two buttons that held the corners of the collar down.

"They play no practical part," his companion answered, knowingly. "They're just for decoration."

Another was attracted by the narrow coat lapels; they were much narrower than the Russians'.

However, it was the station wagon that concerned the Russians most. "How much does a car like that cost?" one asked.

"Twenty-five hundred dollars," the American answered.

The crowd showed its astonishment. At the government rate of exchange for Russians, this amounts to only 825 rubles, which, Nila whispered to me, is much cheaper than the cheapest Soviet car.

How many gallons does it get to the mile? another asked.

How much is the down payment? How much are the monthly payments? What are the carrying charges?

As these questions were asked and answered, some people strolled about the station wagon. One man, shaking his head disapprovingly, growled, "Such a beautiful car and such dirty windows." And one short, fat woman was entranced with what she called "the big, lovely jars" behind the back seat and was absolutely staggered when Nila told her they were only tin cans for the emergency supply of gasoline.

The Russians also asked the American how much it costs him to go to school, how long boys and girls are required to remain in school, whether there are TV sets in United States schools.

The youth answered questions until his lips were dry and chapped. Frequently he closed them tightly and drew them in as if to wet them.

"You've had a lot of failures with your sputniks, haven't you?" one Soviet citizen called out.

"Yes. And how about you?"

"We don't know," came the amazing reply. "They don't tell us."

A momentary interruption occurred when one Russian, who had been practically hypnotized, discovered that the ice-cream tart he was taking home in a pasteboard container was melting onto the sidewalk; muttering, he hurriedly wormed his way out of the crowd. Instantly, though, the crowd re-formed and the session continued; and it was still going strong when Nila and I decided that we, too, must worm our way out and dress for dinner. However, it would have had to end soon, for when we reached the dining room the young man was already there with a middle-aged, distinguished, successful-appearing man. We stopped to congratulate the boy on his performance and learned that his name is Robert Bolton Hughes and he goes to Yale, and the older man is his father, Dr. Bolton Hughes of Philadelphia.

Dr. Hughes was delighted with the curiosity and warmth of the Russian people. He and his son have had huge, questioning crowds around them everywhere they stopped since crossing the Finnish-Russian border. Today they weren't even able to get into the station wagon; they've had to do on foot what little sight-seeing they've done.

"I think we'll stay here ten or twelve days longer than we'd planned," Dr. Hughes declared, "and do the city block by block. Why, this station wagon is enough to put an end to the Revolution."

"Have you the permission?" Nila asked.

"No, but the Russians are so friendly I'm sure they won't mind."

"*Bozhe moi!*" Nila exclaimed. "*Bozhe moi!*"

Dr. Hughes gave her an unconcerned glance. Evidently he didn't know that *Bozhe moi* means "My God!"

Nila and I excused ourselves and went to a movie, *Gay Boys*, which was made by the Russians more than a quarter of a century ago and is now showing in two or three or maybe more theaters in Leningrad to packed houses.

We went to the second show at nine o'clock and we walked the six or seven long blocks alone with no one paying the slightest attention to us, though at first Nila couldn't believe it. All the way, she kept looking nervously over her shoulder and whispering, "Willie, I don't see anybody following us— and don't think I wouldn't know it if somebody was. I've been followed too often in my life not to know it." And finally, under the lights of the marquee, she said in wide-eyed awe, "Can imagine—here we are in Russia, going and coming at night just as we please, and nobody caring? I simply wouldn't have believed it. Just wait until I write Robert!"

Suddenly, while waiting in the lobby for the doors to open for the second performance, Nila grabbed my arm and whispered, "My God, Willie, I think I see my 'bottle' sister!" With her eyes and head she indicated a short woman with huge calves, tapering to fairly small ankles, directly in front of us; but then the woman turned around and Nila relaxed her hold. She was a stranger.

The movie was the most outrageous slapstick comedy, but the Russians laughed so uproariously I found myself now and then laughing, too.

HAVING TOLD RHETA we wouldn't need her any more, Nila and I set off right after breakfast to prowl about the city. We went first to Leningrad's largest department store, Gosteny Dvor, which covers a full block of fashionable Nevsky Prospekt, and Nila immediately was tremendously impressed by the fashion magazines for both men and women and the patterns for women's clothes, which, she said, never existed in Russia in her day.

Thumbing through the women's magazine, she was amazed. "Could be written here *Vogue*," she exclaimed. However, *Vogue* could never command the price. One issue sells for the equivalent of five dollars in Russian money. On the front of the men's magazine were swank gray-haired figures, one wearing a tuxedo and one a brown tweed sport jacket—"Two things the Russian man needs for everyday," Nila commented wryly. With the tuxedo were shown a white tie and a white vest.

There was also a brand-new do-it-yourself magazine (we saw the second issue) for women who want to learn to make their own clothes.

Nila also studied the patterns. The dresses were slim and stylish and the directions complete. "These will revolutionize the way Russian women look," she predicted. "Just give them a little time until they learn how to use them."

Near the pattern counter is a curtained-off area where women can bring their material and have it cut. Here "fashion experts" will choose the proper style and cut a simple dress, suit or even raincoat for nine rubles—less than two dollars at the Russian exchange. To cut a more "shoo-shoo" (Nila's translation) dress costs ten rubles.

But the prices of material are something else again. Enough material of a good quality will cost between $70 and $100. Naturally at these prices there were very few customers and so Nila and I were able to carry on our research in a cloisterlike seclusion; but, as research under the most favorable circumstances is to me mentally fatiguing, I dragged Nila into the more frivolous cosmetics department. And here, believe it or not, were those *nye kulturnye* items, lipsticks. Not a big selection, you understand, but enough to brighten my day. Also perfume, powder, toilet water and soap. And every ounce of everything, of course, was made either in the Soviet Union or in one of the "social democracies." The clerk didn't care to admit it, though. When, smiling innocently, I asked for Arpège, she said she was just out of it. (Lord knows what I would have done if she'd been in it.)

This clerk and all the others wore brown sateen uniforms with small pins, embossed with the name of the store, on their shoulders.

Nila and I next gave the eye to the sports department and for a minute or two I thought I was in Abercrombie & Fitch. All over the place were tennis racquets, volleyballs, tennis balls, tennis nets, soccer balls, sport shoes, dominoes and enough sets of chess to supply all the Republican clubs in the United States.

Then suddenly Nila and I were in the midst of a milling mob. Mamas and papas were buying school supplies like mad. "Oh," said Nila, "I saw an editorial in *Pravda* this morning, reminding parents that school starts the first of September and to get their children ready."

Nila and I made it to the counter and got into a conversation with a man I judged to be in his late thirties. He had an open, lean face, brightened with the most alive black eyes. He bought a book satchel for 58 rubles ($14.50 to him, remember), six notebooks, a copybook, and a pencil box full of assorted pencils. The clerk totaled the bill on an old-fashioned abacus and it came to well over 100 rubles. Yet he earns, so he told us, only 1,000 rubles a month.

"But there is nothing too good for the child," he said hurriedly, and he looked down at a little girl by his side, his face and even his narrow shoulders seeming to melt with love.

A Russian, I thought to myself, isn't supposed to look at his child with such tender affection.

The little girl had on a white-and-blue-checked dress and a round skullcap "embroidered" with white braid, and she carried two "perhaps" bags, a quarter full of tomatoes and cucumbers.

"She is the best pupil," he went on, unconsciously straightening his narrow shoulders, "and so I buy only the best for her. She makes all fives."

"Fives is the very highest mark," Nila explained to me quickly, "and one is the worst mistake."

"I congratulate you," I said to him. Nila interpreted it, but he didn't hear her, so the little girl pulled at his shabby, shiny coat and said, "Papa, the lady congratulates you."

"Ah, I thank you," the man exclaimed, his face radiant.

Then he told me the child's name is Linda and he has two other children, a boy, ten, named Paul, and a girl, four, named Lena. The boy also makes "fives," and the father hopes the littlest one will, too, when she starts to school. In addition to the "supplies," he has to buy schoolbooks, but they aren't expensive. "And even if they were," he said, "I wouldn't mind. I don't mind sacrificing everything for the children."

He works on a machine in a textile factory; but at night he goes to a technological institute to study to be an engineer. He has been doing this for five years and he has one more year to go.

Eying me sharply with his bright black eyes, he asked, "Does anybody in America work in the daytime and go to school at night?"

"My very own son-in-law does," I answered proudly.

He looked taken aback for a moment, then recovered and told me that he gets his education and medical attention free, though he does have to pay for his books, which, unlike his children's, are very expensive. He added that he could read them in the library but preferred to have them "under the hand," as Nila interpreted.

Then he asked about my family, unemployment in the United States, movies and books. "I'm sorry I've read so few American books," he apologized. "I've read only Dreiser and Longfellow. I like Dreiser very much."

He then declared he and all Russians are anxious that the Russians and the Americans be friends. "We fought together like brothers against fascism," he said with the greatest seriousness, "and we must continue to be brothers. And our children must be friends, close, close friends." He hooked his two little fingers together to show how close the tie must be.

And a moment or two later, when we parted, he crushed my hand and sent his regards to everybody in the United States and special regards from Linda, Paul and Lena to my children and even my grandchildren.

In a glow Nila and I sauntered on until we came to the infants' department, where I admired an elaborately embroidered linen envelope in which to slip a baby. Thinking I might bring a half-dozen home to young mothers I know, I asked the price and was told it cost 270 rubles ($27 in my money).

"Gosh, it's so terribly expensive!" I said.

"Yes," the clerk agreed. Then she added the now familiar words, "But there's nothing too good for the children."

Walking by the shoe department, which has no conveniences such as clerks, chairs or stools, but only one woman behind the counter, we saw a woman stoop over and thrust three pairs of brown rubber-soled shoes with cloth tops, similar to tennis shoes, into a suitcase spread open on the floor, and we stopped beside her and Nila inquired how she could afford such a purchase.

With no show of resentment at the question, she said they were for her and her two sisters. "We live in the north of Russia," she explained, "where there is nothing to buy, so one of us must come to Leningrad and shop for all."

We moved on and arrived at what might be called the on-wheels department. Children's tricycles, bicycles and baby carriages cluttered up the floor, and a huge red banner with letters of gold hung from the ceiling. "They have overdone their selling quota," Nila said. "Last month they sold seventy baby carriages."

A pretty, black-haired clerk demonstrated for my special benefit how the wheels of one model, descending a flight of stairs with a mama at the handlebars, let down automatically at each step, saving the mama's arms from being jerked from their sockets and the baby from being all shook up. (A flight of stairs was right there for the demonstration.) She also folded the carriage into a suitcase-sized package for storing.

"It's very thoughtful of the Communists," commented Nila, "to keep the small, crowded apartments in their busy minds."

The clerk ran after us as we were leaving and, shaking my hand and bowing repeatedly like a small tree in a storm, said urgently, "Please come back and bring all your friends with you. All come. All are welcome. And please give my regards to all the American people."

We hadn't begun to see the entire department store, but we'd had enough for one morning and so we departed and went to the Kazansky Cathedral, which is now an antireligious museum. Several groups, made up mostly of school-age children, were being shepherded from one exhibit to another by earnest lecturers. The young listened attentively, their eyes wide and glinting, their mouths frequently open.

"The Russians want to learn everything," Nila said. "Willie, you will see it for yourself. They have the greatest thirst there is for knowledge."

Nila and I joined one of the groups, but I learned very little. Nila couldn't interpret for me without disturbing the others and, besides, she didn't comprehend many of the religious terms used by the lecturer. "Whew," she groaned at one point, "I will have to develop a brand-new field in my language."

I did understand that the lecturer, tapping with her ruler on the Bible and at illustrations on the wall in one alcove, listed what she termed the "conflicts" in the Four Gospels with well-known historical facts, and in another alcove, pointing to the Egyptian, Indian and Japanese illustrations of God in three persons, declared that the Christian church hadn't even bothered to invent anything new when it presented to the world the Father, Son and Holy Ghost triumvirate.

We didn't follow the group long, but wandered about on our own, gazing into the many cabinets holding the priceless objects taken from the Russian Orthodox Church at the time of the Revolution. The purpose, of course, is to show the people the tremendous wealth of the Church under the czars in spite of the abject poverty of its downtrodden peasant members. There are miters, Bibles and crosses, laden with emeralds, diamonds, rubies and sapphires bigger than thumbnails; robes of the high priests, stiff with threads of gold and ropes of pearl; and ikons fashioned entirely, except for the faces, of pearls and other precious stones.

In one cabinet, documents set out that the Church had been second to the state in wealth and that despite this the state had given it sixty million gold rubles a year.

A panel containing the images of three hundred saints excited Nila exceedingly. "When you had troubles in the old days, and of course everybody had troubles," she explained, "you could come, light candles and pray to any one of these saints." She got up close to the panel, narrowed her eyes and studied the saints, one by one. "Here is the saint you pray to if you are afraid of fire . . . and here is the saint for the headache . . . and here for the teeth . . . and here when you give birth to the baby and want it not to be so hard . . . and here is rain for the harvest . . . and here for the household problems. Can imagine, Willie, three hundred of these saints?"

The exhibits went on and on, but Nila and I didn't. We rode an escalator hundreds of feet underground, caught the subway and visited seven or eight—I lost count—of the most fabulous subway stations in the world, I'm positive. Nila told me Moscow has some fine ones, too, but I don't intend to go near them. Those of Leningrad are enough; in fact, they are too much. They are more lavish than the most lavish ballrooms I've ever seen, including those on stage and screen. I kept expecting somebody to ask me to dance.

They have shiny floors of the finest marble and the finest stone and not one cigarette butt or Milky Way wrapper or old newspaper or wad of chewing gum or anything to mar their pristine cleanliness. And they have marble, granite and glass walls and marble, granite and glass columns and they are lighted with hundreds of candelabra and chandeliers. In one station there are thirty (I counted them) huge crystal chandeliers with chimneys of the most heavenly shade of dark-blue glass. Some of the chandeliers hang right over the tracks where the trains run. Altogether the chandeliers in this one station hold 50,000 electric-light bulbs. And the columns supporting the vaulted roofs are made of two layers of glass, etched with bas-reliefs and circled with strips of bronze.

"Who invent things like this?" cried Nila, echoing my sentiments exactly.

6   Evening

NILA AND I WERE in the hotel dining room, waiting for our supper to be served, when the waiter ushered to our table a pink, plump-cheeked, blond-haired American of medium height and indeterminate age. Swiftly he eyed Nila and me, and though he made no outward sign it was plain to see he shied from us inwardly. Without a doubt he wanted to be with someone young and Russian, and here he was being planked down with two anything-but-young females from his own country.

"This is Nila Magidoff," I said brightly, waving my hand toward Nila, "and I'm Willie Snow Ethridge."

He muttered his name—I caught what sounded like Ward—and glumly studied the menu. He was so unhappy he was almost rude.

Then another American landed unhappily at our table. He was tall—at least six feet—dark, handsome and young. Again I introduced Nila and myself, and then suddenly, excitedly, this paragon looked straight at me and said, "I know you—you're the woman who wrote the book about that Russian . . ."

By this time Nila had her napkin over her head and was pretending to slide under the table. Nevertheless I said with a flourish, "And here is that Russian right here."

Well, the young man is Peter Gillingham, the nephew of Mrs. William Cotton of Louisville, my friend and right hand during the years I was Kentucky chairman of Russian War

Relief. Peter himself came once to my home—and Mark's too, of course—to confer with Mark about writing some newspaper article about a flying stunt he had under consideration. He is from Los Angeles and is a student of law at Yale.

Ward perked up now that we'd been joined by this most presentable young man, and shortly Nila told him and Peter that after supper we were going to a Park of Culture and Rest and if they would like to come with us they'd be welcome. In this park, she explained, as in all Parks of Culture and Rest throughout the U.S.S.R., there are bands playing, people dancing, movies showing and other forms of entertainment going on. Yes, they said, they would like to come.

So we hopped into the Intourist car that was waiting for us and set out. On the way—which was very beautiful, for we drove along the Neva, where the Winter Palace and other big public buildings and the bridges crossing the river are gold-washed with many lights—we learned that Ward's name is not really Ward (I had misunderstood him completely, but it suited him and I decided to continue calling him by it); that he's in his forties, a bachelor and, of all things to be in the Soviet Union, a broker; and that Peter is on a fellowship, studying some phase of Soviet law, and speaks Russian.

The minute Nila heard of Peter's knowledge of Russian, she announced that he would do all the interpreting that was necessary during the evening and that she would be an American tourist who didn't understand one word of the language.

On reaching the park on the far side of the Neva, we got out of the car and hiked down wooded paths toward a dance floor. We could hear the music a long way off. At the gate in the high fence surrounding the floor, we discovered it costs five rubles apiece for admission; but Nila refused to let us pay it. "The Russians will let us in free," she said. "I know their psychology and they want to do everything for the tourists." And she rushed up to the ticket taker and talked very fast in English. And, sure enough, we were swept through the gate with no exchange of filthy lucre.

At least a thousand young people were dancing on the rough floor of unpainted planks. Many girls were dancing with girls and many boys with boys, and the boys, as Nila was quick to point out, weren't "basic black."

As we stood on the outer edge of the dancing multitude, a nice-looking woman in a gaily embroidered peasant blouse and skirt topped with a long white coat, came up to us and, after introducing herself as the hostess, asked Ward, who was smoking a cigarette, not to smoke. It is not allowed, she said. Ward snuffed the cigarette out and put it in his pocket. And he a capitalist, remember!

The director of the orchestra announced that the next dance would be for girls only and Nila said, "Willie, let us go into the act." So we took our places with a hundred or more "girls" lined up two by two, hands joined, and when the orchestra swung into an old-fashioned waltz we took two steps forward, "one, and two," and turned around on "three." "This dance is called Pompadour and no man dance it," Nila told me.

When the music stopped, we found our two men sitting on a bench on the sideline, watching a wrinkled-faced hunchback as he invited one girl after another to dance with him and was refused.

Then the orchestra crashed into "Yes, Sir, That's My Baby" and Nila and Ward jumped to their feet and began "gingerbugging," as Nila has always called jitterbugging, with the abandonment of two fifteen-year-olds, directly in front of Peter and me. The jitterbug has been Nila's favorite dance since she learned it the first Christmas she spent with Mark, the children and me in Prospect, and she threw her whole self into it. And so did Ward. He drew his shoulders together, kept his upper arms tightly to his sides and made quick, short, rather squirming steps.

At least one third of the Russians stopped dancing to stare at the two with serious, concentrated faces. They formed a huge circle, leaving only a small gap in front of the benches.

Peter and I were still seated when suddenly the hunchback flung himself across us and plunged to the edge of the open dancing space. Squatting there for a few minutes, he swung his deformed body and snapped his fingers in perfect time to the music; then he leaped to his feet and reached out his hand toward Nila.

Quickly she turned away from Ward and began to dance with this gnomelike creature. The crowd was electrified, tense. It grew larger and larger.

A whistle shrilled above the music and a militiaman plowed through the circle. Arriving on the front line, he halted abruptly, a look of absurd shock on his face. It was evident he had expected to find a fight to the death.

The music stopped. The hostess pushed forward and introduced a thin young man, neatly dressed, to Nila and Ward. He is in charge of the entertainment at the dance hall and he asked, "Will you be so kind as to tell me what dance that was you demonstrated?"

When they told him the jitterbug, he wanted to know the names of the other new dances in the United States. They mentioned the samba, mambo, conga, cha-cha, and then the thin young man bowed and asked Nila would she give him the pleasure of the dance. Nila was still pretending she didn't understand Russian and so she just smiled and glided off in his arms. Then a boy no older than eighteen, with wild, long, curly black hair, asked her to dance. And then another came and broke in. And then the curly-black-haired one returned. The orchestra by now was playing, or rather "murdering," as Ward growled, "I Love Paris."

Finally the evening was over. Nila put her hand on the arm of the black-haired one as if she were walking in to dinner on the arm of an ambassador and came over to Peter, Ward and me. Her face was flushed; her gray eyes twinkled.

"Only once before in my life have I had such success," she crowed, "and that was at that debutante ball in Boston where all my partners were Republicans by tradition."

Ward was not nearly so enthusiastic about the evening as Nila. "Do the Russians call this fun?" he asked glowering. "Here I have spent a long evening dancing without a cigarette and with no place, damn it all, to get a drink. God knows it doesn't take much to make the Russians happy."

IV

Moscow

<u>1</u>   August 10

CHILLED TO THE BONE, I woke up very early this morning on the crack train, the Red Arrow, that runs between Leningrad and Moscow. I spread my coat over me and stared out the train window.

A little after midnight last night, immediately after the dance, Nila and I rushed to the hotel, grabbed up our already packed suitcases, bade Ward and Peter farewell and caught this fancy streamliner.

At least, it would be fancy if it had a toilet connected with our compartment and blankets on the beds. As soon as we got on Nila and I tried to locate the toilet. Between our compartment and the adjoining one is a good-sized closet as brilliantly lighted and spotlessly white as an operating room, which looked as if it certainly should contain a toilet; but none was apparent to the naked eye. There were a huge washbasin, fresh towels and a big, shiny mirror, so, we felt, the toilet must be somewhere. Nila and I, ably assisted by the occupants of the adjoining compartment, Dr. and Dr. Segal (a husband and wife who are both doctors) of New York City, pushed, pulled and kicked every handle, knob and panel in the place; however, as Nila expressed it, "nothing doings." We have to go to the end of the car and use a toilet that, in spite of looking clean, stinks

112

worse than a long-dead rat. "I'm positive it's something they did from the hygiene point that makes it smell this way," Nila said.

As I was gazing at the fast-passing landscape, Nila got up, complaining of the cold, too. "The Russians know summer starts from such and such a time and lasts until such and such a time, so no matter what the weather is we must sleep under cotton blankets, which in Russia are called 'piqué' blankets. My God! I nearly froze. But worse than the cold was the sink in the middle of the berth. All night I consider who travels in a car like this and it comes to me only big, important people. And they're all fat, fat like Bulganin and Khrushchev, and they lie on this one—" Nila shoved her fist angrily into the offending mattress—"and they make like this sink in the middle."

Still disgusted with the mattress, she flung it back, evidently to see how deep the trough ran, and there, folded up neatly, were the wool blankets we needed so much in the night.

We dressed, then both sat by the window, looking out. At intervals on the track embankment, printed with pebbles, were the words PEACE AND FRIENDSHIP TO THE WORLD.

Shortly we arrived at Ostankino on the outskirts of Moscow and saw blocks and blocks of big, new brick apartment houses, five, six and seven stories high. "Look at them, Willie," Nila commanded, awe in her voice. "Just a wood of houses as far as you can see. When the people move here I hope they move to separate apartments." She rubbed her hands briskly together. "Ah my, this is something! It is unbelievable!"

The train moved swiftly, silently, gliding by whole communities of new buildings. On the first floor of some are spaces for shops.

"Written there is a department store," Nila told me, "and a grocery store. It is, as we would say in the United States, a shopping center. I certainly am impressed. And, Willie, this is only the beginning. Now that they start to make apartment houses, they will go like mad. And I'm sure they will build subways to all these and they will be no distance at all from Moscow."

And we were no distance at all, either. In fact, we were there. A young man from Intourist met us and informed us we are staying at the Leningradskaya Hotel. Nila was annoyed. Though this is one of Moscow's few skyscrapers and was only opened in 1954, it is in the suburbs and Nila had set her heart on being downtown. She frowned and muttered unhappily to me, but said nothing to the Intourist representative. "I didn't want to attract attention to ourselves," she explained when we were settled in the car without him.

The Leningradskaya is really something. It is twenty-six stories high and has 350 singles, doubles and three-room suites and two restaurants. *A Short Guide to Moscow* by A. Kovalyou says, "the interior is overly sumptuous," and I agree one hundred per cent. The lobby is spacious, with marble floors and marble columns and huge lamps on filigreed bronze stands as big around as telephone posts. The elevators are at the rear of the lobby with three steps leading to them under an elaborately gilded archway, similar to the altar entrance in a Catholic cathedral. Involuntarily both Nila and I genuflected as we passed through it.

There are two elevators, and we crowded into one and finally reached our floor, the eleventh; but then almost immediately we were unpacked and ready to descend to the lobby again.

In the vestibule between the elevators, a Russian was sitting on a sofa with his legs crossed and his spine relaxed against the back. He must be mighty lazy, I thought to myself, to sit down while waiting for an elevator—which just goes to show how foolish a girl can be.

Nila and I punched the down buttons on both sides and waited. After five or six minutes Nila joined the man on the sofa. I punched the button again and waited. But it was like ordering food at the Hotel Europe in Leningrad—nothing happened. Finally I said to Nila, "Let's walk down. We can't spend the day here."

"All right," Nila agreed, and she went over to the woman at the desk on our floor and asked where the stairs are. When the woman answered, Nila turned back to me and said, "There are no stairs."

"What do you mean, there are no stairs?"

"That's exactly what the woman says—there are no stairs."

"Nila, you had to have misunderstood her."

"I suppose I know what she said, but if you insist, I'll ask again."

She did and got the same answer, except the woman added there were stairs as high as the sixth floor.

"How about fire escapes?" I asked, gasping.

"I already asked and there are no fire escapes."

"Then we will move to the sixth floor or to one of the floors below the sixth," I announced with positiveness. "Just suppose there should be a fire."

"I already thought of that, too. If there is a fire, it is the fate and we are ended."

"Not so as you can notice it," I said elegantly. "I didn't come to Russia to have my bones charred in a hotel fire."

I could see Nila considered this most unreasonable of me; but when the elevator did come she consented to accompany me to the registration desk and make my desires known to the woman there. There was a considerable to-do; the woman didn't understand my unreasonableness any more than Nila. Nevertheless, she did at last bury her head in her records to find us a new room and Nila whispered to me, "I explained to her you had once been in a terrible hotel fire where many people burned to death and that is why you're so particular and insist on stairs."

This was news to me; but I didn't feel it was the time to set the matter straight.

While the registration clerk was still puzzling over her records and Nila was hovering at her elbow, an excited American, red of face and hair, hurried up and asked the address of the Moscow Baptist church. He wanted to attend the morning service and he couldn't find the address. (This was the first hint that Nila and I had that it was Sunday.)

"Why don't you look in the telephone book?" I asked.

"There is no such thing as a telephone book in Russia," he said.

And once more I went into my routine—"What do you mean, no telephone book?"

And he declared it an absolute fact; they don't have telephone books in Russia. The Communist commissars may have directories, but not the common people.

The registration clerk left off her search for rooms long enough to tell the man where the Baptists hold forth and, murmuring his thanks, he went away; but in a minute he was back. He needed to get in touch with a friend in the hotel, who is accompanying him to church, and he'd decided (with brilliance, I must say) not to use the elevator but to try the house telephone. Would Nila help him? He couldn't make the operator understand.

He and Nila withdrew into a corner of the lobby and were gone long enough to get a call through to Louisville. "What took you so long?" I asked Nila when she returned.

"To get a room number in the hotel," she explained, "you have to dial a number outside the hotel; then this number rings the hotel and then the hotel connects you with the room."

It was on the tip of my tongue to say, "What do you mean?" but the clerk interrupted. She had found rooms on the sixth floor. However, as she handed the keys to Nila, they had a brief confab.

"What were you saying?" I asked Nila as we walked toward the elevator.

"She was telling me that though there are stairs to the sixth floor, they are kept locked at all times."

"What do you—?" I caught myself and started over. "Did you say locked?"

"Yes, locked; but, as you saw, Willie, I argued with her and she agreed that since you are so nervous she will unlock them during our stay."

"Well, thank God for that," I said with relief.

2   *Later*

Now THAT NILA and I knew it was Sunday, we decided just to take a ride around the city and so we went to the Intourist office of the Leningradskaya to ask for a car and were informed by the one person on duty this semiholiday that there were no guides available.

"That's perfectly all right," said Nila. "We won't need one anyway before three o'clock tomorrow afternoon."

"Why then?" I asked her when we left the office, for I knew she knows Moscow well.

"Just to be like other tourists," she answered.

Nila is familiar with Moscow, for she spent the greater part of her life there, either in or out of prison. She arrived in Moscow first when she was eighteen years old, "a very simple peasant woman," to quote her own words, "a *baba*, something ignorant, stupid, not good-looking, no manner, no standing, no nothing." She worked in an agricultural exposition and in a tea factory and then she met "an exceedingly good-looking man," to quote her again, "named Karl Gahlin, who everybody called Karel, with very revolutionary ideas." He courted her "heavily" and finally they were married.

A few years later, when Stalin began to make his claim for power, Karel joined Trotsky and other leaders in a counter-revolutionary organization known as the Oppositionists and this soon led to his arrest and, eventually, to Nila's. They both spent many, many months in prison, though only once in the same prison, and in Siberia, where Karel finally died at Kolyma.

Then in November 1936 she met Robert, who was in Moscow for a year to gather material on Russian folklore, and they were married. Robert extended his stay in Moscow. First he became an assistant to the chief of the AP bureau, then chief of the NBC bureau. Then came the war and you know the rest.

After her ten-year absence from Moscow, the drive this morning was a highly emotional experience. As we rode down a fairly wide street toward the heart of the city, she grabbed my arm and whispered, "At the next corner, Willie, look to the right and you will see the first house I lived in when I married Karel. Look quickly, Willie, there—that little gray house in the middle of the block."

I barely caught a glimpse of a two- or three-story house and then we were past the street.

"This is the most interesting thing that has happened," Nila said excitedly. "The driver could have come into the city by millions of routes, yet he chose this one. How very, very strange. . . . Ah, Willie, here is the grocery store where I bought the sausages when I was poisoned. I was all blue and white. They took me in an emergency ambulance and they pump me. It was when I worked in the tea factory and the next day it was in the whole Moscow paper that I was poisoned. Gosh, that was something! Everybody read about it. Was I glad I was poisoned. The last line in the paper read, 'The suffering human being was saved.' "

It was a poor section we were driving through. Most of the houses looked centuries-old and a few had tumbled-down walls as if from bombings. Many people thronged the streets and an amazingly large number of men were carrying bouquets of mixed garden flowers. All the stores were open and the people were hurrying in and out of them or standing in long lines waiting to get in. They were weighted down with open, bulging satchels, huge, shiny pocketbooks and "perhaps" string bags. The driver said that the stores selling clothes, shoes and other wearing apparel stay open on Sundays until seven o'clock and the food stores until ten o'clock in the evening. They are usually closed on Mondays.

Nila's fingernails dug into the flesh of my upper leg and her voice was low, tense. "Willie, look, there on the left is the Lubyanka prison."

I followed her directions but saw only what looked like a large office building.

"The prison is on the inside," she said, her voice still low and tight. "They don't want the people outside to know. As I told you, Willie, it is the most horrifying prison."

I bent over and stared at the high dirty-yellow walls. Nila's words came back to me: "Everything terrible is there: secret-police officials, prisons, everything. It is the most known, the most horrifying name there is. You don't need to say 'prison,' you just say 'Lubyanka,' and you already say the most horrifying place. Everything that human being can fear was concentrated in this one word, Lubyanka."

Nila gripped my leg again. "There, right in the middle, is the yellow door where I saw Karel for the last time."

Eyes fastened on the heavy, blank boards, I could see Karel as Nila had pictured him. "He stood there for a moment," she had told me, "took off his hat, put his hand to his mouth. Then he went inside and the door was closed."

We drove on and shortly passed the famous Bolshoi Theater, which like almost everything in Leningrad is "under repair."

And now directly ahead of us was the Kremlin, a group of simple, many-windowed buildings painted the softest shade of yellow, and three ancient cathedrals with soaring steeples balancing like seals a dozen or more onion-shaped, twinkling golden balls, and all surrounded by a high brick wall. It is beautiful! Absolutely beautiful! Even the brick wall is beautiful, for it is rose-colored and crenelated and broken at frequent intervals by twenty of the gayest, fanciest towers, fashioned, so they seem, for fairy-story castles. How could anybody ever call the Kremlin "grim"? I realize, of course, that the acts committed there have been grim; but the buildings are among the loveliest in the world.

Nila echoed my exclamations of delight; still she was not as carried away as I was. She'd seen it, of course, many times and, besides, she was still living in her past.

Suddenly she clutched me again. The chauffeur had driven to Arbat Square and from there she saw the window of the room where she was living when she met Robert. "What a shock," she said, gripping my wrist until it hurt, "the driver comes right to the door. There I lived—" she pointed her finger—"on the second floor, in a divided room, but it was very nice."

We continued to ride and I saw many big hotels and public buildings and fantastically colorful Orthodox churches and innumerable statues and streets lined with small trees and, between the trees, cement bowls of petunias and geraniums; but I was vague about everything, for Nila was so tense, watching for old familiar places, she didn't want to talk. Once, when I asked her to inquire of the driver about a many-storied apartment house, she answered, "Please, Willie, don't involve me now."

We turned down a street running alongside a park and Nila put her fingers, stiff as claws, over my knee. "Right there, across the street, was where I was walking when the man came up behind me and said very quietly, 'Don't turn around. Just keep on walking and listen to what I'm going to tell you. I was in Kolyma and I saw your husband working there. It was very cold and he was in this thin, ragged coat and he got pneumonia and died. I myself saw him dead.'"

Nila leaned her head on the back of the front seat, put her hand to her cheek and wept.

I felt helpless, so I turned away and looked out the window at the park. It is a lovely park, extending down the middle of the street for several blocks. Young, lacy trees and flowers grace it, and handsome stone benches line a wide walk that runs its full length, and grownups sit on them watching small children play.

When I turned back Nila had straightened up and was once more ramrod-stiff, staring with feverish eyes at the houses and buildings we were passing. And in a few minutes she said, "Right there in that big green building is where I went to inquire about my brother, Nikolai, when he was sent away to prison and my mother didn't hear from him for a whole year. Remember, Willie? It was after the war when I returned to Moscow and put on such a performance in the white gloves?"

"Yes, I remember."

Nila sighed heavily. "I don't know whether I can take much more."

"Don't try," I said.

3   *Evening*

NILA AND I DIDN'T do anything in the afternoon except rest and write. After dinner, at which we took up with a very charming middle-aged investment banker, Mr. Comstock Clayton of Boston, who was put at the table with us, Nila announced she was in a terrible mood and wanted to be left alone.

"But pay no attention to me, Willie," she advised. "When I can decide what is best to do about finding my family, I will be more pleasant. It is this indecision that is giving me a nervous breakdown. To be in New Hampshire and be helpless is one thing; but to be in Moscow and helpless is an entirely different thing."

So we were quiet, but with the coming of evening Nila threw off her dark mood completely and was unusually gay in anticipation of the ballet *The Left-handed Smith*, for which she, Mr. Clayton and I had tickets.

"The book of *The Left-handed Smith* was written by N. Leskov in the last century," Nila animatedly told Mr. Clayton and me at an early supper. "Leskov was a very broad-minded intellectual with very revolutionary ideas and he was always making jokes on the police, the military and the governors. What he wrote was so applicable to what began to happen in Russia under the Communists that his books were not favored by the Soviets. And now to find that the Russians are using him!" Nila clasped her hands against the base of her throat. "Can imagine?"

We began supper with a crabmeat salad and ordered beer to go with it, but when it came it was warm and I suggested putting some ice in it. Nila and Mr. Clayton opened their eyes in surprise—not at the idea of ice in the beer, though that did shake them, but the idea of ice in Russia. It was true I hadn't seen a lump since leaving Copenhagen; but surely in this new skyscraper hotel they would have ice.

Yes, indeed, there is ice, the waiter said; he would bring some immediately. He disappeared and in ten or fifteen minutes reappeared with a dozen small chips of ice on a flat, salad-size plate and presented them for our approval just exactly like Mr. Tiffany himself showing a choice selection of unset diamonds to valued customers.

As we were doling these out, the red-faced, red-haired American who was trying to get to the Baptist church eons past (it certainly couldn't have been just this morning) and his hard-to-contact friend appeared, pulled up chairs from a neighboring table and joined us.

(Really, Russia is the finest country I've ever been in to get acquainted with strange men. In spite of Venice and the way Katharine Hepburn got ahead there in that movie *Summertime*, Russia has it all over Italy. I can't see one good reason why all old maids who want to get married, widows, and other lonely hearts don't put it at the very top of their where-to-travel list.)

The Baptist churchgoer introduced himself as the Reverend Mr. Harry K. Zeller, Jr., of McPherson, Kansas, and his friend as Mr. William Murstein of Hamilton, Ohio. We explained to them we had to hurry with our supper as we were going to the ballet, and of course instantly they wanted to go with us. But there were no tickets. When Nila got ours and Mr. Clayton got his, they were told they were the last tickets to be had. Nevertheless, Mr. Zeller and Mr. Murstein were determined to go and try their luck at the box office.

The ballet, because of those repairs to the Bolshoi Theater, was at what is referred to as the "offspring" of the Bolshoi, the Filial Theater.

Mr. Zeller and Mr. Murstein were in luck. Nila found a Russian in the line in front of the ticket window, waiting to turn two tickets back, and quickly bought them.

The Left-handed Smith was the most heavenly ballet imaginable. The scenes were typical old Russian scenes—at least, they were what I've always thought of as typical—the dances were native Russian dances, and there was the youngest, sweetest love story with such exquisitely tender dancing by the beautiful hero and enchanting heroine I broke down and wept.

I was sitting alone, but during the first intermission Nila, who was just two rows behind me, joined me. Her anticipation of the production had been more than fulfilled.

Also, Nila had discovered that the ballet company is from Sverdlovsk, where she spent so many months in jail with "hardened criminals." "The city was nothing then," she said. "Absolutely nothing. And now they build a big theater and this company is from that theater."

She was further delighted by a conversation she'd overheard between a young man and woman in front of her. "These two Russians talk between themselves," she recounted, "about a man sitting across the aisle from them, who has propped his feet on the back of the gold-velvet-covered seat in front of him. One of them said, 'I wonder what nationality he can be to act like that.' And the other answered, 'I'm sure I don't know, but he certainly can't be Russian. A Russian would never act like that; it is so nye kulturnye.' "

At the end of the second act, which was even more glorious, if possible, than the first, Mr. Clayton made his way down the aisle to Nila and me and asked Nila if she knew the composer's name. Mr. Clayton is a charter member of the Friends of the Boston Symphony Orchestra, and he was enjoying the music this evening, he said, more than any ballet music he could remember and he wanted very much to know the name of the composer.

Nila, after searching diligently through the program, found that the composer's name is Alexandrov, but she dismissed him with a loud "Never heard of him."

We went out then and joined Messrs. Zeller and Murstein in the spacious lobby. Practically all the audience was there, parading up and down and talking with animation. They were dressed in their best, it was plain to see, and they were better groomed than the people I'd seen on the street. There was a vibration, a gala, keyed-up feeling, in the air.

The bell sounded and we made our way back to our seats; but I was scarcely in mine before Mr. Clayton was at my elbow. He had learned from a neighbor that the composer of whom Nila had never heard was sitting directly in front of her and directly back of me. Elated, he introduced himself and then Nila and me to Mr. Alexandrov. Nila acted as if she had never heard of the "never heard" remark.

Then the curtain went up on the third and final act. When it was over, pandemonium broke out. There were shouts for the hero and heroine. Sheaves of flowers appeared. The director took bow after bow. There were cries for the composer. The composer came. The director kissed the composer. The composer kissed the director. The entire company took a bow. The director kissed the hero and shook hands with the heroine. The hero kissed the director.

It was wonderful!

Without suspecting it, we had sat through the premiere of a new ballet.

4   August 11

As soon as Nila was dressed this morning, she tried the door to be sure it was locked, glanced behind the furniture as if she expected to find dictaphones, and then beckoned me to come close to her in the middle of the room.

"Now, Willie, I've decided on my plans," she said in tones so secretive I could scarcely hear her, "and I feel better."

"Good," I answered, "but why are you whispering?"

"Sh-sh-sh." She put her finger to her lips and held my eyes with hers. "You never know in Russia who may be listening."

I felt she was being overly cautious and dramatic. The Russians had appeared so friendly and so relaxed since we landed in Leningrad that my fears had completely vanished and I couldn't believe that anybody was spying on Nila, especially here in the bedroom.

"As you see," she continued in the same hushed voice, "I'm wearing my Russian dress which I made with this day in mind. It will permit me to melt unnoticeably into the background."

It was true. She was wearing a blue cotton print, which looked similar to thousands we'd seen on the streets. She also had on open-toed and open-heeled sandals.

"I'm going to the house of a friend who I believe will know where my sister now is. I'm afraid the address I have on that envelope is too old; she probably has moved to a new place."

It interested me that Nila didn't mention her mother. I've suspected since the seemingly long ago morning on the *Batory* that she has very little hope, if any, of finding her mother still alive; this, though, was the first time she has intimated as much.

"We will get a car from Intourist," she whispered, "and we will ask the driver to take us to a beauty parlor that is in walking distance of this friend's house and I will tell him you want to get a manicure and that he can go away and come back for us in an hour. Then we will go to this friend's apartment."

"Me, too?" I asked excitedly.

"Sh-sh-sh." She looked hurriedly about the room as if, with my loud voice, I might have brought somebody through the walls. "No, not this morning. I must find out first will she see me and give the permission to ask you in. You see, Willie, she might not want to see me."

"But why, Nila?"

She stared at me as if I were the biggest fool in the world. "I'm the wife of a man accused of being a spy of the United States. Have you forgot that?"

"No, but I'm sure the Russians have."

"Hah!" She tossed up her head and smiled a crooked, bitter smile. "The Russians don't forget."

"But, Nila, Robert wasn't guilty."

"My God, what has that got to do with it? They accused him of being a spy, didn't they? And they gave him forty-eight hours to leave the country, didn't they?"

"Yes, but—"

She cut me off. "So, my friend might not want to see me."

I couldn't believe she really believed this; nevertheless, I kept quiet. I realized I didn't understand all the undercurrents here and that anything I said was liable to be wrong.

"You will just walk with me until we get to the house," she said, "and then you will continue to walk very slowly until you come to the end of the street and then you will turn around and come back. I'll be waiting for you."

So, just as she planned, we drove to the beauty parlor and then, when the car was out of sight, we started walking. As it had been raining during the morning, we were wearing our raincoats and berets; however, now the rain had let up and the sun was trying to come out.

Nila was extremely nervous. She ran the long fingers of her left hand over her thumb. "Remind me," she whispered, "to take off my pearls when we come in sight of the house."

"All right," I agreed.

She looked over both her shoulders. "We're not being followed. I know how to watch."

We turned down a street lined with apartment houses. Nila's face was drained of all color; her lips were an ashy purple. Constantly, her eyes darted behind her and from side to side.

"You told me to remind you to take off your pearls," I said.

"I've already done it," she answered and I saw that she had; but she must have done it very stealthily, for I had been watching her and I hadn't noticed her doing it.

"Which do you think looks less foreign," she asked me suddenly, again running her fingers over her thumb, "my raincoat or my dress?"

"Neither one looks conspicuously foreign," I assured her.

"That's right—I see many people in raincoats."

We walked on in silence for some minutes and then she said, "Willie, will you take my handbag or are two too heavy for you to carry?" She lifted up her plain dark-blue leather bag and eyed it disapprovingly. "This handbag really looks foreign."

"I can carry it, of course," I said, "but I really don't think it looks foreign. Look, there's a Russian woman with one similar to yours."

"It isn't so nice. It's not real leather."

"I know, but nobody is going to notice the quality of the leather."

"Maybe not," she answered, but her voice dragged with doubt.

"But, Nila, maybe mine looks less foreign," I suggested, and I held it out in front of her. It's a simple black bag.

She stared at it for some seconds as if she had never seen it before. "No, I'll take my own."

Her fingers slid over her thumb again and again.

Finally she said very, very quietly, "Soon now, Willie, I will leave you. Remember, you are just to keep on walking to the end of the street and then walk slowly back. I may be gone only a minute."

Then, suddenly, she darted to the left and disappeared.

I continued on, forcing myself not to look back, until I reached the intersection; then I turned and retraced my steps.

Nearing the spot where she had disappeared, I saw her running toward me, her raincoat flying out behind her. I started running to meet her and when I reached her she flung herself into my arms, sobbing frantically, oblivious of the people on the street. For many minutes she was unable to speak; she wept as if her heart was breaking.

I was frightened. I was sure her friend had told her that her mother, sister and niece are dead; but at last, when she quieted a little, she said her friend has heard nothing of them in nine years. "Nothing! Nothing! Nothing!" she repeated wildly. "But she did have a later address than the one I had."

Also, as she had said she feared, the friend and her husband, who was at home ill, had told her that they never wanted to see her again, and that her other friends wouldn't want to see her, either. They said they didn't want to run the risk of endangering their present security by associating with the wife of a man accused of being a United States spy.

I was shocked. Evidently Nila had been right to be apprehensive and I had been the simple, naïve one.

This was even more evident when we went by the main office of Intourist in the National Hotel and Nila received two letters that had been opened. One was from Robert and one from a friend in New Hampshire who had enclosed a small snapshot that she had taken of Robert.

"God damn!" Nila muttered, seeing the picture. "God damn!"

Both letters had been carelessly resealed with Scotch tape.

5   Later

WHEN DINNER WAS OVER, Nila was sufficiently recovered from the blows of the morning to take an interest in our next sightseeing tour and, also, our next long jump, which was to be two days hence to Odessa on the Black Sea, so we went to the Leningradskaya office of Intourist to inquire about our guide for the afternoon and our railroad tickets.

The Intourist office, now that it was in full swing, was a madhouse. A half-dozen or so Russian women and men sat behind big desks and told weary, confused travelers from France, England, Sweden, the United States, Canada and all over that they were addressing their requests to the wrong persons.

It is to this room, you see, that every tourist in the Leningradskaya who is not an official guest of the government must come to get tickets for the ballet, the opera, the theater, the puppet show, the circus, the Kremlin Museum and what have you in Moscow; to check on reservations for planes, trains, ships and hotels; to arrange for his Intourist car and secure its license number, which changes with almost every expedition (the car, not the license) and to meet his guide.

So he stands in line in front of an unmarked desk until he comes face to face with an Intourist representative who, nine times out of ten, will say, "I'm so sorry, I don't handle that matter; you'll have to see the young lady behind that desk over there," and she will wave her hand vaguely to the right—or to the left. I'm sure many people reach their full allotted time and die in this room and are buried in a common grave.

Nila made the rounds for us and I crept into a corner to write a letter. When she at long last located the young woman who was handling our reservations for Odessa, the madhouse tempo increased alarmingly. Instead of train reservations, which Nila and I had instructed Cosmos to get for us, we had plane reservations, and this enraged Nila. In fact, she announced vehemently that we would not go at all if we had to go by plane.

"We will stay right on here in Moscow," she declared, shaking her fist.

(Naturally, Nila and I have nothing against planes, but we chose to make this trip, as well as all others inside the Soviet Union, by train or boat so that we would have an opportunity to meet and talk at leisure with the Russian people and really see the countryside and small towns.)

The Intourist representative was frightened. It was plain to see, even from my corner, that she didn't want Nila to remain one minute longer in Moscow than was absolutely necessary. She telephoned people and talked long and earnestly; she raced with sheaves of papers in hand from desk to desk; and she held repeated conferences with Nila.

Finally Nila joined me, her eyes glowing triumphantly. "My God, Willie, what a fight, but I won!" She rubbed her palms scratchily together. "First she tells me this is the height of the Black Sea season and the reservations on all first-class trains are taken for many days. 'All right,' I say to her, 'put us on a second-class train.' That's quite impossible, she says. It's a thirty-six-hour trip to Odessa on a fast train; on a slow one, half passenger coaches and half mail baggage cars, we will leave at twelve-forty at night and will not arrive in Odessa until two-forty in the afternoon of the second day. And not only are there no sleeping cars on these trains, but no restaurants. 'That's okay,' I say. 'We will carry our own food.' But she still say it's quite impossible. Nevertheless, Willie, I continue to argue and finally, in absolute desperation, she throw up her hands and agree to let us go. I tell you, I almost kiss her."

Immediately Nila headed for the dining room to put in the order for the food. Since we weren't going for thirty hours, it struck me as being a bit previous, even in Russia, but I didn't mention it. I sat on quietly in my corner, waiting for the guide. For some reason, he was very late.

When Nila returned she was bursting with her success. "I order fifteen hundred rubles of food," she said, her face beaming. "I already see us eating every meal with twenty Russians. I order cheese, black bread—but just a little for you and me, Willie, I order mostly white bread for the company—smoked salmon, sliced ham, hard-boiled eggs, wine, vodka and a hundred candies to give the children. The waiter was completely on our side. As you know, we already give him three packs of cigarettes. In Russia there's a wonderful word, translated means 'throw in.' The waiter said, 'Let's throw in some sardines.' Wasn't that sweet?"

This mission accomplished, we were both anxious to start our sight-seeing; but still there was no guide. Standing in the middle of the room, the backs of her hands on her hips, Nila announced impatiently and loudly in English, "We don't give thirty dollars a day to spend the time in this damned room."

Several people threw looks of gratitude her way, but not the young woman in charge of guides. Her flushed face showed clearly she could chew Nila up and spit her out. However, as that was not practical, she chewed the guide up when, a few minutes later, he put in his appearance. And, heaven help us, he chewed her right back. And both of them in English, yet. The dozen or so tourists still waiting about stood with their mouths open and their eyes bulging.

"What do you mean, coming in here late like this?" she screamed at him.

"It's not my fault," he answered stoutly. "I was not notified until thirty minutes ago." He's a personable, intelligent-looking young man, with broad cheeks, dark complexion, black eyes and a short, bristling crew cut, and he was dressed neatly in a well-pressed dark-blue suit, a white shirt and a tie.

"It's your business to look after the tourists," the representative shouted angrily. "As you well know, you are supposed to be with them whenever they need you. Here these two have been here since yesterday morning and you show up at four o'clock this afternoon!"

"I told you I wasn't notified." The young man's voice was high and angry, too. "It's not my fault; it's your fault."

"You know very well it is the party line that everything be done for the tourists. And here you—"

"I told you it wasn't my fault," he interrupted hotly. "Can't you understand English?"

"Of course I understand English; I speak it very well."

She was still in a rage, but suddenly it was apparent that this absurd exchange between two Russians about understanding English startled her. Like a high-strung horse, she gave a quick, jerky look about the room; then, head up, she whirled away from the young man.

It was too late now to do much serious sight-seeing, so we did it again mostly from the back seat of a ZIM. We drove along one of Moscow's most exciting thoroughfares, Bolshaya Kaluzhskaya Street. In just the past few years it has been widened from 58 feet to 148 feet, so it bears little resemblance to the narrow, rough road over which Poland's troops in 1612 and Napoleon's Grand Army in 1812 entered and retreated from Moscow. The many large, stolid structures lining both sides of it were put up by what is called the "conveyer building system," whereby thirty-five to forty-five buildings are built simultaneously, instead of one by one.

Bolshaya Kaluzhskaya leads into Kaluzhskoye Chaussée, which leads to Russia's tallest, most conspicuous structure, Moscow University, on the Lenin Hills. According to our guide, whose name we finally learned is Victor, everything about the university is the biggest, even the clock on its main tower.

"It's the biggest clock in the world," he bragged, and Nila and I hung out the car window to get a good look at it.

And having got a good look, I said, "Victor, I'm sorry, but you're surely mistaken about that clock being the biggest in the world. I know somebody must have told you that, but you shouldn't repeat it. The Palmolive clock in New Jersey in the United States is much larger; even the Palmolive clock in Jeffersonville, Indiana, is larger."

His black eyes regarded me skeptically. "This clock is thirty feet in diameter and weighs four tons. How big are those clocks you're talking about?"

And there I was lost. "I'm not sure," I confessed, "but they're huge. Absolutely huge."

He shrugged his shoulders. "I'm sure this one is bigger."

Nila smiled at me and whispered, "Willie, you mustn't forget it comes into the Russian blood and mind and soul to be proud of their achievements and it helps them to live. I remember a story Isaac Stern told Robert and me when he returned from a visit to Moscow. He said he had a little radio about the size of a brick and one Russian looked at it and said, 'We have better. What is it?' Everything the Russians have is the biggest and finest. They really believe it."

Having bested me in the clock argument, Victor rattled off figures so "irregardlessly," as we say in Kentucky, that to follow him I had to resort to a guidebook called *Going To Russia?* by an Englishwoman, Kathleen Taylor. The central building of the university is thirty-two stories high, with an eighteen-story wing on each side. Altogether there are 45,000 rooms and over 18,000 students.

Miss Taylor pants: "If you entered the University as a new-born child" (but, I ask you, what newborn child would want to?) "and spent a day in each classroom you would be sixty years old by the time you left it." (And no doubt feel a hundred and sixty.)

We drove away from the 45,000 rooms along the edge of a handsome park adorned with flowers, shrubs, a fountain and statues of Russia's twelve leading scientists. Then shortly thereafter Victor ordered the driver to stop the car and we got out and stood on a steep, curving bluff above the Moscow River.

With my back to the bluff, I saw new apartment houses everywhere. Many were already completed, but many were in the process of building. The grasshopperlike skeletons of cranes cut the sky into hundreds of blue, lopsided squares and triangles. Here, without a doubt, the conveyer building system was in full swing.

"Cranes, you might say," Victor remarked importantly, "are the insignia of Moscow these days."

Turning around I gazed afar off, across the river, to the flat, crowded older sections of Moscow, though they're really not very old. It was only 146 years ago that Napoleon set fire to Moscow. We were standing, Victor told us, on the very spot where he stood to watch it burn.

Nila was unusually quiet on the return drive; evidently her rise in spirits in the Intourist office after the ordeal of the morning had faded, and when we reached the hotel she said she didn't care to have supper with Mr. Clayton and me and see Moscow by night, as we had planned.

So, Mr. Clayton and I dined alone, except for two or three hundred Hungarian and East German delegations, and talked scintillatingly about our grandchildren; then we took a car and motored into the city and circled the lovely, floodlighted, castlelike walls of the Kremlin. At night they are even more beautiful than in the daytime, for five of the spectacular towers lift into the luminous sapphire-blue sky large, double-faced, lighted-from-the-inside red glass stars that turn with the wind.

After our fill of the Kremlin, we stopped for a glass of champagne at the Metropole Hotel, which doesn't look like much from the outside but has the reputation of being The place to stay in Moscow.

Heading for the front door, we saw a big group of Russians and in the middle, holding forth, our friend Bill Murstein. He was wearing a white golf cap and was speaking German, which a Russian youth was translating. Catching our eyes, he called to us to go on into the dining room and he would join us in a few minutes.

The dining room is mammoth and square, with a round marble fountain in the middle, circled by the dance floor, and roofed over by a colored glass dome. The floor was comfortably filled and practically every table was occupied. Dr. and Dr. Segal sat with friends at one. The band was playing "I'm Forever Blowing Bubbles."

After a few rounds of dancing and glasses of champagne, Mr. Clayton and I gave up hopes of Bill Murstein's joining us and got up to leave; but then he came, mopping his face and sighing wearily. He had just that second been able to get away from the Russians; they had been questioning him about the United States for more than two hours. He was so exhausted he could repeat for us only one question and answer:

"They asked me, 'Are you a capitalist?' and I said, 'Yes I am and thank God for it.' "

6 August 12

NILA AND I GOT UP early, each had some yogurt sweetened with cherry preserves, some black bread and coffee, in our room, then started out.

Nila had in her bag a letter to her sister. It was addressed to Penza, a little town a hundred miles from Moscow where her friends had said her sister lived the last time they had heard. She had written her sister that though she was in Moscow she was leaving on a tour, but that she would be back

August 29 for a nine-day stay and hoped the sister would come to Moscow to see her. (We had planned the tour on purpose so that the sister would have time to get leave from her job and make other plans necessary for the trip.)

After waiting longer than usual for the elevator I suggested to Nila that we walk down; but she demurred. Why have stairs, I argued, if we don't use them? Then she confessed that they were still locked and, what was more, they were sealed. I had to see this to believe it, so she led me to the rear of the sixth-floor lobby and sure enough the double doors opening onto the stairs going down were bolted and tied with a piece of cord to which a gold seal was attached. I looked at Nila accusingly.

"I know I lied to you that everything would be done," she said hurriedly, "but I was in front of the dilemma—you, Willie, on one side and the sealed stairs on the other. I didn't want to be hostile to the hotel woman and attract any more attention, so I just decided to tell you they would be unlocked. I saw if a fire came I could break the glass in the doors with no trouble and here we would go."

"But why are they sealed?"

"Why? Oh, it's very, very Russian. The management reasons the servants might have keys and unlock the doors, but he knows they would never dare to break the seals. Also, he was thinking of the people who don't live here and might slip up the stairs and go into the rooms. They, too, might unlock the doors, but they'd never break the seals. They are a real security measure."

Finally reaching the main lobby, we met Victor, who was to conduct us to the Kremlin, and we started for the front entrance, but on the way I saw a mailbox and, making toward it with my own letters, said to Nila, "Give me the letter for your sister and I'll mail it for you."

Well, if I had said, "Let me cut you up in little pieces and stuff you in the box," she couldn't have recoiled more. Her eyes flashing, she flayed the air with one downward stroke of her clenched fist and rushed on toward the door.

While Victor was locating our car, I asked Nila, "Don't you want to mail the letter to your sister?"

She gave me a long, hard look. "Won't you ever understand? I certainly don't want to mail it in a hotel lobby mailbox and in front of an Intourist guide."

A small Russian boy approached Nila with some cheap lapel pins left over from the 1957 Youth Festival. He wanted to exchange them for chewing gum. "I don't use it," Nila said haughtily.

Victor was in a chatty mood. He has an American pen pal in the state of Washington who has sent him some jazz records and three plays of Tennessee Williams, *A Streetcar Named Desire, Cat on a Hot Tin Roof* and *Baby Doll.* He said he has enjoyed them immensely and is now hoping his pen pal will send him some of Arthur Miller's plays.

I asked him how he found this pen pal and he said there is an organization to which Russian and American boys and girls who want to exchange letters can write and tell about themselves. He read the Americans' letters and from them selected his correspondent. "And I haven't been disappointed in him," he concluded smugly, revealing more satisfaction in his own good judgment than in his pen pal.

Victor is studying at an institute to become an economist. He is a guide-interpreter only during the summer months to pick up extra money.

We got out of the car at a towered gate in the Kremlin walls and strolled along winding paths, tree-shaded and bordered with pinks, roses, geraniums, gladioli and many other flowers. A hundred or more other people, the vast majority of them Russians, were strolling, too.

We entered the wide doors of the Armory, where the museum is housed, and I was immediately dazed. Everything is here. From the thirteen hundreds on, Russia's czars and princes avidly collected the objects that are now under this one roof. The first mention of some of the treasures here was made over six hundred years ago in Ivan Kalita's will. There are fabulous precious stones, elaborately decorated arms and accouterments, glorious fabrics and embroideries, magnificent royal robes, utensils and gold and silver pieces. Indeed, Victor says, and I don't contradict him, that the Kremlin's silver and

gold collections of both the Russian and the English silver-
smiths of the sixteenth and seventeenth centuries are the finest
and most complete in the world.

From the Armory, we visited the three cathedrals, absolutely
plastered with ikons, within the Kremlin walls. Then a heavy
rain caught us and we ran for shelter under a porte-cochere.
A dozen or more Russians were also gathered there, laughing
and talking animatedly.

Nila's eyes, I noticed, were feverishly bright and she was
extremely restless. She walked to one end of the shelter and
peered through the iron gate into a courtyard where overalled
women, even in the downpour, were unloading heavy timbers
from a truck and mixing cement. I followed and stood close
beside her. Her hands gripped the iron rails so tensely they
were white.

"Willie, I'm so excited I can't tell you," she said in strained
tones. "I don't know whether you realize it or not, but this is
the first time I've ever been inside the Kremlin, and though
I was impressed by the beautiful things in the museum and in
the cathedrals, they are nothing to the way I feel, seeing people
walking topsy-dopsy inside the Kremlin, taking pictures against
the Kremlin palaces, against the Kremlin churches, against the
Kremlin walls. Willie, I even saw one man taking movies inside
the Armory. It's worth all the emeralds and diamonds to see
the people waiting happily out of the rain here—" she tilted
her head over one shoulder—"right here in this most restricted
place. Before, even if it had been stones falling, the secret
police would say, 'Pass, citizen! Pass, citizen!' My God, one man
is standing there, laughing and joking, and he is using his
plastic raincoat to play hide-and-seek with his child.

"Once when I was living here, I was just walking by the
Kremlin walls, not inside, of course, but outside on the sidewalk and my shoelace came untied and I stopped for a second
to tie it and two NKVD men appeared as if from the underground and asked, 'Citizen, what are you doing?' 'Just tying
my shoelace,' I said, and they said, 'Pass! Pass!' And holding me
like this—" Nila drew her elbows stiffly to her sides—"they
threw me forward.

"Do you notice today, Willie, there are no NKVD men? Just a few militiamen standing about, quietly smiling, to help the people. As I said, I've never been inside the Kremlin before, but I can swear no militiamen were ever inside in my time; only the NKVD."

The rain stopped and the clouds, as if they had been rinsed in bluing, billowed above the shining golden balls and the star-tipped towers.

We then joined the long, long line shuffling across Red Square to the mausoleum holding the bodies of Lenin and Stalin. The head of the line was at the door of the mausoleum; the end was God knows where. Nila related that the favorite story in Russia is that "so many came, for they want to be sure for themselves that Stalin is dead."

Foreigners are permitted to go to the head of the line, but as Nila and I were more interested in the people waiting to get into the mausoleum than those two dead ones inside it, we took our turn.

When we were about halfway there, a loud-speaker mounted on a car touring the streets announced that no more people could join the line. The capacity of the mausoleum, fifteen thousand, was complete for the day.

The crowd was on the young and female side. There were hundreds of school-age girls, their long plaits tied with white ribbon bows, and about half that many boys. Most of them belonged to conventions and delegations and they cradled ornate arrangements of flowers to lay against the outside walls of the mausoleum.

Nila, Victor and I were in the midst of the delegation from the Young Naturalists Organization. Six hundred of them from all the republics of the Soviet Union were holding a convention in Moscow. One of the leaders, a heavy-set, well-poised woman, was in front of Nila and me. She and her group are from Siberia and, slapping her hands against her high-lifted chest, she told us, "You must come to Siberia and see our accomplishments."

When Nila translated the invitation for me, she added in a whisper, "I want to tell her, 'Thank you, no; one time in Siberia is enough.'"

At last we were walking down the steps into the plain room in which the two corpses lie on slabs side by side. Then we were moving slowly, slowly, along a raised platform at their feet. Then, quick as a flash, my pleasure in the occasion vanished. My eyes fixed on Stalin's mustache, or, to be exact, on his upper lip, and I saw he had no mustache to mention. I had expected a big, droopy, reddish-brown mustache and here was a sparse gathering of close-cropped hairs. Had moths got into it, I wondered, or had I always had Stalin confused with two other people? When I got too far past to look back, I realized it could have been the lighting; but whatever it was, it absolutely spoiled the occasion for me.

Walking to the Metropole, where the car waited, we braced ourselves against the waves of people dashing into GUM, Russia's largest department store. People were rushing toward it like baseball fans to the World Series.

"A man from the United States," said Victor, "told me that the store owners there would be mighty envious of these crowds."

"Yes," I agreed, but I added, "We have many department stores, you know. People don't have to shop in just one."

"It's not only that," he said surprisingly. "We have not so many goods. People have to come again and again to find what they want."

"We saw beautiful materials in Leningrad," I said. "Lovely silks and cottons."

"And the prices?" he asked, a gleam in his black eyes.

"They were very high."

"Hah!" he exclaimed as if he had caught me out. "And what about the woolens?"

"I don't remember seeing any woolens."

"And you won't, either. Our woolens aren't very good."

High-heeled, two-toned shoes in one window knocked Victor out. He laughed at the ridiculousness of them until his shoulders shook. There was no danger, though, he said, of any Russian woman wearing them. They were in the windows just to impress the tourists; there weren't any inside the store.

After these carefree minutes, the day went into a tailspin.

On reaching the Leningradskaya, we learned that somebody higher up in Intourist had heard of our day-coach traveling plans and had put his foot down. Magically reservations for the de luxe train leaving at eight o'clock next morning had been produced.

Also, we learned we are to have a guide-interpreter for the Black Sea tour. Suspecting it might be Victor, as we have noticed other women tourists with young-men guides, and hating the idea of having any kind of any sex, we protested on the ground that a young man would be a terrible nuisance to us; but we got nothing except the assurance that we will have a female. The trip will be very complicated, the Intourist representative argued, with many changes from trains to ships and from ships to trains, and we need someone to tend to the reservations and tickets.

So, a few hours later, we met Jenna, a twenty-two-year-old girl with huge, slightly popped brown eyes, a pleasant, narrow, long face the color of faded white silk, and an unkempt, shoulder-length bob of black hair.

We put her to work immediately to contact our ambassador, Mr. Llewellyn Thompson. We had promised Robert and Mark we would acquaint him with our travel plans as soon as we reached Moscow and we hadn't yet done it. Jenna got through to the embassy and the next thing we heard she was asking for "Comrade" Thompson. Fortunately "Comrade" Thompson was out.

Nila and I decided to skip the embassy, but then Mr. Clayton persuaded us to accompany him there. He'd been once, but he needed in the very worst way to go again. On the first visit, the wife of a member of the embassy staff had given him a box of Tide to do his laundry, but he had already used it up. His washbasin, just like everybody's washbasin in the Leningradskaya, has no stopper and so he has had to wash his two nylon shirts in the bathtub. To cover the shirts takes five inches of water, which, he has figured carefully, as a dealer in stocks would, equals ten gallons of water, and ten gallons of water, he has also figured carefully, takes five handfuls of Tide. It sounded to me like a mighty lot of Tide for just two shirts; but who was I to advise a broker?

Mr. Ambassador was in his office by the time we arrived, and he received us politely; but when Nila asked him if he had any advice to offer her about how she should go about finding members of her family, he wasn't very helpful.

"I've only one thing to suggest," he answered slowly. "Don't attempt anything behind the Russians' back. If you decide to inquire about them, go to the proper officials and inquire."

He then explained it is impossible to predict these days how the Russians will react to such requests. In some cases, he said, they go all out to try to locate the persons' families; in other cases, they ask the persons to leave the country within twenty-four hours.

Though considerably sobered by this visit, Mr. Clayton, Nila and I went when evening came to the famous Puppet Theater directed by that genius, Sergei Obraztsov. As Nila remarked, "It is more than magnificent—it is terrific."

While watching the performance it was impossible to re-member the puppets were puppets. They looked like people and they talked, sang, played the piano and the violin, acted, tangoed, made speeches and trained lions like people. And there were not just a few of them on the stage, but five and six, and once there was a whole choir of them as large as Fred Waring's singing gloriously a cantata programmed as "The Vitamin Cantata." The basses sang, "Take vitamins," the sopranos sang, "Take vitamins," the tenors sang, "Take vita-mins," the contraltos sang, "Take vitamins," and then every-body sang, "Take vitamins and you'll live until you die."

However, the greatest hit with the Russians was a parody of an American TV singer. Wearing a long, skin-tight black evening dress, elbow-length red gloves and extremely high heels, she wiggled onstage, cradled the microphone in both of her caressing hands and sang, "Who . . . who . . . who . . . who . . ." Then she stepped back from the microphone while the orchestra played a little stomach music; then she swayed forward again and sang, according to Nila's interpretation, "Darling . . . darling . . . darling, where you are?" The Russians shook the walls with their roaring laughter.

Still our day wasn't over. We were invited to the apartment of the John Milkses (he's the head of the Associated Press's Moscow Bureau) for a drink and an after-theater snack. Getting out of the car, I was surprised to see a Russian militiaman standing in a sentry box a few feet from the apartment house door; but Mr. Milks said, when we were seated in his and Mrs. Milks's big living room, that the militiaman was no surprise to him; he was always there.

The Soviet government claims the guard is there for the protection of the Americans who live in the apartment house. Nevertheless, he keeps close watch and makes notes on everybody who comes and goes.

On leaving the party, we gave a lift to a young man connected with the Associated Press, and as he stepped out of the car Nila slipped him the letter to her sister and murmured, "Would you mail this for me, please?"

Cold feet crawled along my spine. All day Nila had carried that letter in her handbag and had been afraid to walk up to a mailbox and drop it in, or even allow me to do it, for fear somebody might be watching. Her years in prison and in Siberia have surely left their mark.

V

Odessa

<u>1</u>   *August 13*

WHEN WE DROVE UP to the station to catch the train for Odessa,
I abandoned all hope of making it. There was a terrific mob
on the sidewalk, blocking the entrance. I thought there must
have been word of an army approaching and that Moscow was
being evacuated; but not at all. It was just that everybody had
to pass through one small door, as if he were going to the
theater, for everybody must have a ticket whether he is catching
a train or only seeing somebody off.

Jenna did manage by brute force to push her way through,
Nila and I in her wake, and once inside the station it wasn't
bad, except there were no porters and I had to stagger down the
platform with the Greek bag, which was as heavy as if it held
the last Czarina's jewels, around my neck and with a rain coat,
a cashmere coat, four large tomes, a suitcase and a pocketbook
in my hands. I thanked God that we had canceled that two-day
supply of food that Nila ordered for us and the twenty Russian guests.

We had a four-berth compartment, which was clean but
stuffy, with red plush curtains at the window.

The train pulled out on the dot.

Suddenly music poured out of the walls. Somewhere a radio
was playing and sending music through loud-speakers into the
compartments. "It will play until evening," said Jenna.

"I'll go crazy," Nila cried with vehemence. "Can imagine this music all day with my nerves shattering around anyway? I'll break it, that's what I'll do. I'll break it."

"We will do it." Jenna agreed, and she laughed delightedly.

However, she learned from the conductor that the music can be turned off with the push of a button under the table. Nila pushed, leaned back and murmured, "Ah, the luxury of silence."

The conductor is a dumpy, hard-faced woman in what, I presume, passes for a uniform on Soviet trains. On her dyed, soot-black hair is a navy-blue cap with a visor; around her short, fat neck, a string of amberish beads; on her body, a shiny blue serge suit, the hammer and sickle sewn on the coat lapels; and on her feet, short, striped socks and open-toed black suède shoes with medium heels.

After a brief exchange with Nila about the tickets, she said, "You speak Russian very well." (I don't know which accent Nila used—her English, French or Chinese.) Nila, with a straight face, answered, "Thank you."

The conductor not only takes up tickets but vacuums the floor every moment she isn't taking up tickets. She has a brand-new electric sweeper and it's worth your leg to walk down the aisle.

We passed through a picturesque village of little wooden houses with roofs as steep as inverted V's and with a grove of fluttering, dark-leafed, silvery-trunked birches partly screening them from the railroad track. A woman in a shapeless ink-blue dress was walking through the grove carrying a pail, and two flocks of geese and a half-dozen goats were nibbling at the bright-green grass growing with surprising thickness between the silvery trunks. Much of the grass had been cut, no doubt with scissors and shears, and was raked into small mounds. Queen Anne's lace, just like in Kentucky, bordered the tracks. It made me a bit homesick.

The train butcher appeared with books for sale.

We came to a good-sized town with TV antennas shooting thickly from the roofs of large apartment houses and long lines of clothes flapping in the breeze.

Shortly the director of the restaurant arrived with sheets of paper in his hand, to find out what I, the American, would like for dinner. He introduced himself as Vasili. He is a young-ish, lively fellow with bright-blue eyes which he cuts about at me in a flirtatious manner. His hair is blond and he wears it brushed sleekly back in a long pompadour (I had seen this style frequently in Leningrad and Moscow); his teeth are mostly false and of bright chrome steel, and he has an elaborate tattoo on the back of his right hand. And though his nails are very dirty, they are polished. He was wearing a checked shirt, open at the neck, a cheap tweed coat and black, bell-bottomed trousers.

"For the guest everything the best," he said, and so I suggested starting dinner with caviar.

He clasped his hands, pumped them to and fro and cried, "Allah! Allah! Allah! All that the American tourists dream of is caviar and I have none."

Jenna translated for him and this called forth an apology for his ignorance of English, but if I will come back in a year, he said, he will be speaking it. He has already made his plans to start studying it September first.

"There is an old Russian joke," he recounted, grinning. "If you want to speak English, boil three potatoes, put them in your mouth, talk Russian, and English will come out." He chuckled gaily.

Nila invited him to sit down and he did with alacrity.

Then he suggested that I, perhaps, should study Russian.

Gesturing at my gray hair, I said I was too old to learn anything new.

"Gray hair doesn't mean people are old," he denied quickly. "Age depends on the heart." He narrowed his eyes to gleaming slits of gaiety and wickedness. "There is a Russian saying, 'Gray hair here—' he patted his blond head—'the devil here—' " and he poked himself in the side and rocked back with laughter.

I decided it was time to get the conversation away from me and onto him. It was easy; he loved talking about himself. He lives very well, he said. He has a liberal pension from the government, for he served in the Navy and was seriously wounded four times. He has fourteen medals under the ikon at home. And, besides his pension, he has this "responsible" job with the railroad which pays him a minimum of 1,200 rubles a month and 1,400 rubles when the restaurant goes over its quota. He and his wife and three sons have three rooms and a kitchen in Odessa.

"My oldest son," he boasted, beaming, "is taller than I am. When we walk down the street people won't believe I'm his father; I look too young."

This led back to his years in the Navy. He has been everywhere—except to the United States, but this doesn't mean, he said, that he hasn't known American sailors and also American soldiers.

"The Russians are much better lovers," he threw in as if in parentheses. "In every country where the Russian Army and Navy were, the women will remember them with pleasure. For somebody we like—" he threw out his hand—"everything the best, even to watches. I noticed during the occupation of Germany when Russians and Americans came together, they made love very differently. Russian men, even when it is a short love, try to make it beautiful; but Americans just make it short."

"He's real sailor," Nila said to me in a quick aside. "So boastful and wide-natured."

Vasili always got along fine with the Americans, though. "They liked me," he said frankly, "and I liked them."

But a year ago he saw some American sailors in Sweden and they snubbed him dead. "Though I was as anxious as ever to be friendly," he told me, his alive face clouding over, "they were no longer friendly. I didn't understand it then and I don't understand it now."

Then I let him have it. I hated to, in a way; he was such an outgoing, warm human being; but I felt it was my duty. "No doubt those American sailors resented what the Russians did to the Hungarians," I said. "And before that what they did to the Bulgarians, Rumanians, Poles and the other people of the so-called social democracies."

He was shocked and so was Jenna. I believe sincerely shocked. They both talked at once. Russia had to go into Hungary because, according to the Warsaw agreement, she had promised to uphold the Hungarian government. It was the government the people wanted, the government the people had elected. Those who tried to overthrow it belonged to the old, discarded regime who had been outside the country and had come back in with arms.

I harked back to the close of the war and told how cold-bloodedly Russia had imposed Communism on Hungary and the other countries she occupied; but they didn't accept a word of it.

"It's impossible to push over governments unless the people want them pushed over," Vasili declared hotly. "We've never interfered in other countries' politics. We have never needed to. It's true that at the close of the war there were only a few Communists in those countries, but then the people learned what real democracy meant and the Communists grew and grew."

The arguments became heated. Our voices rose. Nila argued, too. Indeed, the two Russians and Nila got so involved at times, none of them would stop long enough to interpret for me what was being said.

At last, however, Vasili remembered his restaurant duties and announced solemnly, "We went away from the menu."

I said I would leave it to him.

"You'll not be sorry, madame. I'll prepare such a meal for you you will cry 'Allah!' "

I returned to my window gazing. The land was far-spreading, empty and bright green. Nothing stopped it until it was pinned down by the blue-gray horizon and nothing relieved its emptiness except modest areas of small trees, mostly pines, firs and birches, and dainty pastures of pink, yellow and blue wild-flowers.

"It's like they were planted," I said enthusiastically of the flowers.

"Yes, by God," Nila answered.

A little later I said I loved birches and that Russia seems to have so many of them.

Nila nodded her head. "No other trees," she said, "was ever said so much about and sing so much about by Russians."

Jenna told me we were now crossing the Russian steppes, the southernmost part of that vast prairie stretching east and west across the Soviet Union from Eastern Europe to the Pacific Ocean, and I was amazed. I'd always thought the Russian steppes were forever buried under sixteen feet of blinding, crusty snow with never a tree or flower in sight.

At long last dinner was ready and verily, verily, it was a meal over which to cry, "Allah!" Single layers of onions were cut like Shasta daisies, cucumbers were cut like roses, and tomatoes were cut in quarters. Then there was a nest of slaw, and, over everything, sour cream sprinkled with the chopped green tops of onions. On a side plate were thin slices of "summer" sausage. Also there was sunflower oil for the salad, if we wished it.

"Oh, I haven't had any sunflower oil in such a long time," Nila declared, her face aglow. "It is the best oil in the world. It is much better than olive oil."

Next came big bowls of steaming borsch. It was made, said Vasili, hovering over us, of the very best beef, red cabbage, fried white onions, fried green tops of new onions and halves of potatoes.

Then kasha arrived and Nila rolled her eyes heavenward. "Kasha is the most traditional and most common Russian dish," she gloated. "I don't understand why we don't have it in the United States. It is simply dee-licious! You cook it in a pillow the same as rice—"

"How's that?" I interrupted, having never in all my Deep South days heard of rice cooked in a pillow.

"Oh, you know, you put one cup of rice in two cups of water and you cook it until the water is ended . . ."

"Yes, that I know."

"Well, you put the kasha—I believe in America you call it buckwheat—in water the same way and when it comes to a boil you take a pillow and put the kasha still in a pot inside it, and it continues to cook. The pillows are the same as a double boiler."

"Really?"

"Of course, but nobody in Russia in my time ever saw a double boiler. My mama used to cook kasha early in the morning, put it between the pillows and go on about her work. Then when we children came home from school in the afternoon it was done and simply dee-licious."

The meal was served by a plump, pink-cheeked maid wearing a crocheted "crown," which she had made herself and starched stiffly, and a red print dress. The butcher, who had had a hand in the preparation of the meal, sat across the table from us and eyed us intently to gauge our enjoyment. He could play the role of Mephistopheles without make-up. He had a bullet-shaped, completely bald head, a lean, dark, flushed face, a generous quota of gold teeth, and narrow, devilish gray eyes.

After the kasha, we wanted only coffee. "Mrs. Ethridge takes her coffee without sugar," Nila said to Vasili, who had long ago pulled up a chair and joined us.

He reacted as if an acute pain had clutched him and asked Nila, "What has she—diabetes?"

"Oh, no, she watches her figure."

Immediately he recovered from the pain, shook his head at me disapprovingly, made a big circle with his two arms and said, "Russian men like their women so."

Now for many miles the track was lined with little fir trees, just the perfect size for Christmas. Frequently a crow sat on the tipmost top which at home we reserve for the angel.

The train stopped at the town of Brijansk for ten minutes and Nila and I got off and walked up and down. Many men from the train were also walking. They were in silk pajamas of various colored stripes, which didn't shock me too much, for some years back I had seen men traveling in pajamas in the daytime on trains in Turkey. One papa strolled hand in hand with a boy about ten or twelve years old and both of them were in pajamas, striped, but in different colors. Another man wore a raincoat over his pajamas. And why not? The day was cloudy and cool and the pajamas looked thin.

Crowds of women from the town pressed about the steps of the restaurant car, where the waitress was selling loaves of white bread. Eagerly the women grabbed the loaves out of the basket, thrust the money into the waitress's hand and rushed away. Some had two loaves, some three and four. Their faces beamed with triumph.

Returning to our compartment, Nila and I talked with Jenna. She is a responsive, happy-natured girl and has a comical way of rolling her big eyes about in their seemingly well-oiled sockets. She has a terrific crush on the pianist Van Cliburn, and when she mentions him her pupils disappear completely into the recesses of her head. Like an American teen-age fan of a movie idol, she has begged three pictures of Cliburn and has them tacked up in her room at home.

There are six members in her family: mother, father, brother, sister and grandmother. Her father is a lawyer and her mother is secretary to the editor of the magazine *Soviet Culture.*

"Not *Soviet Kulturnye?"* I exclaimed.

"Yes, *Soviet Kulturnye."*

Practically all Russian women work, Jenna said, unless they have very small children and no grandmother or kindergarten to care for them. Usually women return to their jobs when their babies are two months old.

Jenna belongs to the Komsomol, the organization of the young between fifteen and twenty-five years of age who meet regularly to be indoctrinated in the Communist line. She will be automatically dropped from membership when she's twenty-five, and then, if she wishes, she can apply for membership in the party. She doesn't believe now that she wants to be a member of the party—not that she doesn't believe in it, but membership carries so many responsibilities and she will have to pass stiff examinations on the party's doctrines at home and abroad. She fears she cannot measure up to the requirements. However, she measures up in one—she doesn't believe in God.

Listening to her talk, I understood better why there are only approximately 7,000,000 Communist Party members out of a population of 200,200,000. It's one thing to believe in what the party stands for and quite a different thing to belong to it. Jenna's father is a party member and her brother and sister also belong to the Komsomol.

Talked out, Jenna took off her good black suède shoes and put on some comfortable yellow sandals, which were imported from Czechoslovakia and cost 180 rubles. They were much cheaper than the black suède, which are Chinese and cost 500 rubles ($125); that really took a bite out of her salary of 800 rubles a month.

Outside the window, the landscape grew more beautiful. It was beginning to roll very gently now, like an old-fashioned biscuit quilt, alternating green swatches of trees and grasses with golden swatches of ready-to-harvest grain. Now and then there were little gray log houses with thatched roofs perched upon them, looking as if children, playing dolls, had set them up and run off and left them.

Nila and Jenna made up their berths with sheets and pillowcases that were sealed with small tags to show they hadn't been used since they were laundered, and announced they would take naps; but they found it impossible. Loud shouts and whoops of laughter came through the walls from the adjoining compartment. The occupants, a woman and three men, who, according to Jenna, were strangers when they got on the train, were playing cards.

Again the train stopped, this time at a large town, and Nila and I hopped off. Booths selling soft drinks, candies, newspapers, magazines and books were strewn the length of the platform. A half-dozen men—in striped pajamas, of course— were jockeying in front of the booth and several of them made purchases.

"The Russians love to read," Nila commented. "Everywhere, Willie, you will see them buying books."

A woman from the town pulled down the knitted pants of her baby boy and he squatted right on the platform and relieved himself. His blond face was radiant as he got up and peered down at his considerable accomplishment.

The train once more moving, Nila and I stood at a big window in the vestibule and stared in some amazement at the countless number of railroad tracks, at the modern buses passing on elevated bridges and at the cranes silhouetted against the sky. Then, almost immediately, there was another town, or perhaps it was a continuation of the same town. There were even more railroad tracks and, high above them, many towers holding huge sets of floodlights.

A Russian standing beside me said something to me. I shook my head and murmured, "Amerikanka."

"Russky," he said.

I held out my hand and he gripped it crushingly hard. I tried to pull it away, but he continued to hold it tightly.

"He is so friendly," I whispered to Nila.

"And so drunk," she answered matter-of-factly.

Of course, I should have known. It's been well over a quarter of a century since anybody who wasn't drunk took to me with such fervor.

<u>2</u>   *August 14*

WE WERE COMING into a handsome station of yellow stucco when I woke up at ten minutes of eight. Many people got off, a goodly number in pajamas, loaded down with baskets, bundles and cheap pasteboard suitcases. A woman carried a small child on her shoulders, his feet dangling against her big breasts, and a gaping satchel in each hand. A man with a little green pail dangling from his fingers hurried to a spigot against the stucco walls, rinsed out the pail, filled it with water and hurried back to the train.

Leaving the town behind, the engine gathered speed and I saw fields much more intensely cultivated than those we passed yesterday. Some were honey-colored with wheat, oats, rye or some other grain; some were deep green with potatoes; but most of them had been recently plowed, as if the harvest had already been gathered and the stubble turned under. The land was so black it looked as if it had been burnt over. Not even in the Mississippi Delta had I seen land blacker. We were now in the Ukraine, the breadbasket of Russia.

Before I finished dressing we arrived at another huge railroad station. It was a pale green and was adorned with many pots of flowers. A woman came through the train selling hot *piro-*

chki. They are something like popovers, filled with rice, meat and chopped hard-boiled eggs. Nila bought three.

Brushing the crumbs from our laps, we went to the restaurant car for breakfast. A tightly jammed case of fresh, loud flowers— pink cosmos, orange marigolds, dark-red dahlias and feverfew— and asparagus fern decorated our table.

Across the aisle, three men were drinking vodka and eating hard-boiled eggs, tomatoes, onions, cucumbers and caviar, which they evidently supplied themselves. A deep male voice was singing "Auld Lang Syne" on the radio. It—the voice—belonged to a famous Ukrainian bass, according to Jenna.

The clock on the restaurant wall was wrong and I called Vasili's attention to it. "No, it's not right," he agreed pleasantly and casually. "But everybody in Russia has a watch, so we really don't need public clocks."

"It's very interesting about the Russian nature," Nila said in an aside to me. "The economy of the country is going by the number of watches."

Vasili pulled the fourth chair out from our table and sat down. I showed him a picture of Adlai Stevenson and Khrushchev, on the front page of a copy of the European edition of the New York *Herald Tribune* that John Milks gave me before we left Moscow. He got excited, and I, thinking he might like to have the paper because of the picture, offered it to him.

He first accepted, then hesitated and asked Nila if there was anything in it which would make it bad for him to have it. "He means," Nila explained to me, "if there is anything against Russia in it. You don't have to say much in Russia; we understand each other."

Nila turned the paper over to Jenna for censoring and very casually she went through it, said it was okay and gave it to Vasili. Then, without one glance at Messrs. Stevenson and Khrushchev, he turned to the back page and buried himself in the cartoons and funnies.

However, he came out of them quickly when a Russian in pajamas appeared and started to sit down. It's *nye kulturnye* to eat in the restaurant in pajamas, he told the man. Without protesting, the man left and in a few minutes returned looking rather handsome in a light-colored sport shirt and dark pants.

Nila, Jenna and I had another *pirochok*, yogurt and coffee and talked with Vasili, the butcher, the maid, the three vodka drinkers and the re-dressed man. (We were the only people in the restaurant; everybody else seemed to have brought his own food and was eating it in his compartment.) I spent most of the time answering questions: Why doesn't the United States import goods from Russia and why doesn't Russia import from the United States? Do we have free TV? How much is our income tax and how does it work? Again I fervently wished I'd taken a course in economics before dusting the good dirt of Kentucky off my feet.

Between questions I stole glances at the countryside. It really couldn't have been lovelier, which was hard for me to accept. I wasn't prepared for Russia to be so beautiful. The land was still gentle, but somewhat hilly, and practically every foot of it was under cultivation. Here, on a rounding slope, a field of corn; here, sunflowers; here, fruit trees; here, potatoes; and here, the freshly turned-up land.

Nila decided this was a good time to give presents. She presented packs of American cigarettes to Vasili and the butcher, and they, bowing low, gave her and me packs of Russian cigarettes.

Nila was deeply touched. "It's impossible, as you can see, Willie, to give Russians anything without them giving you something in return. Isn't it sweet?"

Then she gave the maid that fancy can of spray which Kick Erlanger sent to the *Batory*, the one that turns to powder the minute it touches the body. Ah, what a sensation! An absolute sensation! Not only did the maid spray her arms and hands, but everybody, including the four strange men and Jenna, sprayed some part of himself. The butcher even sprayed his bald head.

We escaped from the restaurant just as the train stopped at a large town and everybody sprang off. Women in long bathrobes and the men still in pajamas swarmed over the platform, buying armfuls of apples and pears from the heaped-up stalls. Many foresighted passengers had brought along their "perhaps" bags and others had brought big baskets. One frantic woman, with neither, purchased a whole water bucket of apples, rushed to her compartment, dumped the apples in the unmade berth and dashed back with the bucket. I feared for her heart.

As the engine snorted and made for the open country, I saw that the Ukraine, too, has small wooden houses with thatched roofs; these, however, are painted, most of them blue but a few pink and white. Farmers, both men and women, were gathering some kind of grain, or maybe the stubble of the wheat, in old-fashioned, steep-sided unpainted wagons pulled by big horses. There was not a tractor or any other piece of machinery in sight. At the road crossings, women in blue uniforms stood at attention, holding in front of their noses small yellow flags folded around short staffs.

A Russian officer shared my window. He wore an olive-green blouse piped in raspberry, two stars on the shoulders, and vivid blue pants, lighter than navy. His eyes were a soft, light brown and they gave his face a gentle look.

"California?" he said hesitantly to me, nodding his head toward the hills that were now taken over by regiments of fruit trees, and I, pleased, said, "Florida and Georgia, too." Then, having used up our common vocabulary, we turned back to observing the landscape.

By the time we arrived at Odessa, we'd been on the train almost forty hours, but it hadn't seemed long. I left it with the same feeling I have when I leave a ship, and I wasn't surprised, as we were struggling through the maelstrom of flower-laden people meeting relatives and friends, and of grimy, ragged porters, to see Vasili and the butcher hanging off the restaurant platform, smiling at us warmly and waving farewell.

3

August 16

BEFORE DAWN, Nila and I got up, woke Jenna and dressed for a long day's journey. Last night when we returned to the hotel from the Odessa Opera House, where we had heard a spirited performance of *Rigoletto*, we learned that a delegation of the British-Soviet Friendship Society had arrived at our hotel and were going early this morning to visit a collective farm about seventy miles away.

We learned this exciting piece of news almost accidentally from our broker friend, Ward, with whom we spent that last gay dancing evening in Leningrad. Ward arrived in Odessa within a few hours of us and he was in the hotel dining room when we, dehydrated from sitting in the third balcony with our heads against the dome (they were the only seats available) dropped in for a cooling drink of mineral water.

Now, Nila and I had been wanting to visit a collective farm ever since we got to Russia. We had asked Jenna just the day before about seeing one while we were in Odessa and she had said it was impossible. Yet here this group of English Soviet sympathizers were being whisked to one right under our noses.

Our hackles were up; but as it was nearing midnight when Ward told us, and his guide and Jenna had gone to bed and the Intourist Bureau was closed, we could do nothing but sip, seethe and listen to the orchestra play "My Heart Belongs to Daddy" and "Oh, Susannah, Don't You Cry for Me." However, we determined right then and there those British friends of Russia wouldn't leave us behind without a fight.

So, with the coming of daylight and Jenna on her feet, we urged her to telephone the head of Intourist and ask her to come immediately to the hotel and make arrangements for us to go. Then we invaded the dining room, had a quick breakfast, ordered a picnic lunch to be packed and went into battle. At first it ran against us. The Intourist representative explained the English were traveling in a bus and there was no room for us; their Intourist guide objected personally to having me in the party, for she understood I'm violently anti-Soviet; the head of the Collective Farm was having a banquet for the guests and he could not take care of five extra people with no notice.

We fought back furiously. We would take an Intourist car; I promised to make no anti-Soviet demonstration; we didn't expect to be invited to the banquet—we were carrying our own lunch.

Finally, victory was ours and we gathered on the sidewalk in front of the hotel to depart. Everybody of both groups was present except Ward's guide. She hadn't appeared so far this morning.

The bus arrived and the English piled in. There were about fourteen of them, both men and women, and they were a run-down-at-the-heels lot and all but two of them were old, older than sixty-eight, I'd say. There were plenty of vacant seats for us if they had desired our company.

As the bus disappeared around a corner, Ward's guide showed up. She was apologetic; she had overslept. She is a sweet-faced girl, with long, narrow, appealing gray eyes heavily fringed with black lashes. Her hair is black, too, and straight. She wears it pulled back and caught with a barrette at the nape of her neck. Her name is—well, I'll say it's Ruby; it's just that American.

It was clear to see that Ward is much taken with her. "How are you feeling, Ruby?" he asked solicitously. "Did you sleep well, Ruby?" . . . Is your room comfortable, Ruby?"

She smiled at him slowly from beneath those thick lashes and answered in a soft, almost lisping voice.

How interesting, I thought to myself as we got into the car and started off, that Intourist gives this attractive girl as a guide to this traveling-alone American. For a month she will go wherever he goes, stay in the same hotel, eat three meals a day at the same table—even, maybe, a midnight snack. She is forbidden by Intourist to enter his room, but she can be with him everywhere else.

This wasn't the first time I'd noticed this custom of Intourist, and once I said to Nila, "It strikes me as being pretty stupid of Intourist to throw their young girls for such long periods with men tourists—that is, if Russia wants to keep them pure." Nila answered, "Maybe Intourist is innocent like your Mark. It doesn't have an ugly thought."

The day was brilliantly sunny and the Black Sea, on which our hotel faces and along which we drove for several blocks, shimmered like the linked material from which coats of mail are fashioned. A park, bordered with acacia trees and stamped with flower beds, lies along these blocks, separating the buildings from the edge of the bluff that drops steeply to the water.

Shortly we were in the country—the same mildly rolling country that I saw the other day from the train. My eyes lighted upon stacks of golden wheat chaff, as big as airplane hangars, hundreds of cattle, shepherds, ragged as scarecrows, watching herds of goats, women pitching hay, flocks and flocks of geese, and fields of cabbage so startlingly blue-green that I thought at first they were lakes.

The road was terrible, or rather I should say the roads were terrible, for usually one or two branched off from the main road and snaked across open fields. Some had a thin layer of badly broken blacktop; some had only dirt, pocked with holes and veined with ruts. Even though it had rained all day yesterday it was very dusty.

We passed a cemetery in which all the graves are marked with blue crosses and a village in which practically all the houses are painted blue. "It is easy to have everything blue in Russia," Nila commented. "They just mix the indigo into the water and there they go."

Coming to a field of sunflowers bent almost to the ground, Nila asked the driver to stop the car and she and Ward got out and rushed about madly searching for heads with the seeds already ripe. Grinning like children escaping from a watermelon patch just ahead of an irate farmer, they returned bearing in their cupped hands the big black-brown centers of the flowers. The petals, of course, had long ago shriveled away.

They broke off small pieces and passed them about, then sat picking out the tiny seeds from the sections they had left. The seeds tasted like matchsticks to me, but Nila was in seventh heaven.

"There is a wonderful game you play in Russia with sunflower seeds when you gossip," she told us. "Without throwing out the husks after you've sucked the meat from them, you make them into chains, and the one who makes the longest chain wins."

I didn't understand this at all and said so.

"All right," said Nila. "Just watch me and I'll show you."

I watched, and shortly out of her mouth and down her chin

dribbled a chain of husks that somehow she had stuck together with her tongue and palate. However, it was a very short chain, for, as she said, she was out of practice.

After passing through several more villages, we arrived at the collective farm of Bondarny, a dozen or so small, one-story stucco houses straggling along two or three unpaved streets.

The vice-chairman of the collective farm greeted us side by side with the English-Soviet friends and ushered us into a modest office building. By the doorway a poster proclaimed: "Peace to the world"; and in the bare hallway another: "Good Morning, Happy Day and Peaceful Night"; and, in the room in which we landed, still another: "Three Holy Words: Friendship, Happiness and Peace."

A desk was at the front of this room and straight chairs were lined up facing it. The vice-chairman sat behind the desk and we sat in the chairs. The vice-chairman is a short, heavy-set man with a big, handsome head on a thick neck. He told us about the collective farm.

There are 9,130 acres and 1,800 people, 750 of whom are able-bodied farmers, living in three villages. In each village there are field brigades, cattle-feeding brigades and orchard and vineyard brigades.

Last year the farm planted 2,750 acres of winter wheat, 1,625 acres of corn, 375 acres of sunflowers, 500 acres of grasses, 250 acres of millet and eighty-seven and a half acres each of potatoes and vegetables. They also planted a little barley.

Besides, there are 265 acres in vineyards; 200 acres in forest, including protection belts; 1,650 head of cattle, 600 of which are milk cows; 3,000 pigs; 1,300 sheep; 1,040 horses; 18,000 poultry and 150 hives of bees.

The total income of the farm last year was 9,345,000 rubles, which at the Soviet exchange for its own people amounts to $2,336,250. With this lordly sum, it pays the expenses of the farm, including, among other items, the wages of its farmers. Now hold your hats. The net income of the farmers of Bondarny last year totaled $500,000. Some farmers made as much as $7,500 each.

The farmers live in their own private houses, which they can

do with as they like, even to selling them. Seventeen own automobiles and many have motorcycles, radios, gas and electric
stoves. The farm doesn't furnish running water inside the
homes, but if a farmer wants it and can pay for it, he is
welcome to it.

Besides his wages, each farmer is alloted a private plot of
one and a quarter acres. On this he can raise one cow, two
heifers, two sows and as many piglets, poultry and vegetables
as that small plot will take, and he is allowed to do what he
pleases with what he raises.

Both women and men work, of course, usually from eight
to ten hours a day in harvest time, eight hours in summer and
six hours in winter. The children work after they finish secondary schools and during the summer vacations.

And guess what? They don't have any infectious diseases,
except dysentery now and then. No measles, no mumps, no
chicken pox, no Asiatic flu? I wanted to ask; but there was no
time. The lecture was over and we were on our sight-seeing
way.

We strolled leisurely down a black dirt road, the vice-chairman at our head. We had to keep a watch for plops of horse
dung. The houses, some white, some faded pink and some faded
blue, sat behind low fences in grassless yards, though here and
there were small patches of many-colored, insignificant zinnias.

We stopped at a gate and the men disappeared behind a
white wooden building, and then the women. Everybody was
headed for an outdoor privy, but I got no farther than the
door. The privy was filthy. Some children—at least, I trusted
they were children—hadn't bothered to use the hole.

"It is sickening," cried Nila, who got in before anybody
else and now stood on the path, her face screwed up in disgust.
"It makes me throw out."

One of the Englishwomen, a tall, scrawny creature with a
huge beak of a nose, a leathery complexion and tight, tight
plaits about her head, took exception to Nila's remark. "I've
seen just as bad in the stations in Paris," she said hotly.

"Maybe you have," Nila retorted, "but that's no excuse for
this rich, model collective farm having such a one."

"You must remember this collective farm is young."

"It's thirty-seven years old. Do you call that young?" Nila flung at her; then she took off, I following, to face the vice-chairman himself. "You are such a wealthy collective farm," she told him, "why don't you take five hundred of those nine million rubles you made last year and build a decent toilet and hire a man or a woman to keep it clean?"

Naturally, the vice-chairman was taken aback. He opened his mouth to say something, but Nila rushed on like a flash flood. "I realize clean toilets aren't important to the Russian people. I know they have never been interested in such things. They care more for the well-being of their cows and pigs—I understand that. But here you receive foreigners who do care about clean toilets and for their sakes you ought to have them."

The vice-chairman finally broke through. The collective farm is now in the process of building a toilet, he said. He held up his hands, the backs of them to Nila, and pushed them to and fro excitedly. It will have marble to the ceiling and running water and all modern conveniences.

We took another stroll and came to a building housing the machinery that generates the electricity for the farm. Nila gave one engine a searching look, then announced in her biggest voice, "I didn't come all this way to see a diesel engine from Oakland, California."

With this off her chest, she and I streaked across a rough, un-kempt field to a big cow barn and began to talk to two women just inside the entrance; but in a twinkling another came up, bringing two milking stools for Nila and me to sit on. Un-fortunately she placed mine under the head of a cud-chewing cow, who doused me with suds of saliva at every rotation of her slow-moving jaws. Then five more women came.

Nila asked them do they ever long for the city and they didn't even know what she meant; she had to amplify the question. Then, their weathered faces showing plainly their surprise, they said no; they belong here. They have their homes here and they have all they can eat here. "In the city," a girl in her teens said, "you have to pay for every piece of bread; even for pumpkins you have to pay." She had on a brown bag of a dress and as she talked flies crawled thickly over her bare legs. They have movies, she said, a theater, an orchestra and a dance every Saturday night.

"And a church?" I asked.

She and all the others again showed surprise. "No, there is no church," she answered, "but if anybody wants to go he can go to a nearby village where there is a church. But only old people are going."

Nila questioned them about their families. Two of them are divorced, two are widows, one has a husband away in the Army and the other three are single. So many Russians, they said, were killed in the war that many women are unmarried, even young women.

And how about their work, I asked. All on the milk brigade, they answered; milk fourteen cows three times a day.

Glimpsing the vice-chairman and his followers disappearing around the corner of a faraway building, Nila and I decided we'd better catch them. By the time we did, they were hiking down a country road with a field of cucumbers on the left. Nila popped into the field and began hurriedly to gather in a modest harvest, but a man rode up on a bicycle and ordered her out. Nevertheless, she held on to those she had.

The vice-chairman led us into a building where they make "the best wine in Russia." He ordered the manager to fill the few available glasses; then he disappeared into the cellar.

When the glasses were brimming, I started to take one, but Nila, frowning, stopped me. "You can't drink before the vice-chairman returns," she whispered, biting off a sizable hunk of cucumber.

"No?"

"Of course not." She bit off another hunk of cucumber. "It's not done."

Nobody else, though, understood this fine point of etiquette and the glasses were soon empty. The manager rinsed them in a bucket of water and refilled them.

When the vice-chairman reappeared, he asked, "Shall we continue our sight-seeing tour or shall we have dinner?"

"Have dinner." Nila, deciding instantly that the invitation included us, shouted louder than anybody else.

At the door of the dining room, which was in the same small white building behind which we went to the privy, we took turns washing our hands beneath a spigot over a washbasin and drying them on a communal towel held by a buxom woman.

"They think of everything, don't they?" A member of the English party asked me in tones of awe.

We were at one long table, the vice-chairman at the head and Ward at the foot. A water glass of wine was at each place and food was everywhere: platters of torn-off chunks of white bread ("To give the black bread is not polite," Nila murmured); cut-glass compotes of pears and large, pale-green plums; herring with slices of white onion and little black olives, covered with sunflower oil; two kinds of cheese, a yellow and a white cheese called Brenza, made from goat's milk; Polish sausage; honey ("Where to eat it?" Nila questioned); green peppers cooked in sunflower oil and sprinkled with fried onions; cold green peppers stuffed with carrots, onions and tomatoes; sliced onions and tomatoes; and butter fashioned into fancy designs.

As we were about to dive into as many of these dishes as our plates would hold, the vice-chairman got to his feet and made a speech. He apologized for the absence of the chairman; it happens that the chairman at this very minute is with a Soviet delegation visiting farms in the United States. The occasion would be much better, the vice-chairman declared gallantly, if the chairman were only present. Then he talked again about the achievements of the collective farm.

"Today there are still many bad things," he said. "We have made many mistakes; but—" he paused for emphasis and spread out his big arms—"but the theme of all Russia is, What is bad today will be better tomorrow, and the next day it will be excellent."

Nila, who had been eating plums steadily through the vice-chairman's speech, though she kept her eyes fastened on his face, put her mouth to my ear and whispered, "So deeply he believes in it, what's a one-hole toilet?"

The vice-chairman continued and I wished I had the nerve

to eat a plum. I felt I could only roll small pieces of bread into pellets and slip them stealthily into my mouth.

At last, however, he reached his peroration. "In spite of differences in beliefs and in spite of differences of opinions, we all, I'm sure, have one thing in common—the desire for world peace."

We stood, lifted our water glasses of wine and drank.

Then we plunged into the hors d'oeuvres.

Following the hors d'oeuvres came big bowls of soup with "unborn" eggs and pieces of chicken afloat in it. Then while we were still eating the soup course, the waitresses brought in platters of stewed goose and breaded veal cutlets. As there was no room on the table for them, they put them down on top of the platters of hors d'oeuvres. Then they brought in baked chicken spread on mounds of homemade noodles; then meat balls and rice.

The vice-chairman called to his side a rawboned woman with red, rough patches of skin across her high cheekbones, who had been standing in the background supervising the waitresses. "Dear guests," the vice-chairman said, waving his arm toward her and smiling broadly, "I want you to know that our cook is the most distinguished woman in this collective farm. She is decorated by the order of Lenin and was a delegate to the Communist Festival in Moscow. I propose a toast to Nadia."

We stood and drank to Nadia.

Nila started a Ukrainian song. Immediately Nadia, folding her heavy arms under her heavy breasts, joined her in a high, piercing voice. They sang in parts. Nila stopped, Nadia started, Nadia stopped, Nila started. Then the vice-chairman came in; but shortly he gave a gesture of disgust. "There are not enough voices catching on," he said.

Quiet reigning and the water glasses refilled with wine, the vice-chairman delivered another speech. Beginning with the surprising statement that at the beginning of the meal he had made only a very few brief remarks, out of consideration for our hunger, and that now he would make a real speech, he launched into a more detailed account of the collective farm's progress.

"Such a power and such a poise, that man," Nila whispered.

Finally he closed with another reference to the chairman's visit to the United States. "They have told him," he said, "that he can learn everything that is good in American farming and bring it back to us here at Bondarny."

This moved me to my feet and, raising my glass, I said, "I, too, will carry back all I've learned good in Russia to the people of the United States." Then, realizing this was no proper toast, I added, just like that, "To peace and friendship."

Then Ward, his plump, pink cheeks pinker than a sun-bathing baby's, strode swiftly to the head of the table, put his arm around the vice-chairman's broad shoulders and pronounced this a historic occasion. Here he, a Wall Street broker, a capitalist, no less, sits at one end of the table and the vice-chairman, a Communist and a day laborer on a collective farm, sits at the other end.

He spoke with ease and Nila and I were impressed until the very moment he made his toast, and then he blundered terribly; he mentioned that unmentionable name in Russia. Flourishing his glass slightly above his head, he said, "God bless us all and keep us in friendship."

Every English-speaking person gasped; but the interpreter "saves him," Nila whispered as we pushed our chairs back and got once more to our feet. "She's smart and quick. She didn't translate 'God bless us,' she just said, 'May we keep in friendship.'"

Balancing his hands in front of him, the vice-chairman led us in a rendition—and I do mean rendition—of "Auld Lang Syne." We linked arms, raised our voices in the Ukrainian, Russian, English and United States versions of this nostalgic number and swayed gently from side to side.

When we finished, the vice-chairman himself went around the table, refilling everybody's glass and saying, "Drink up! Drink up!" Then, back at his place, he focused his eyes on Nila and announced that because some people were so hungry he hadn't got to show us his summer and winter theaters, but maybe we could visit them now. Also, we were welcome to visit in the people's homes.

Immediately the interpreter-guide of the British group threw cold water on these suggestions. We must leave at once for Odessa; her people had tickets for the evening performance of Aïda.

So, without further ado, everybody got up and shook hands with the vice-chairman and the waitresses; but then a few decided they must take pictures of Nadia. She posed with the bored air of a Hollywood queen.

"You look as if you had already got tired of having your picture made," Nila said to her.

"Yes, I have it made all the time." She sighed deeply. "All the time."

Walking to the car Nila excitedly pointed out to me the significant part the awarding of medals and the displaying of photographs in public places plays in Soviet life. "Everybody wants to have his accomplishments recognized," she declared. "Remember the glass case we saw yesterday showing the pictures of the best people?"

(Yes, I remembered. We saw on the outside of a public building this large case, like a photographer's show window, displaying the names of Odessa's Board of Honor—the top collective-farmers, teachers, engineers, lawyers, workers.)

"Well," Nila went on, "those honorary people are happier than the people Ford gives a million dollars to. When I lived in Moscow in this huge apartment building, the cleaning woman invented some kind of brush to wash the windows and the superintendent called a meeting of all the people in the apartment house and gave her a piece of dress material for her contribution to the motherland. Willie, I wish you could have seen her face. Tears flowing. That moment she experiences the highest feeling a human being can get. 'I promise you I'll invent more and more for our dear country,' she said. Can imagine everybody standing there clapping?

"Now here's Nadia. She went to Moscow; maybe she is in the Kremlin; maybe Khrushchev himself shook hands with her, and here she comes back with a beautiful medal. So everybody says to himself, 'I, too, can do something for my country. I, too, can go to Moscow and shake hands with Khrushchev. And so everybody works and works."

As we got into the car, Nila said to the driver that she hoped he'd had some food and wine. "Yes," he answered, "but, pshew, the wine is no good. I had eight glasses and they have had no effect."

Nevertheless, his eyes were glassy, his face flushed and before we could even shut the doors he slammed the gas pedal to the floor and we were off.

Frightened out of my wits as I was, still my admiration for the flexibility of the Russian car grew by leaps and bounds. Approaching the fork of two roads, the driver waited until the very last possible moment, then swerved at a ninety-degree angle into the one that looked best. We tumbled like empty boxes from one side of the back seat to the other. And as for slowing up for anybody or anything, he never heard of it. The sight of one truck passing another inspired him to even greater bursts of speed so that he could swish between them.

When I had abandoned all hope of ever seeing my loved ones again, steam began to rise from beneath the hood and he resorted to a new technique. He gave the car the gas, got it to its maximum momentum, then turned off the ignition and coasted. Finally, though, this technique failed. Steam geysers covered the windshield and we simply had to stop and find water. The radiator had a serious leak.

We stopped by a small marsh of mud and slimy green water, but the driver had no bucket or other utensil with which to dip it up. Then we remembered the lunch we had brought in case the collective farm didn't feed us, and we got out a bottle of mineral water. The radiator gulped it down and panted for more. The driver descended to the marsh, lowered the bottle and waited patiently for it to fill; but finally, when only mud went in, he gave up and drove slowly on until he spied a fairly clear pond.

By now we knew that filling the bottle would be a slow process, so we got out, too, stretched our tense muscles and smiled at two teen-age boys pedaling by on bicycles. They smiled back; then, evidently realizing we were foreigners, they turned around and dismounted. They were unusually handsome youths, one a brunet and the other a blond. The brunet had a chrome-steel tooth clumsily fitted into the front of his mouth.

"The dentistry in Russia is upsettingly bad," Nila muttered.

The boys told us they are in school, but for the summer they are working on the docks and in their hours off they are practicing for a soon-to-be-held bicycle race.

"Did you make the money to buy your bicycle?" I asked.

"Who else?" the brunet answered as if he considered me touched in the head.

Then they began asking questions about us and Nila told them Ward is a capitalist. Their eyes widened and traveled from Ward's head to his feet, disbelief written clearly on their faces. Ward was wearing a white shirt checked in yellow, with no tie, a dark-gray drip-dry coat and gray-and-white seersucker slacks.

"He doesn't look like a capitalist," the brunet protested, finishing his careful scrutiny.

"Not looking like a capitalist is one of the best things about being a capitalist," Ward said, grinning. "A capitalist doesn't have to dress up to make an impression if he doesn't feel like it; a capitalist can dress any way he pleases."

The boys weren't convinced, but we couldn't argue further. The driver had hit on a new scheme for gathering up and carrying water: He had removed the hub cap from the right rear wheel.

"Please give our regards to the people of America," the boys said simultaneously as we got into the car.

_4_   August 17

WHILE NILA AND I were waiting for breakfast to be served in our room, there was a knock on the door and the hotel porter came in, bringing the suitcase I had entrusted to him for mending, as the cloth had pulled away from the leather binding.

"It was very poor workmanship," he said, clucking his tongue, and I was embarrassed for my country, for he spoke only the truth. "But now it will carry stones. It will live longer than you."

Though neither one of these prophecies cheered me, I offered him money, but, to my amazement, he refused it. My eyes and Nila's met. It was the first time since we reached Russia that our money had been turned down.

(This matter of tipping has been a constant source of irritation between Nila and me. Since Soviet propaganda pretends that Russian workers do not accept tips, I am in favor of not giving them. If they accept the credit for being so noble as to be above gratuities, then why not let them enjoy their nobility? But this attitude of mine enrages Nila. "You tip American waiters and porters," she argues hotly. "I've even seen Mark give a waiter a five-dollar bill. So why shouldn't you tip Russians?")

As soon as we finished breakfast, we put our bathing suits on under our dresses. Today is Sunday and we'd heard that practically everybody in Odessa would be at the beach. Then we waited on the sidewalk in front of the hotel for Jenna, Ward and Ruby, who were going with us.

Another woman was also standing there and she began to talk to us. Her name is Mrs. Ratoff and she's from the United States, though she was born in Russia and lived there until she was ten years old. She talks in a high, nasal, rather grating voice, with an accent. Her hair is suspiciously black and her cheeks, which are sallow and cut off from her nose and mouth by two deep wrinkles, are heavily rouged. She looks as if she is in her late sixties and has had a hard life. In fact, she told us she has had a hard life. She has worked in the garment industry since the day she landed in the United States. When she was scarcely tall enough to reach the work tables, she was cutting cloth. Now she's the supervisor of a large cutting room and almost every summer she travels abroad—"My children say to me, 'Mama, go ahead and enjoy yourself' "—but this is her first visit back to Russia.

When Ward, Ruby and Jenna showed up, we headed for Odessa's finest beach. The road leading out of town was clogged with sheep coming into it; with open trucks loaded with people, the women's heads covered by orange babushkas; and with jammed streetcars. The people from nearby farms, said Jenna, were on their way to Odessa to shop.

The beach of beige-toned coarse sand was already crowded when we arrived, though it was not quite ten o'clock. Most of the women were sprawled in the sun in the very wee-est of bikinis and the men were in short-short trunks; but some had already been in swimming and were changing into dry clothes right out on the open beach, for there were no bathhouses. My eyes popped.

"But why?" asked Jenna, sensing my shock. "There is nothing new to see."

She was right, of course; nevertheless, I was shocked, but also fascinated. I watched one woman closely. First she wiped all around the bikini strip that barely covered the tips of her bosom; then she spread the towel over her shoulders and arranged her dry brassière around her waist just below the bosom; then, quickly, she whipped off the strip and pulled up the brassière. This accomplished, the rest, of course, was simple. She put on her dress, which was voluminous, took off her wet pants, dried herself, and drew on her dry pants.

Usually, though, the women put on dry brassières only. For hours they sat in cheap sateen chalk-pink or baby-blue brassières and wet bathing pants. Evidently it is considered harmful to the bosom to leave a wet strip about it for any length of time. And I must say I don't blame them for being careful about their bosoms. If anything went wrong with them, it would be a big, big pain. Ninety out of every hundred women, sitting with their breasts encased in that shiny pink and blue sateen, looked as if they had balloons suspended on strings about their necks.

"Didn't you tell me on the *Baltika*," I said to Nila, "that Russian women aren't supposed to show even a fraction of their breasts?"

"Ah, that's when they have on clothes," she answered, shrugging. "On the beach it is entirely different. They aren't supposed to be covered up. They are here to get the sun."

"I see," I murmured. Then I added, "You'd agree, wouldn't you, that the majority of the women are pretty fat?"

"Practically all the women over thirty are hefty as prize hogs," she said with a flash of anger. "It is because it is not fashionable to eat vegetables. Just wait until they learn to eat correctly; then this extra weight will melt."

We strolled a while close to the sea. Children, naked as angels, were building castles; watermelons and bottles of beer and mineral water were buried in the sand where the waves barely lapped them. The watermelons were the little, round kind, no bigger than honeydew melons.

We found an unoccupied space, pulled off our top clothes and stretched out to sun. Ruby, her face pillowed on her arms and her head covered with a big white sheepskin hat with fringe around the edge, was asleep almost instantly. Nila said the hat is from Kirghiz, but Jenna said that though it looks Kirghizian it is manufactured in China. Almost every other person on the beach had one; the rest wore coolie hats. They too, of course, are from China; also Jenna's and Ruby's bathing suits and their pocketbooks and raincoats are Chinese. I couldn't help but wonder what the Chinese people have left for themselves.

Boats, weighted down with passengers, arrived every ten or fifteen minutes from Odessa, unloaded at the end of a long pier and steamed back, plumes of black smoke waving behind them. A few—a very, very few—cars brought people. The drivers parked them far back from the sea and covered them completely with cloths to protect them from the sand and spray.

Our Capitalist, casting forlorn glances at sleeping Ruby, boasted to Jenna about fabulous Jones Beach on Long Island. "There are between forty and fifty thousand cars there every Sunday in the summer," he said. "And there's a boardwalk there with everything you can think of to entertain the people: archery, games of chance, bowling alleys, bingo; it even has a nine-hole golf course."

Jenna rolled her eyes about as if surprised; but she wasn't seriously impressed.

A woman came by selling shucked corn on the cob. She had

170

it between the folds of an old comforter in a satchel to keep it warm. "The same way Mama and I used to keep the pancakes warm," commented Nila, "when we sold them at the railroad station."

Many people bought ears, including a group of exceptionally lovely-looking young people sitting next to us. The girls were slim and had very light gray and light blue eyes, black hair and high cheekbones. They are typical Ukrainians, Nila said. The Ukrainian women are noted for their beauty.

Seeing them eating corn made me hungry and I asked Nila to buy me an ear; but before she could even get to her feet, a tall, trim, blond young man stepped over and gave her and me ears bigger than any that Man o' War ever ate. Then he passed us salt in a piece of newspaper.

I bit down on mine and shuddered. It was feed corn and was old and hard. I thought, What am I going to do? Luckily Ward broke off an end, but still I had more than I could ever eat. I offered Jenna a piece but, grinning wickedly, she refused. I bit and chewed, bit and chewed. All the young Ukrainians were watching me eagerly.

Ward asked them how they got to the beach and they said in a truck. He shook his head dolefully and gestured toward his seat.

"He's a capitalist," Nila explained, "and he thinks a truck is too hard for his soft capitalist behind."

They roared with laughter, then asked Nila just what does a capitalist do. Nila was at a loss for a moment but then remembered that Ward works in Wall Street. They nodded their heads; they were familiar with Wall Street.

As for them, they attend an agricultural institute in the town of Kishinev. The blond one who gave me the ear of corn is studying ways to prevent diseases that attack vegetables. Another is studying the cultivation of apples and grapes, and the others are studying similar subjects.

They asked if grapes grow in the United States. Yes, said the Capitalist, in California and New York. They shook their heads; they didn't know where these states are. Ward smoothed out the sand and drew a very respectable map of the United States and put pebbles on California and New York.

And what about oranges and apples?

Ward answered Florida and California for oranges and I answered Georgia for apples.

They laughed elatedly. They thought I was referring to Russian Georgia and they wanted to show me they appreciated my attempt at a joke; but the Capitalist told them it was no joke and put a pebble on Georgia in the United States.

By now the group had grown to huge proportions. People wormed forward like snakes on their stomachs and lay prone, their chins in the palms of their propped-up hands; others crawled forward on all fours, then eased down to the sand, and still others walked up boldly and peered over our shoulders at the map and listened intently.

What state do I come from, the young agriculturists asked; and when I said Kentucky, they wanted to know what grows there. I mentioned corn from which bourbon is made. "You have good corn in Iowa," one interrupted, but he was hushed quickly by the others. What else is in Kentucky? Race horses. They had to know what kind of races, who takes part in them, what can they win, are people allowed to bet. They were terribly quick and earnest.

To change the subject, for I was over my head, I said that Kentucky, like the Ukraine, is famous for its beautiful women, but, unfortunately, I was born in Georgia. Then they really went to pieces. I could see my brand of humor hadn't been properly appreciated all these years at home.

The blond boy and another handsome young man got out their cameras and took pictures of us Americans completely surrounded by Russians, and Ward got out his camera and started to take pictures, too; but first everybody had to examine the camera, exclaim over it and ask dozens of questions. Ward took down names and addresses; he will send copies to all the people whom he takes pictures of as soon as he has them developed. Then the Ukrainians took down our names and addresses. They will send us pictures, too.

172

Finally we all went swimming. B-r-r-r, it was freezing. "It is the coldest water in the world," I said.

"Have you ever swum off the Cape?" the Capitalist asked.

"No."

"Then I wouldn't say it was the coldest water in the world until I swam off the Cape."

When we returned to our places in the sand, practically everybody except the young agriculturists and us was eating watermelon. So, quickly, Nila and Jenna went off one way and Ward and Ruby, who had finally awakened, another, to see if they could buy some, and I was left alone with the Russians.

As I stood drying myself off, the blond boy came over and offered me a drink from a glass. Thinking it was mineral water, I took a big swallow, then gasped for breath. It was warm vodka. I blinked the tears from my eyes and saw at least a hundred people watching me, smiles of friendly amusement and pleasure on their faces. Hurriedly I sat down.

The agriculturists gave me a hunk of Polish sausage and slices of bread. I struggled to make conversation, but without Nila and the interpreters I was up against it. Then a small boy ran by on his way to the water and I was reminded of my grandchildren and, with many gestures, began to talk about them. Miraculously, they understood me and asked their "nomens." I began with those named Mark—Mark I, Mark II, Mark III. Their eyes grew big and, laughing, they shook their heads; I had lost them completely; but then Nila and Jenna, their arms piled with watermelons, arrived and Nila explained that all my children who have boys have named one for their grandfather.

Then Nila told them what she considered a big joke on me. She and Jenna, on returning to the beach with the watermelons, couldn't see me anywhere and so Jenna said, "Let's stand perfectly still for a minute and listen for Mrs. Ethridge."

And though these young Ukrainians had never seen me before today, they laughed uproariously as if they appreciated the joke fully. I didn't understand it.

We cut the melons and passed them about and everybody ate them the way I used to eat them in Georgia—the ends poking into my ears. Then the Capitalist and Ruby came with more. We all ate until our chins were chapped with juice and we were foundered.

Finally it was time for us to return to the hotel, for we had to catch a boat for Yalta in the late afternoon. We shook hands for a long time. People who hadn't even been on the outskirts of the party hurried up to shake our hands.

"Please come to Kishinev next time," the young agriculturists urged. "We will give you the best apples and grapes."

"And you all come to Kentucky," I urged in return, and I saw the look of wry amusement in their faces, for the remark was as absurd as if I had said, "You all come to the moon."

VI

Yalta

<u>1</u>   Late afternoon

SIXTEEN HUNDRED PEOPLE, all Russians except Ward, Nila, Mrs. Ratoff and me, crowded onto the Black Sea ship that is to take us to Yalta. They came on foot mostly, having been dumped off street cars at least a mile away. They lugged innumerable suitcases, overstuffed, gaping satchels, and those ubiquitous net bags, lumpy with watermelons and yellow melons similar to our cantaloupes, sausages, bread, tomatoes and hard-boiled eggs.

As usual I leaned on the rail and watched them pour like a flooding river down the long, long pier. The seven o'clock hour of departure grew very close and still they came. Many would be left, I felt sure; yet nobody hurried. They just plodded steadily, heavily forward.

On the stroke of seven the gangplank swung up and the ship sidled slowly out and, amazingly, everybody seemed to be on board. Then an excited porter dashed to the edge of the pier with a suitcase covered in ersatz leopard. He held it aloft. He shouted wildly to the sailors at the head of the gangplank. He ran to and fro. The owners of the suitcase and their friends and acquaintances along the ship's rail yelled and waved their arms.

The porter spied a rowboat with a fisherman at the oars near one corner of the wharf. He rushed toward him, talking and gesturing. Evidently, he persuaded the fisherman to row

175

the suitcase to the still barely moving ship, for hurriedly he hoisted it up and tossed it toward the boat. But, alas, it missed the boat and fell into the sea!

As one man, the passengers at the ship's rail clasped their hands and groaned.

The fisherman tried to reach out for the suitcase, but it floated away. The porter danced madly up and down. The fisherman plopped back into his seat, grasped the oars and rowed after the bobbing rectangle of leopard. Would he reach it before it became waterlogged and sank? For many minutes it hardly seemed likely. The tide was sweeping it swiftly out. Inch by inch, though, he gained upon it, and finally he was on top of it and succeeded in dragging it in. The rail watchers cheered. However, the fisherman hadn't a chance now of catching the ship. We were a goodly distance from shore and plowing purposefully ahead.

On entering our cabin, I found Nila ecstatic. "Look at these beautiful towels!" she exclaimed. "Look at the beautiful linen sheets! You scarcely ever see these any more. And look at the wood!" She strode across the room and laid her hand on the highly polished veneer of the walls. "I think this is even better than the *Batory*. I never traveled in Russia in such a style."

We unpacked hurriedly and joined Ward in his stateroom for a drink of vodka or mineral water. He was lounging in a big chair, a twinkle in his blue eyes and a glass in his hand, while Jenna and Mrs. Ratoff's Intourist guide stood in the middle of the room, literally wringing their hands.

Mrs. Ratoff had been assigned to share the Capitalist's cabin and she refused to do it. She was now sitting in the lobby of the ship, her suitcases and other belongings stacked about her.

There were only two de luxe staterooms on the ship and we four Intourist tourists had them and there were no unoccupied cabins. Mrs. Ratoff's guide was frantic, but Ward was relaxed and amused and Nila and I, I must say to our everlasting discredit, were amused too.

Mrs. Ratoff's guide hurried out but in a little while returned with the news that she had located a man who had agreed to consider moving in with Ward and giving his cabin to Mrs.

Ratoff. "May I show you the man?" she asked Ward most deferentially.

The Capitalist nodded and in due time she returned with the man, introduced him and urged him to have a seat. He was a rather distinguished-looking elderly man, his skin saddle-brown and his hair and bushy brows black with flurries of white. A Russian by birth, he now lives in Turkey.

After some minutes of solemnly and silently regarding Ward, he got up and, without even murmuring a by-your-leave, went out. He had decided, so Nila said with a burst of giggles, against rooming with Ward.

And so it turned out and the guide had to search for some other solution. Finally, she located an empty berth in a cabin with three Russian women.

Mrs. Ratoff is lucky at that. I've never been on a ship half so jammed. Taking a turn around the deck I realized that the vast majority of the passengers were spending the night right there, some in hard chairs and some on benches, but most of them curled on the floor over their suitcases, cloth bundles and "perhaps" bags. Some were even stretched out on the slightly raised hatch cover, with the huge hook that lifts out the cargo swaying and creaking only a few inches about their heads. One old woman on the floor sprawled her upper body over one suitcase and held with clutching hands to two others. Her eyes were wide and apprehensive.

"She makes herself uncomfortable on purpose so she won't fall asleep," Nila told me as we stepped around and over her. "She's afraid if she falls asleep, somebody will steal her things."

2   August 18

YALTA REMINDS ME of the cities of Greece and of Italy and other Mediterranean countries. Most of it is on flat land that hugs the U-shaped harbor, but some of it clings to the precipitous slopes that circle it from shore to shore. Flooded with brilliant, yellow-white sun, oleanders, palms, banana trees and other semitropical plants flourish everywhere.

Nila and I have a spacious suite on the third floor of a small, unpretentious hotel—a big living room, two bedrooms, a bath and two balconies. Extremely tall, slender cypresses shoot like rockets right past our windows and I feel tempted to crawl into one and nest there indefinitely. Between the cypresses, we can glimpse the navy-blue (I wonder why it is called Black?) sea.

On the balcony next to ours, when we arrived at the hotel shortly after noon, was a group of very gay, well-dressed, important-looking men and women having dinner. The table was elegant, with a fresh white tablecloth, tall-stemmed wineglasses bubbling with golden wine, and a large cut-glass compote heaped with fruit. From snatches of conversation we overheard, Nila decided they were members of Russia's movie world.

After Nila and I had our own dinner, we started on an expedition along the rocky coast to see the famous castle built in 1846 by Count Michael Varansov in the village of Alypka.

Jenna had deserted us temporarily for a hotel in the heart of the city, and a local guide with the lovely name of Larissa accompanied us. She is a very pretty, dainty blonde with large, golden-brown eyes and the most aristocratic features I've seen in the U.S.S.R.

Winding up the high hills, the Black Sea on our left, we passed many huge stucco buildings which the Communists call sanatoriums, though they are really more like resort hotels. It is true some ill people come to them, but the majority are in good health and come solely for a rest and vacation. I saw several of these sanatoriums in Odessa; here on the rim of the mountains are many more. In fact, there are 112 of them in Yalta alone.

The people who stay in these sanatoriums pay only thirty per cent of their expenses; the remainder is paid by their trade unions. (And, of course, everybody who is anybody in Russia belongs to a trade union.) If they are actually ill or run down and need doctors' treatments and a long rest, they can stay three months, six months or just as long as necessary and still pay only thirty per cent of the bill. Invalids from the war are the only exceptions; they pay nothing. The usual length of stay for the hale and hearty is two weeks.

The castle is all a castle should be, even to the sharp-toothed, crenelated walls. The architect, who was an Englishman, tried, so Larissa told us, to catch the feeling of the pointed gray crags that rise up almost perpendicularly behind the castle in what she called the walls' "tusks."

At the base of its long façade stretches a beautiful garden teeming with pink-blossoming oleanders, crepe myrtle (the Russians call them Chinese lilacs), pomegranates, figs, laurel, box and other familiar plants; and below the garden—hundreds of rocky feet below—rolls the sea.

Though the wings of the castle could be transplanted to England and be perfectly at home, the central portion is Moorish and over the curved main doorway is written in Arabic, "All the Power is from God," a shocking proclamation in this heathen land.

We had to tie felt-soled slippers over our shoes to slide across the floors, for they are exquisitely fashioned from many small pieces of wood into intricate designs. We were permitted in only those few rooms on the first floor that are now a museum; all the others have been taken over for one more sanatorium.

Every room is beautiful, but I liked best the handsomely paneled dining room that extends across the front of a goodly part of the central building, its three huge windows, from ceiling to floor, overlooking the water.

"And we in the United States talk about picture windows as if they are something new," Nila remarked.

I started to reply, but a Russian standing on the edge of a group listening to a lecture turned and growled, "Comrades, behave yourselves."

Coming outside, we walked in a perfect English park of thirty-seven and a half acres. Crimean and Mexican pines, holly, acacia, sequoia trees and hundreds of others that I didn't recognize grow on the slopes of the craggy peaks.

A poorly dressed Russian woman eased to Nila's side and said with a pleased grin, "Those rich aristocrats sure had the best of everything, and now we, the people, are getting the benefit."

Churchill occupied the castle during the Yalta Conference in February 1945, and he liked it so much, according to Larissa, that he offered to buy it from the Russian government. I liked it, too, but not that much. After all, it is a little out of the way from Kentucky.

Motoring back to Yalta, we passed cars with fancy curtains draped inside across the rear windows, blocking completely the drivers' rear view, and cars in parking lots outside the sanatoriums encased in plastic covers.

We made one stop at a sanatorium that is truly a sanatorium. It treats practically all ailments, but specializes in heart, respiratory, bronchial and nervous diseases. It was erected in 1955 and is an impressive, grandiose structure of 230 rooms, with an adjacent building of 100 rooms. There are wide porches where patients sleep in the open, overlooking the sea, a mammoth swimming pool under glass, shuffleboards, tennis courts and even a boathouse full of canoes. And what's more, the canoes have red paddles. They looked very gay, flashing in and out of the water.

Come evening, Nila and I sat for a while on our balcony amidst the cypress spires and watched young people, predominantly girls, dance on a cement court across the street to music from a loud radio. A new moon, as silky and thin as a baby's cut-off curl, and one merry star lay upon the slickly waxed, deep-blue linoleum of the sky.

Then we hiked through the streets, dusty and dark, until we reached the wide promenade that borders the waterfront for a mile or more. Hundreds of people were walking there and other hundreds were sitting on a breakwater. The sound of talk was as muffled and steady as the engine of a running plane.

Around eleven o'clock the crowd began to thin and Nila and I made our way back to the hotel. The new moon had gone in, but the sky was jumping with stars.

August 19

THE INTOURIST CAR arrived early and I went out and found Ward, Jenna and Larissa already in it. Nila had a "bug" and had decided to stay in bed and Ruby has gone away for a few days to a nearby village, to see her parents, she said. Her absence and other matters had got the Capitalist down.

One of the other matters was that he spent an hour last evening lecturing to a large crowd of Russians in front of his hotel on how to make money in Wall Street and he saw by their faces that they thought he was making up every word of it. And he's not accustomed to having his words taken lightly. He is a professor in a school of business, he said, and when he lectures, his students accept what he says as gospel.

His professorship was news to Jenna (it was to me, too, as far as that goes) and she rolled her big eyes and remarked saucily, "The next thing you'll be telling us you are Vice-President of the United States."

Ward grinned at her fleetingly, then returned to his gripes. The crowd was especially skeptical, he said, when he told them he could use any of a hundred textbooks in his classes or he could use none.

Also, he was irked that he hadn't thought to bring a Polaroid camera on the trip. He ran into an American at his hotel last night who had one and who absolutely shattered the Russians every time he snapped and developed a picture. The Capitalist was so envious he could bite himself.

The object of our trip this morning was the Palace of Livadia, built in 1911 by Nicholas II, the last of the Romanov czars. He visited it only twice before he was murdered by the Bolsheviks. Now it is a national museum, of course, and a sanatorium for seven hundred vacationing Russians. However, President Roosevelt and his staff made it their headquarters during the Yalta Conference.

Livadia, like the castle of Count Varansov, sits high above

the Black Sea with the mountains at its back and it, too, has many rooms with glorious mosaic floors. Also very beautiful ceilings and chandeliers.

Shuffling through it, our mouths agape, we passed Mrs. Ratoff and she commented brightly to me in her high, scratchy voice, "Those old Russians surely lived the life of Riley, didn't they?"

This juxtaposition of the Romanovs and the Rileys took me so by surprise that, quick-witted as I am, I could think of no response.

From the palace we jolted down a narrow, rocky road to a public beach completely covered with smooth gray rocks about the size of hen eggs, which in turn were completely covered by sun-bathers and swimmers. The women had small paper cornucopias over their noses to protect them from the sun. There wasn't a bottle of cream or suntan oil the entire length of the sea-washed strip.

We joined the sun-bathers. The rocks were almost as hot as turned-on gas burners. Shortly I noticed that many of the women had angry-looking red circles on the exposed parts of their bodies. Poor souls, I thought to myself, they are afflicted with ringworm or some similar disease; but when I got up my courage to ask Larissa the name of this terrible blight she laughed hysterically and said they were only the marks caused by the rocks when the women lay upon them.

Baked through, we sauntered to a pavilion and Jenna and the Capitalist went to buy four bottled soft drinks while Larissa and I found an unoccupied wooden table. Ward was more put out than ever when he and Jenna, carrying the bottles and tiny paper cups, joined us.

"It took twelve minutes for that girl to serve four people," he complained. "In the United States she could have served twenty-four in the same length of time without even trying." He shrugged his heavy, broad shoulders. "But I understand it. The girl here knows she is just going to pass out bottles so many hours a day all her life and so why should she hurry. She has no incentive."

Jenna and Larissa listened with serious faces but made no comment.

Then the Capitalist took note of the paper cups. "My God, Mr. Lilly would turn over in his grave if he saw these tiny, flimsy objects."

This time he went too far for Jenna. "Why, these paper cups are a terrific achievement," she said with spirit. "I never heard of such in Russia before."

Ward refused to be squelched. The drink was warm and tasteless, he growled. Also Russian champagne is tasteless. He tried some last night and it was terrible.

Feeling uncomfortable at his continuing criticism of Russian products in front of Jenna and Larissa, I said to them, "I must compliment you two on your wonderful dispositions. I don't believe Americans would be so tolerant if Russians came to their country and found fault with so many things."

"It's their job," Ward said quickly. "They are carefully chosen to associate with tourists because of their tact, common sense and good dispositions. You never saw an airline stewardess get angry with a passenger, did you?"

The two girls kept quiet until Jenna, flashing her impish smile about the table, ordered, "Drink up, everybody. I'm going to return the bottles and make some money, too. The Capitalist is not the only one who knows how to make money."

"You'd better be careful," retorted Ward, chuckling. "If you become a capitalist, you'll be liquidated."

Ward's show of good-humor was short-lived. Zooming around sharp curves on the road back to Yalta, we saw signs announcing: MOTHERS OF THE WHOLE WORLD FIGHT FOR PEACE and WE ARE FOR PEACE and DOWN WITH WARMONGERS and the Capitalist flared out at me because I thought their purpose was to impress foreign tourists with Russia's longing for peace and foolishly said so.

"How can you be so dumb?" he asked, scowling. "There are not enough foreign tourists in this part of the U.S.S.R. for the government to go to the expense of erecting those signs for them." He pressed his lips together and shook his head as if my ignorance was beyond human comprehension.

"These signs and all the other peace signs you've seen are solely for the Russians," he went on. "They are to convince them that their government yearns and works unceasingly for peace and if war comes it won't be the fault of the Soviet leaders, but the fault of the United States and other countries who force war upon them."

Larissa, Jenna and I listened with wide, startled eyes. I'm sure the idea was as new to the guides as it was to me.

"Then," Ward concluded, flinging out one hand, "then, of course, the Russian people will fight happily to the death to save the innocent motherland from the barbaric invaders."

We rode on for several minutes in silence, everybody except the Capitalist evidently pondering his theory; then Jenna asked do we have such signs in the United States and I answered, no, not exactly, but in the South sometimes at dangerous curves we have billboards that shout PREPARE TO MEET THY GOD.

This struck her, agnostic that she is, as hilariously funny, and from then on, every time the car swerved on two wheels around a mountain shoulder, she turned from her front-seat perch and, making fearsome faces, cried, "Prepare to meet thy God."

4   Afternoon
—

BY AFTERNOON NILA had recovered from her indisposition, and so we traveled into the mountains in the opposite direction from the one we'd been taking and spent several heavenly hours in the most beautiful, elaborate botanical garden I'd ever seen.

The garden was started as far back as 1812 by Czar Alexander I and has everything in it—I mean it, everything! Well, maybe, on second thought, no Gordonia. There is even a handsome library with 1,000 volumes on botanical subjects. Then there are acre-sized beds of begonias, starry with dainty pink blooms, the kind I have three pots of at home and tend with such loving care with no results; 800 different kinds of roses ("You should see them in June," said Larissa); cedars of Lebanon in much better condition than their sad, straggly ancestors in their native habitat; Japanese bamboo; 500-year-old yews and sequoias; white lotus and pink water lilies blooming madly in square and round pools; weeping cedars somewhat similar to our weeping willows; a garden of all types of cacti ("A Little Bit of Mexico," a sign reads); madroña trees which change their bark four times between spring and fall, first brown, then red, then pink, then white—the Russians call them "shameless trees"; hibiscus; great sweeps of purple heliotrope and pale-blue lantana massed together; hydrangea . . .

In all, the garden covers forty-five acres and every acre is lovely. Its director makes 7,000 rubles a month, which is one of the top salaries in Russia; but, after all, as Larissa pointed out, he is a scientist and all scientists are paid well.

In the car, heading back toward Yalta, our talk veered from salaries to property, and Larissa and Jenna got into an amazing argument. Larissa contended with all sincerity that Russians can own land, as well as houses; but Jenna insisted they cannot own land.

"But," Larissa argued, her golden-brown eyes candid and troubled, "I sold my house and the land it stood on and the gardens and orchards around it when I moved from Kiev to Yalta."

"You couldn't have sold the land," Jenna contradicted her. "The state owns the land. The state gives you the land to build a house on and to plant a garden and orchard on, and the house, garden and orchard are yours; but not the land."

Larissa shook her lovely blond head bewilderedly. "Perhaps you're right, but I never realized I didn't own the land."

"Well, for all practical purposes you did," said Jenna, "but in theory it belongs to the state. You can do anything with the house you want—sell it, rent it, even tear it down; but the state retains the right to the land."

"Can you build any kind of house you want to?" I asked. "That is, any kind you can afford?"

"Yes," Jenna answered promptly, "and the government helps you to build it. The government will lend you ten thousand rubles and you needn't start paying it back until one year and the first payment then is only one thousand rubles. All these houses here on these slopes—" Jenna waved her hand to the right—"are privately owned."

We were on the outskirts of Yalta, though still high above it. The houses that Jenna referred to stick like eagles' nests on the narrow shelves of the mountain ridge. There are so many of them, and the land is so steep, they seem to perch on one another's roofs; but they were almost unnoticeable in the late-afternoon light, for their low stucco façades are smothered in fig trees and cypress and in grape and morning-glory vines.

❦   ❦

5   ❦   August 20

THE CAPITALIST, NILA, Larissa, Jenna and I took a picnic lunch and caught a boat to the fishing village of Gurzof, crouching beneath the muzzle of Drinking Bear Mountain, to spend the day on the beach. The Capitalist needed only a camel to look like a Moslem chief setting out with his four wives.

The boat seemed powerfully small to me to be sailing out to sea. It was only thirty-six feet long and was completely open except for a narrow strip of roof. Two rows of benches, facing each other, ran along both sides and they were packed with gay, vacationing Russians.

We'd scarcely got under way when a young woman asked me, "Are you English?" and when I said, "No, I'm American," she glowed like a floodlight. If I had been Rita Hayworth and Marilyn Monroe rolled into one she couldn't have been more pleased. With Nila interpreting, she told me she is studying to be a surgeon and has only one more year in the medical institute. Her father is a doctor and so was her grandfather. Her grandfather, of course, had private patients, as he practiced before the Revolution; but her father works in clinics for the government at a fixed salary. However, in his time off he does have a few private patients and she, too, hopes to have some.

Then another young woman joined in and wanted to know how long a person has to go to school in the United States to be a doctor; then another asked how long does a person have to go to school to be an engineer. And here once again I was wishing I'd learned more about my own country before I set out to learn about Russia.

Then a most dashing figure, wearing on the back of his blond

186

head one of those big white sheepskin Kirghizian hats, chimed in and asked, of all things, about our Civil War.

Believe it or not, I told him, the Civil War, as he called it, though I myself as a Southerner preferred the name War of the Federal Invasion, was before my time.

He opened his mouth wide, showing two even rows of beautiful white teeth, without a gold or steel one among them, and laughed heartily.

Just what did he want to know about the Civil War, I asked him, and he answered, "Did the South treat the slaves as terribly as Harriet Beecher Stowe said in *Uncle Tom's Cabin?*"

I counted ten real fast and then told him as unbiasedly as I could about the treatment of the slaves and the real causes of the war. It was quite a lecture. My history professor at Wesleyan would have been amazed. In fact, anybody who knew me would have been amazed.

Then, of course, the next question was about the treatment of the Negro in the South today. And don't think I didn't sweat blood and tears over that one. I first told him about the peaceful integration of the schools in Kentucky; but then I had to talk about Mississippi, Alabama, Georgia and Arkansas. He had read all about Little Rock.

"And what is happening in Little Rock now?" he asked.

"God only knows," I replied from the heart.

By now a dozen people were listening eagerly, their eyes alert. If I could only ask them questions; but they gave me no chance. A woman who had left her seat at the rear of the launch and was standing at the edge of the crowd called out, "Can any American come to Russia who wants to?"

"Yes," I answered innocently, "if he can get a Russian visa."

"She means," Nila explained, "will the United States allow anybody who wants to come to come."

"Absolutely," I said proudly. "Didn't the United States permit Paul Robeson to come?" Then I told them about the Supreme Court's last ruling that the State Department has no right to deny a United States citizen a passport because he is a Communist or holds other beliefs inimical to our form of government.

Yalta

"The Supreme Court ruled," I concluded, "that to deny such a person the right to travel is contrary to the Constitution, which guarantees every citizen freedom of speech, freedom of religion, freedom of assembly—"

"Yes," interrupted the dashing young man in the sheepskin hat, "we in Russia are guaranteed those freedoms, too."

I looked at him searchingly and decided he really believed this. Having never known freedom as we know it, he wasn't conscious of being denied it. And he's typical, I'm sure, of the vast majority of the citizens of the U.S.S.R.

The boat docked in the shadow of the towering Drinking Bear and we spent several happy hours of sunning on a rocky beach and swimming in the sea; and then it was time for lunch. We spread our tomatoes, hard-boiled eggs, hunks of brown bread and sausage on the paper they were wrapped in and started to eat; instantly a militiaman materialized from nowhere and said it is not permitted to eat on the beach; but when Jenna and Larissa explained that they are Intourist guides with three American tourists, he smiled politely and withdrew.

Then, just as on picnics in Kentucky, black clouds not much larger at first than boxing gloves began to swing about in the empty arena of the still brilliantly lighted, gold-blue sky; the wind quickened and the waves grew big. We had better gather up our belongings quickly, we decided, and hurry to the dock. A boat left every hour and it behooved us, we could plainly see, to be on the next one. We couldn't afford to be caught on this distant spot; that is, Nila, Ward and I couldn't afford to, for we were scheduled to sail at six o'clock for the Black Sea resort of Sochi.

The launch was already at the pier when we arrived, and the captain and his assistant were busily putting up canvas curtains on the sea side. They had a struggle keeping their balance, for the waves were very high by now and were slamming the hull against the pilings of the dock.

The horn blasted off again and again. It sounded as if the captain was warning all the vacationers they had better take this last chance to get to Yalta. A dozen or so came running. With the help of the strong arms of the captain and his assistant we got aboard and huddled in the rear of the bow, close up against the enginehouse.

The launch ventured forth and immediately, out of the protection of the land, plunged into swells, splitting the crests in two and tossing spray high into the air. The canvas curtains and the strip of roof were no help. The water swept in, slapping our faces like wet rags. One woman raised her umbrella, I put on my bathing cap and everybody except the Capitalist wrapped bath towels and anything he had handy about his shoulders.

But the Capitalist took off instead of putting on. He stripped off his pants (fortunately, he still had on his bathing trunks) and slipped off his shoes, then perched on the rail. He was ready to jump at the drop of a wave.

Then Larissa was ill and threw up over a goodly portion of the deck. Then we sighted a man in a rowboat skiing over the swells and falling into troughs right across our bow. As we came nearer, he stood up, swaying, and held a rope aloft. He wanted us to catch it and tow him to land before he foundered.

The captain slowed down; the man swung the rope with all his might. The captain grabbed it, attached it to our stern; then, as if nothing unusual had happened, he started up the engine at full speed and headed toward a pier reaching into the sea. The pier was spotted with people. It is the sea station for the botanical garden where we spent yesterday afternoon.

The minute Ward realized that the captain was going to try to dock there and take on passengers, he sprung into action. Hopping off the rail, he stood, legs spraddled, in front of Nila, Jenna and me and talked fast and vehemently. We must get off the boat, he said. It was terribly dangerous and foolish to try to make Yalta on such a little craft in such a rough sea. He was a Marine in the Pacific for thirty-seven months and he knew how easy it is for a boat the size of this one to capsize. Just let one big wave wash over it and let the water left behind shift suddenly from one side to the other and the boat would go down. He, for one, was not going to risk it and if we cared anything about our lives we shouldn't either.

The Lord knows Nila, Jenna and I didn't want to sink with

the boat, but how would we catch the ship for Sochi if we got off so many miles from Yalta? And if we missed this one, who knows when we could catch another?

Ward announced that Larissa would get off with him, as she was too sick to go further, and they would climb the mountain to the botanical garden, find a telephone and call Intourist to send a car.

But that would take hours, Nila, Jenna and I argued. It would take an hour to climb the mountain and find a telephone, another hour for the car to come and another hour to drive back to Yalta.

No matter, the Capitalist said, he was getting off.

So, as the launch rocked and beat against the pilings, he climbed onto the pier and dragged white-faced, silent, trembling Larissa behind him. I had the feeling I'd never see the Capitalist again and was quite saddened. He acts like a spoiled rich bachelor at times, but then don't all spoiled rich bachelors?

With Larissa out of the way, Jenna staggered to the captain, borrowed a bucket with a rope attached, and lowered it over the side to get water to wash away the vomit; but just as the bucket touched the sea a wave reared up and jerked it from her hands. Her huge eyes popping with shock and her arms clutching her stomach, she looked around at Nila and me and, for a moment, we lost our fears in hysterical laughter.

Then once more our boat was racing like a highly bred jumper through the sea. As the swells rose, it, shuddering mightily, gathered all its strength to lunge over them, but never quite made it. Each time it splintered the top of the watery wall, then tumbled heavily into the yawning ditch beyond.

The Russian men joked and laughed in a forced sort of gaiety. One young, rather cocky fellow clowned continually. "As soon as we reach Yalta," he shouted at one point, "I'll take everybody someplace for a drying out."

Nila, Jenna and I certainly could have used such a place when we finally disembarked, but we had no time for a "drying out." With our soaked skirts clinging to our legs, water dripping from our hair and chins, and self-conscious grins on our faces, we hurried on foot through the streets to our hotels.

190

VII

Sochi

<u>1</u>

THE FIRST PERSON Nila, Jenna and I saw when the Intourist car dropped us near the foot of the gangplank of the ship which is to take us to Sochi was the Capitalist. His round, pink-blond face, circled in grins, and his right hand, holding a glass, hung out the small window two or three decks above us.

Gosh, I thought to myself, something was certainly tickling the Capitalist's funny bone. I'd never seen him in such fine fettle. Could it be that his coup in getting aboard ahead of us after we had predicted he would never make it amused him so?

We waved and his head shrank back into his big shoulders and his chuckles spilled out. We didn't hear the chuckles—he was too far away—but we could see them plainly. What in heaven's name had got into him? Was one of us losing her slip or pants?

At the gangplank a male representative of Intourist handed us our reservations and remarked casually that I was to share a stateroom with Ward and Nila one with Mrs. Ratoff.

Well, if he had said we were booked for the salt mines of Siberia we couldn't have been more horrified. Gasping, I glanced up at the Capitalist. He was now completely convulsed. He looked as if he might even fall out the window, he was that weak with glee. Of course he'd known since reaching the ship that we were rooming together, and he'd been waiting right there in that little window to see my reaction to the news.

I must say he got his money's worth. I went absolutely wild. "I can't do that!" I shouted at the Intourist representative. "It's impossible! Quite impossible! A decent American woman doesn't stay in a room with a man unless she's married to him. I can't do it. You'll have to make some other arrangement. You'll simply have to. . . ."

I talked so fast Jenna had a hard time interpreting for me; but the Intourist representative was not moved. He regarded me as if I were a hysterical child. "It's only for one night," he said in tones of sweet reasonableness.

"But one night is one night too many," I cried. "This is simply not done in the United States. My husband would divorce me. He'd think I'd lost my mind."

The Intourist representative looked as if he was sure I already had. "Oh, why," I could see he was asking himself, "Oh, why does the United States permit such an immature, off-balance female to leave its shores?"

Breathing hard, he repeated again and again that it was only for one night, and I, breathing just as hard, repeated again and again one night was one too many.

Of course Nila was in it, too. She shouted even louder than I did and in Russian, which made it seem louder and angrier. Once she got so undone she yelled that she and I couldn't possibly be separated for we used the same toothbrush, when she meant to say tooth paste.

Finally, it sank upon us that we were getting nowhere; we were only backing up traffic for about a mile; so we adjourned to Ward's—and my—stateroom to carry on the fight.

The Capitalist had pulled his grinning head out of the window and now relaxed in a big chair, sipping his drink. It was vodka, diluted with warm tap water. His bright-blue eyes glinted with devilment.

Nila and I told him right off that he would simply have to move out; it was as little as any gentleman could do.

But where was he to move, he asked, still grinning and not

taking our suggestion at all seriously. He had heard, he said, there wasn't an unoccupied berth on the ship.

Why not move in with Mrs. Ratoff? we asked.

Why did we think Mrs. Ratoff would room with him this trip any sooner that she would the last one? he rebutted.

We had no answer to this, but suddenly I was stricken with regret at my indifference to the plight of Mrs. Ratoff on that last trip.

Then Nila had an inspiration. Why couldn't she stay in the stateroom with Ward and me? That surely would make everything proper. She'd sleep on the couch or on a blanket on the floor and let Ward and me have the two beds.

No, said Ward. He'd sleep on the couch or the floor.

I demurred. I didn't know how proper this arrangement was.

Then Nila had another inspiration. If three of us were going to share the same stateroom, why not ask Mrs. Ratoff to move in with us and let the Capitalist have her room?

This struck us as an absolutely brilliant idea, and Nila and Jenna dashed out to find Mrs. Ratoff's stateroom. It turned out to be next door and Mrs. Ratoff was already unpacked and settled in. (To be sure that she had a stateroom this voyage, she had, no doubt, been on board since early morning.)

Nila sprang her idea upon her, but Mrs. Ratoff didn't take to it. Indeed, she didn't take to it at all. Highly excited, she accompanied Nila and Jenna as far as Ward's—and my—doorway to explain to me why she didn't take to it.

"I've suffered enough," she cried in her thin, rasping voice, her head poked around the doorjamb. "I'm de luxe."

"We know you're de luxe," Nila cried back at her. "Nobody is saying you're not de luxe."

"I've suffered enough, I tell you," she continued to cry. "I shared a cabin with three women last time and I'm not going to do it this time."

"Nobody is asking you to share a cabin with three women," Nila yelled, very angry by now. "We're just asking you to share one with two."

"I've suffered enough. I've already unpacked and I'm not moving for anybody."

"We'll pack and move you," shouted Jenna and Nila simultaneously. "You won't have to lift a finger."

"I won't do it! I won't do it! I'm de luxe and I've suffered enough!"

And with this, she rushed back to her stateroom as if she feared we might try to take it from her by force.

Nila, Jenna and I looked at each other, dolefully shaking our heads, while Ward continued to sip his vodka and water. To see him, you'd never have suspected he was involved in any way.

Then I had an inspiration. If Mrs. Ratoff wouldn't move in with Nila and me, then why didn't Nila and I move in with her? After all, I would be the only one moving in; Nila was already supposed to be in.

Without a doubt, Mrs. Ratoff heard this plotting through the wall, for suddenly her head popped around our doorjamb again and she shrilled out, "No! No! I will not sleep three women in a room!" Her little black eyes were wild and her rouged cheeks were blotched. "I'm de luxe and I've suffered enough!"

Her head disappeared and we heard her feet racing back to her stateroom.

What to do? There had to be some solution, but what was it? At last we came back to our original thought on the matter. Ward had to go. It was the only way. Nila stood in front of him, the backs of her open hands on her hips, and told him there was nothing else for him to do but move out.

For the first time he got worried. "Where's Ruby?" he asked Jenna plaintively. (Ruby returned to Yalta while we were at Drinking Bear Mountain.)

"She's sleeping," Jenna said.

"Sleeping this time of day?" The Capitalist's voice was querulous.

"Yes, I found her sleeping when I took my things to my cabin."

"God, I never knew a girl to sleep so much!"

Nila and I exchanged glances. Nila has been sure for some time that Ruby is pregnant.

Ward put down his glass. "Jenna," he said, "go wake Ruby

up this very minute. If I'm going to be put out of my own stateroom, she's got to find me someplace to sleep. I'm not sitting up all night on deck."

Once more Mrs. Ratoff thrust her head in the door. One thing sure, she hadn't lifted her ear from the wall, for, after giving Nila and me a baleful glance, she pointed her long index finger at Ward and snapped, "I'll take him. I know he's a gentleman and will not harm me."

The softly scuffing patter of Mrs. Ratoff's feet scurrying back down the hall was the only sound in our stateroom for a minute; then the air shook with choking, sobbing noises as we struggled to muffle our laughter.

2   August 21

WHEN NILA AND I went out on deck early this morning, the ship was tied up against a pier running out from the picturesque town of Novorossisk. On the flat floor of the land along the waterfront are narrow streets of pastel-painted shops and houses, closed in by the green walls of mountains.

An East German freighter, the *Falkenstein*, which is so huge with its eight fat yellow stacks that it appears to be two freighters joined together, was pulling out from the other side of the pier. It rode low in the water, very heavily loaded.

In tones of the utmost unhappiness, a Russian standing next to me muttered, "It's loaded with our wheat."

In spite of the earliness of the hour, the Capitalist was already on deck, sitting on a bench reading, and his greeting to Nila and me was anything but cordial. He had had a terrible night, he reported. The bed was hard and as full of lumps as a pile of rocks. Then, too, there had been an embarrassing incident.

Nila and I were all ears.

Mrs. Ratoff, besides stipulating that he mustn't come to bed until after she was in bed and must get up before she woke, had requested that he not turn on the lights, and so, feeling his way in the dark to the bathroom during the night, he had run head on into her, feeling her way back from it.

Breakfast was confusing but gay. We four American tourists and our guides sat at a long table with three young, well-dressed, spirited couples and an unattached, gentle-faced middle-aged man with gold-colored, haunted eyes. Indeed, the couples were so animated, Mrs. Ratoff's guide surmised they are from Odessa.

"Odessa people are so noi-sy," she said in her most precise way. "They think they own the whole world."

However, it turned out they are from Leningrad and are on their way to Sochi for a two-week holiday. The three married men are engineers and the unattached man is a lawyer. All of them, except the lawyer, wore very beautiful, well-tailored plaid shirts with the tails on the outside of their slacks.

Our waitress, in spite of being a chubby blonde, had a mean look and was bossy and critical. When she realized that Nila is a Russian-born American, she snapped at her with a flash of hate, "So, you deserted us for the other side." Then, noticing that one of the Russian wives was wearing slacks, she ordered her to leave the table and put on something more *kulturnye*. The young woman, though, refused to leave. She simply pulled the overhanging part of the tablecloth across her lap. Then, turning to Nila, she asked, "Do American women wear slacks in the morning?"

"Some wear 'em twenty-four hours a day," Nila answered succinctly.

Then Nila announced that Ward, who was sitting at the other end of the table from the Russians, is a capitalist and pandemonium broke loose. The Russians swore they had never seen a capitalist, except in caricatures, and they begged Ward to move and sit beside them so that when they return home they can tell their friends they've talked with a capitalist.

Ward moved, which meant that everybody had to move. Then the Russian wives moved again so that their husbands could hear better what Ward had to say.

And all this time, mind you, we were waiting for food. Finally I ate three tomatoes, one glass of sour cream, sweetened with cherry preserves (this was my own idea), one slice of cheese and a slice of brown bread.

My breakfast, though, was a starvation diet compared to the Russians'. They also began with tomatoes, but then they moved on to canned pickled fish, veal cutlets, mounds of fried potatoes and hunks of bread.

The Capitalist in his tactful way said, "You Russians eat too much."

"We don't eat this much at other meals," one of the engineers answered. "Breakfast is our biggest meal. We have a saying in Russia, 'Eat your breakfast alone, share your dinner with a friend and give your supper to your enemy.'"

Working our way about the packed deck after breakfast, Nila and I saw a very young woman standing near the rail, nursing a baby at her full breast. The baby was wrapped tightly as a papoose in a green blanket, which in turn was wrapped and tied with a rope. Naturally, Nila and I stopped and peeped in the bundle. How, I asked the woman, did she manage to change the baby's napkins with so many layers swaddling it? She doesn't during the day and night she's on the ship, she said. She's afraid the wind will give the baby a cold.

The woman has been on a holiday to see her parents near Novorossisk and is now on her way home. Her husband works in an electric plant and she, before the baby was born, was a maid in a sanatorium; as soon as the baby is a few weeks older, she will return to her job there.

"How many rooms do you and your husband have?" I asked, and she answered brusquely, "A sufficiency."

The baby finished nursing and the mother licked a rubber nipple and shoved it into its mouth.

Many people, hearing me speak English, gathered around us and shortly Nila was holding forth to one group and I to another. A gentleman, distinguished in appearance, with a head as bald as the palm of his hand, a ruddy complexion and very bright, intense blue eyes, interpreted for me. He was wearing a spotless sport shirt that matched his eyes, and gray tweed pants.

"Are you a general?" I asked him, taking a wild guess.

"No," he answered, chuckling. "I'm a retired colonel."

I had no more time to ask questions; I was asked them. An alert eighteenish boy asked, "Are you a Democrat or a Republican?" and when I said, "Democrat," he asked whom I voted for in the last election. And when I answered, "Adlai Stevenson," he asked what is the difference between the two parties.

Agonizingly, I explained that the Democrats are more truly the friends of the "common man," with more advanced social-security, labor and low-cost-housing legislation; but when I finished, the colonel refused to admit the difference.

"They are both devils," he said, shrugging and laughing. "One is just a fat devil and one a thin one. They both represent the same class—the capitalists."

"Oh, no," I protested, but he ignored me.

"They're just faint shades apart," he said in his most authoritative, colonelcy manner. "Neither represents the laboring man—"

"The Democrats represent the laboring man," I interrupted. "Many, many laboring men belong to the Democratic Party."

"*Nyet, nyet,*" spoke up a youth with bright, friendly eyes and exceptionally wide cheekbones. Then he added in surprisingly good English, "The real workers don't belong to the Democratic Party."

"What party do you think they belong to?" I asked.

"The Communist Party."

"Only a very, very few. You won't believe this, maybe, but it's absolutely true. I've never known personally a Communist in the United States."

"How could you meet one when they are hounded, threatened and persecuted?" the youth asked, his eyes still friendly. "Take Paul Robeson . . ."

"No, you take him," I said, grinning.

He flashed me a quick smile, then went ahead most seriously. "Paul Robeson can't even get a hall in which to sing in the United States because the authorities are afraid it will be blown up and, if he does get one, the people won't come to hear him."

"I don't know the truth about his difficulties in getting

places to sing," I answered, "but let me ask you—would you Russians enjoy hearing someone perform who advocates the overthrow of your form of government?"

The colonel broke in quickly. "Do you really believe in capitalism?" he asked me in a voice that implied I couldn't possibly.

"Certainly."

"Do you honestly believe it has a future?"

"Of course."

He flung out his hands, palms upward, and with raised brows looked around at the people as if to say, "What's the use of talking to her? You can't possibly believe her."

Still they went on asking questions and I went on answering until Nila thrashed her way out of her group and gestured to me to break loose, too. "Come," she called. "In spite of your sun tan, you look deathly pale and exhausted."

I shook the colonel's hand and thanked him for interpreting for me.

"I enjoyed it after I got accustomed to your Southern drawl," he said, smiling. "You know, you sound just like a singing waiter."

Nila and I started for our stateroom, but we were overtaken on the stairs by a man in his late twenties or early thirties. After looking furtively around to see if anyone else was about, he asked Nila in a low voice, "Do you sometimes suffer a piercing homesickness for the motherland?"

"I've seen many people who did," Nila answered, her voice also low, "but I have my husband and home and roots in America, and though there are times I long to see the motherland, it is not a life-and-death matter."

"Thank you," he murmured, and he turned and hurried off.

Is he planning to choose freedom? Nila and I wondered.

On reaching the stateroom, Nila sank into a chair and gloated over the success she had had in her "seminar."

"They asked me," she recounted, eyes shining, "Can you describe us the average day of an average worker in an average family in the United States?" and I asked them what they considered an average family, for in this way, Willie, you get the average Russian family, and they answered, a husband, wife, one child and mother.

"So, Willie, I took a modest worker, for I know no matter how simple I make it, the life will be almost unbelievable." Nila rubbed her palms briskly together. "I said, 'He gets up in the morning and goes to the bathroom and shaves and bathes himself,' and already I saw amazement on their faces.

" 'Then,' I said, 'he goes to the kitchen where his wife is preparing the breakfast, and maybe he will help her in little ways. Maybe he will open the refrigerator and get some orange juice. 'Ah, Willie, their eyes got big, for of course very, very few, if any, of them have refrigerators.

" 'Then,' I said, 'maybe he will put two slices of toast in the electric toaster and then he will sit down and have bacon, eggs, toast and coffee.' The Russians never heard of this bacon, Willie, and so I had to describe it—how it comes very thinly cut in a cellophane package and how you pull the slices off and fry them crisp and dry. And as I described it I saw their mouths watering.

" 'Then,' I said, 'he goes out to the garage and gets in the car.' At that a half dozen asked how can he have a car and I explained that almost every family in America has a car; but sometimes the head of the family doesn't drive his car to work; he leaves it for his wife to go shopping in and catches a ride with a friend or neighbor.

" 'Then,' I said, "he takes a lunch box with a thermos of coffee, sandwiches wrapped in wax paper, pieces of celery, carrots and fruit and a paper cup and a paper napkin.' I tell you, Willie, they were absolutely spellbound. That woman with the baby just stood there, her eyes popping out, and when the baby would drop the nipple out of its mouth she'd shove it back in without even looking. They weren't interested in the machinery and the plants; they were interested in what went in that lunch box.

"Then they asked, 'How does he spend his evenings?' and I said, 'He goes home, settles himself in his favorite chair, reads the paper and listens to the radio or watches television.'

" 'Who cooks the supper?' they asked, and I said, 'His wife.'

" 'Doesn't she work?' they asked, and I said, 'Sometimes, but not usually and almost never when there are small children.'

" 'What does the average worker make?' they next asked and, though I wasn't sure about this, I said, 'Approximately one hundred and ten dollars a week.' I tell you, Willie, they were impressed."

Nila was still telling me the people's questions and her answers when the ship docked at the town of Tuapse and practically everybody piled off and paraded along the pier; but Ward was conspicuously missing. Ruby and two other Russian girls had taken pity on him and invited him to make their cabin his home away from home, and he was now trying to catch up on the sleep he lost last night.

The pier was rather terrifying. Edging it are mammoth cranes that uncannily resemble mechanical giants with legs, knees and even feet, and huge towers of floodlights, and stretching back from it for many acres are stacks of steel rails looking like stacks of lumber around a sawmill.

In the shadow of the cranes and towers, an ancient crone, enveloped from head to toe in innumerable folds of white, and an equally ancient man sold bath towels at a temporary stand thrown up for the ship's visit. The towels are from China and the prices are exorbitant, yet they went like the proverbial hot-cakes. A good-sized one with fancy cross-stitching costs forty-five rubles ($11.25 at the Russian rate of exchange).

The boat under way once more, Nila spent the afternoon in a secluded corner, talking to the man with the golden, haunted eyes. When she rejoined me she was as keyed up as she was on the *Batory* after her sessions with the returning-home Russians.

"He asked me, Willie," she related, "how Russia impresses me after my absence of ten years and I told him I'm beginning to feel many things have changed, that there is much more individual, private freedom.

"He answered me, 'Maybe you're right, but sometimes a man can be so terribly hurt it takes him a long time to trust what he sees even with his own eyes. Since you don't know my name and I don't know yours, I can tell you I spent seven years in a gold mine in a faraway place.' Then he said, and I had to laugh to myself, 'You might not understand it or believe it, but every Russian who stayed here will. I spent those years in a concentration camp for doing absolutely nothing wrong.'

"Then, Willie, I said to him, 'I have heard all those faraway places have been closed.'

"And he chuckled, for he jumped to the conclusion that I meant it had been published in the papers in the United States, and he said, 'How I admire American reporters; but how could they know? But then, maybe, they were helped to know.' Then he said the report was true—they were closed. After Stalin's death between six and eighteen million prisoners —only God knows how many—were freed. He said they were freed over a three-year period not to upset the economy and he happened to be one of the lucky ones; he was let out the first year.

"Still, Willie, he came back a beaten-up person, full of bitterness and hate. Only when he talked about his home—two rooms and a kitchen—and his garden and two apple trees and two raspberry bushes did his voice come alive."

It was dark by the time we reached Sochi, and myriad lights were on, which was really something to see. I felt as if I were sailing into a World's Fair or Disneyland or the Tivoli Gardens. Right on the water's edge is a magnificent sea station, topped with a square cream-colored tower that, in turn, is topped with a slim steeple fashioned of colored glass squares that, in turn, is topped with a beacon light that flashes beams in three colors. The still fairly young moon suspended above it looked very shy and unsure of itself.

Intourist cars met us and shortly we were swishing toward the high ridge of land that serves as a backdrop for Sochi. The wide avenues are lined by thickly waving palms and blooming oleanders and closely spaced street lamps with several curving arms holding round white bulbs, which remind me of those old-fashioned flowers, snowdrops.

Through terraced gardens we curved up a driveway to broad, imposing steps that lead to a spacious patio enclosed on three sides by a building somewhat similar to the Shoreham in Wash-

ington or the Boca Raton Hotel in Florida. This is the so-
called Sea Gull Sanatorium. It will be our home while we're in
Sochi.

Sweet, plaintive music drifted down to us, and when we
reached the top of the stairs we saw two dozen or more hefty
men and women sitting on the coping of a fountain, singing.
They belong to a Czechoslovakian delegation on a mission to
the U.S.S.R.

My room is somewhat disappointing after the beautiful
terraces, handsome steps and extremely good-looking façade
of the building, for it's overfurnished with the same heavy,
blindingly blond furniture of the other hotels I've inhabited;
but then it does have a balcony that seems to hang halfway
between the sea, which for once is really black, and the lively,
vivid-blue, moon-and-star-studded sky.

3   August 22

NILA AND I WERE practically the first ones in the dining room
this morning, for as soon as we had breakfast we were taking
off with the local Intourist representative on a full day's excursion to Lake Ritsa in the mountains of the Republic of
Georgia.

The breakfast Nila pronounced "magnificent." Sliding palm
against palm, she gloated, "It's unbelievable—all the things I
like most," and proceeded to gobble up a few slivers of lemon,
which were on her plate as a garnish, a slice of ham, one small
quarter of tomato, a glass of sour milk and a hunk of cold black
bread.

"Ah, Willie, isn't it something?" she asked, coming up once
for air. "The best milk, the best bread, the best everything!"

The Capitalist and Mr. Tim Callahan, a lawyer from New
York who arrived yesterday at the Sea Gull, completed our party
for Ritsa. Jenna chose to spend the day on the beach, but Ruby
who the Capitalist insisted must go as she'd never seen the
lake, which is quite famous, was to his fury left behind at the

last minute because the Intourist representative said there was no room in the car for her.

Immediately, on the outskirts of Sochi, we began to climb the narrow, curving road on the shoulders of the mountain. Both sides are landscaped with palms and oleanders, but between them now and then we were able to glimpse on our right the serge-blue sea with threads of white caps running through it.

Big, open buses with low sides and no tops, packed with sight-seeing Russians, passed us every few miles. "Aren't they sweet buses?" asked Nila.

Because Stalin was a Georgian and had a summer home on the shores of Ritsa and, also, because the scenery is supposed to be breathtakingly beautiful, hundreds of Soviet citizens visit the lake daily.

Some of the men, reddish-brown as American Indians, were without shirts or undershirts, to get as much sun as possible, I presume, and as only the naked upper halves of their bodies showed above the buses' sides, they were startling sights.

After some miles, we dipped down out of the mountains and drove through intensely cultivated land. Three or four collective farms with millionaire incomes are in this area, the Intourist representative said. Many women were in the fields, gathering tomatoes.

We left the Caucasus and entered the Republic of Georgia. "Your second home," Nila said to me, a twinkle in her eye.

The Capitalist, Mr. Callahan, who appeared to be in his late sixties or maybe in his seventies, and I talked United States politics and the guide listened curiously until finally she blurted out, "Are all Americans as interested in politics as you three?" And when we said most of them are, she shook her head as if it was incomprehensible.

Level with the sea again, we arrived at the resort of Gagra. In the old Czarist days, it was a very fashionable spa. Royalty and nobility came from all over Europe on their special trains. A huge wooden chalet-type hotel, which was brought piece by piece from Switzerland and rebuilt a little way back from the sea, still stands.

We got out of the car to saunter through a park along the waterfront. Women were setting out thousands of minute cacti in triangular- and circular-shaped beds. It seemed to me an endless job and threw considerable light on the fact that there is no unemployment in the U.S.S.R.

A sign at the entrance offered to teach the tango, fox trot and slow waltz. The final line urged the public to learn "to perform correctly all ballroom dances." Another billboard was decorated with two painted doves hovering over the head of a pink-cheeked boy; beneath the picture were two words, both meaning "peace."

Althea in full bloom and oleanders and magnolias extended above the wide, sandy walks and cast them into a shadow that appeared dark and cool as a tunnel compared to the yellow brightness of the nearby beach.

We came out of the park at a big rotunda circled with columns, housing a picture show, a dance floor and other places of amusement, but when I said to the guide I wanted to go to a toilet, she answered, "Not here; it wouldn't be clean here."

Settled back in the car, we passed many sanatoriums under construction, a woman driving a pig at the end of a rope, goats, cows and a cemetery. Realizing I had seen only one other cemetery in the Soviet Union I asked the guide why, and she said that many of the Russians are cremated.

We climbed again and drove along a rushing, ruffled, rocky stream crossed by narrow, homemade suspension bridges such as I've seen many times in the Kentucky mountains. Figs, grapes, tobacco and corn grow in the small cleared spaces, and beehives perch on the edge of wooded slopes.

We stopped again and admired for a few minutes a spring as deep a blue as the throat of a blue morning glory, welling from a grotto at the foot of a mountain that climbs sheer, rocky steps to the dome of heaven. If we washed our faces in the water we would have eternal youth, the guide promised, and, though the opportunity came to me a little late, I all but drowned myself.

We continued to climb and the mountains crowded in upon

us and thrust themselves higher and higher, blotting out even the noonday sun. Huge ferns and box—yes, real box like in the old gardens of Virginia, except these are enormous bushes—and mahogany trees grow jungle-thick.

"This area must be really tropical to grow mahogany," commented Mr. Callahan.

"Not necessarily," said the Capitalist with his usual positiveness. "There are forty-five varieties of mahogany and they grow in many different climates."

"Is that right?" said Mr. Callahan pleasantly.

Trucks weighted with logs almost pushed us off the road.

"What kind of logs are they?" I inquired of the guide, but she didn't know.

"They must be mahogany," said the Capitalist. "They are too big for box and, anyway, they wouldn't use box commercially."

"Oh, yes, we do use it commercially," the guide spoke up with shocking temerity. "We use it in the manufacture of lathes in our textile factories."

"Does the Russian government require a tree to be planted every time one is cut down?" Mr. Callahan inquired.

"I don't know," answered the guide.

"It's an excellent method of conservation," Mr. Callahan said.

"Well, then we use it," the guide said without one moment's hesitation.

We came into a majestic canyon, Upshara Canyon, with the mountains like gigantic picket fences closing us in. Once more we got out of the car, bent back our heads and looked straight up.

"Oh, there is snow," I cried, glimpsing a white patch in a saucer on one peak. "Look! Look! I never saw anything like it—ferns and box here and snow up there."

"Have you ever been to Garmisch-Partenkirchen in Germany?" asked Ward.

"Yes," I admitted, and I began to feel uneasy.

"Well, you've seen the very same thing there, except much more snow."

"But not from a valley with such lush, tropical growth."

"Yes, from a valley just as lush and tropical as this."

I kept quiet for a while as my eyes stared at the scissor points of the cliffs punching holes in the center strip of the sky's bright-blue tent; then, never seeming to learn anything, I said, "The canyon of Wall Street certainly dwarfs by the side of this."

And, of course, instantly the Capitalist caught me up. "At some points Wall Street is narrower and the buildings are higher."

Then, bless him, Mr. Callahan said gently, "I don't believe there is a building in Wall Street as high as these mountains."

"Just how high are they?" I asked the guide.

"Fifteen thousand feet."

"No," said Mr. Callahan, "I don't believe there is a building in Wall Street so high."

"Probably not," the Capitalist agreed, and I all but swooned.

The canyon swooshed with the sound of rushing water, and as we walked about, trying to locate the source, we came upon a boulder on which was painted in scrawling yellow letters, "Here was Paul Robeson."

Riding on, we reached Ritsa, lying some 3,300 feet above sea level, seemingly in the mouth of the mountains, for they bare their sharp, pointed peaks, spotted with deposits of snow, all about it. The water is a queer, opaque grayish green.

We shared a motorboat with several Russians and rode around the edge of the lake. Nila and I wanted to see Stalin's house, but when we asked our guide to point it out she shrugged and said, "Who knows which one it is?" and then buried her head literally beneath a big towel.

However, Nila and I kept our eyes peeled and our ears open and suddenly Nila heard a Russian woman whisper to her male companion, "There's Joe Stalin's house." Evidently since Khrushchev downgraded Stalin his house is no longer a shrine to point to with pride.

Returning to the dock, we were greeted by Ruby, who had caught a ride with Mrs. Ratoff and her guide.

We had a gourmet's lunch at a long table in a pavilion

over the water. We began with sardines and tomatoes, which I admit are not too exotic; but then we had small, crisp, sweet lake trout, right out of Ritsa, and French-fried potatoes, and for dessert, vanilla ice cream topped with gooseberry preserves.

The drive back to Sochi was as beautiful as the ride from it—indeed, even more beautiful in the soft, gold light of afternoon. But I couldn't enjoy it to the fullest, for I dared not move a muscle or speak. Ruby, whom Ward ordered to return in the car with us, Intourist representative or no Intourist representative, slept every mile of the way with her dark, sleek head on my shoulder.

Back at the Sea Gull, Nila and I decided to take a quick swim before supper, so we hurried along the paths of the Sea Gull's gardens, admiring the beds of pink, blue, lavender and purple asters, the roses, the gardenias, the crepe myrtles and many other lovely flowers, to the funicular station, from which a cable car drops down the long, steep incline to the beach.

The car's woman motorman, while waiting for a full load, sat with her shoes off, wriggling her bare toes and stitching in pink, red and green threads a pillow top stretched on hoops.

The beach of the Sea Gull is private and quite fancy. It is divided into three sections, one for men and one for women where they can swim in the nude, and one mixed where they can swim—well, not quite in the nude. Bathhouses and pavilions extend out over the water, with bare slat cots, mats and chairs for sun-bathing.

4   Later

WALKING BACK TO THE sanatorium from the funicular in the early evening, I suddenly discovered myself in the midst of forty-one Scotsmen in their plaids, kilts, high socks, dirks and the rest of the works. I tried to carry on a conversation with one of them and found it almost as difficult as talking to a Russian without an interpreter.

"Who are you?" I asked, smiling and waving my hand toward the whole group.

"We're mayners," he answered.

"Marines, you say?"

"No, mayners."

"I'm so sorry, but I still don't understand."

"Mayners, ma'am. Mayners."

"Mailers?" It was a wild guess, but I was hopeful.

"No, not mailers, mayners. We mayne coal."

The light dawned. "Oh, miners!"

"That's right, ma'am. Mayners."

Well, I won't go into the rest of our halting, painful discourse, but by the time we reached the sanatorium I had learned that they are a picked delegation from the mine unions of Scotland on an official visit to the coal mines of Russia and that among their number is a "bund," which is a band, no less, that has won many contests in Scotland and other European countries.

Before supper was over the bagpipes of the "bund" began to wail on the patio, and when Nila, Jenna and I arrived on the scene the Scotsmen had taken over. A dozen or so lads and lassies were shouting and skipping about in their version of a square dance, which was not so different from our Kentucky brand. Then four of the men did an intricate sword dance, the toes of their soft-soled slippers scarcely touching the pavement.

"They are unpleasantly light on their feet," remarked Nila, a look of distaste on her face. "For such big men, with so many muscles in their legs, it isn't becoming."

After this performance, the loud-speaker burst into "Girl of My Dreams, I Love You" and the dancing became general. The Scotsmen, with no timidity, approached the young Russian girls who were sitting about the open square and asked them to dance, and finally, several dances later, one very short, extremely energetic young fellow asked me.

The loud-speaker was now roaring out a samba and the Scot murmured something that sounded remotely like "samba" when we started off, but he didn't do any samba the like of which I'd ever seen or danced before. I'm not sure what a Highland fling is, but if what we did wasn't one, it missed a good chance. Again and again the Scot with one hand flung me—and I do mean flung—under his upraised arm behind his back, then with the other hand whipped me around to his front. Stooping, twisting and turning, I felt like just-washed clothes being wrung out and hung up.

Once, as he threw me behind him, he used his unemployed hand to mop his face, neck and upper chest. Then, as the music went on and on and I went around and around, he asked me several times, "Are you tired, ma'am?" and though I was fast dying I gasped, "Certainly not. Should I be?"

Finally, thank God, it was over and as I sat, panting, eying without one twinge of envy the dancers in the next round, I mused how very queer it was to be kicking up my old heels in the depths of Russia with Scotch "mayners." Maybe when I return to the United States I'll go on that television show, *I've Got a Secret*, and watch the panel beat its brains out in a vain effort to guess what I've been up to.

<u>5</u>   August 23

WAKING UP WITH A fierce stomach-ache and recalling that once in New York I had an attack of diverticulitis that felt the same way and that the doctor whom Mark summoned prescribed castor oil, I asked Nila please to hurry to a drugstore and buy me a bottle of the nasty stuff.

With no arguing she departed; but in no time at all she was back, empty-handed. Instead of going to a drugstore, she had gone to see the doctor of the sanatorium, who refused to let her have the castor oil.

"I explained to the doctor," said Nila, "that you must clean your stomach and want castor oil and she answered, 'No, we consider castor oil must be given only when the doctor will see the patient and even then we rarely advise it.' "

"But, Nila—"

"Wait." She held up her hand, palm out like a traffic cop. "Then the doctor said, 'I'll understand if your friend doesn't want to see me. We know the American attitude toward the Russian doctor. We have had many American tourists who refused to see Russian doctors under orders of their American doctors.' Then, Willie, she laughed sardonically and said, 'I guess they thought we would poison them.'"

Nila took me firmly by the shoulder and started propelling me toward the door. "So, Willie, you're going with me right now to that doctor to show her you are one American who isn't afraid of Russian doctors."

Of course I was a little afraid. However, it took more courage to say no to Nila than to go.

Several men were sitting in the hallway outside the doctor's office, and shortly a nurse appeared and said, "The men will go first."

When my time arrived to see the doctor, I found her very formal, very businesslike and quiet-spoken. She was a fairly young, slim woman with a good, intelligent face and grave gray eyes. She told me to undress completely; she wanted to examine me.

As I stretched out on a table, without benefit of sheet, she poked me gently in many places. My stomach was horribly bloated. (I realize this sounds as if I'm a horse and is most unattractive, but I believe in the truth in reporting at all cost.)

"I've been eating too much," I said apologetically.

She chuckled, then said, "And there are people in the world, you know, who don't think we have enough to eat in Russia."

"Well, I've had enough."

She gave me a light pat on the thigh such as a mother might give a baby and said for me to sit up. Then, to my amazement, she asked, "Why don't you dye your hair?"

"My husband wouldn't like it," I answered.

"Doesn't your husband want you to look young?"

"My husband is rather prudish about some things and dyed hair is one of them."

She shook her head, puzzled. "He must be an egoist. I can't understand a man who doesn't want his wife to look younger."

Then she asked me to open my mouth and she stooped down and peered into it. And so did the nurse. And so did Nila.

I felt more and more like a horse. My stomach was completely forgotten. "Are all those your own teeth?" the doctor asked.

"No," I admitted sorrowfully. "I have two or three false ones toward the back somewhere."

She, the nurse and Nila peered and peered trying to locate them; then, discouraged, they straightened up and returned to the subject of my hair. "No woman in Russia, unless she is really old, goes about with gray hair," the doctor said.

Thinking about it, I believed her. I couldn't recall seeing a woman with gray or white hair. There must be gray-haired women in the Soviet Union, but evidently they don't go around. When they get old enough for gray hair, they must stay at home and take care of the grandchildren.

Exhausting the subject of my hair—it's a thin subject at best, I can tell you—the doctor remembered my stomach. I had been correct, she said—it was overstuffed; and since I was more familiar with castor oil than with other Russian medicines, I could have a dose. In fact, she gave it to me herself, then quickly handed me a piece of hard candy to suck, just the way a certain baby doctor in Louisville hands pieces of candy to his infant patients.

Starting to leave, I asked what I owed her.

"Not a thing," she said, smiling. "All medical care in the Soviet Union is absolutely free."

"That goes for a visitor, too?"

"Certainly. You are our guest."

6   *Later*

SOCHI WOULD BE A fabulous resort anywhere in the world, but in the Soviet Union it somehow seems even more fabulous. The local Intourist representative informed me when I recovered sufficiently to go on a sight-seeing tour (Nila and Jenna preferred swimming to getting educated) that many people compare it to Nice; then she added quickly, "But, as you will see, it is much nicer than Nice."

"Oh, you've been to Nice?" I asked, not meaning to be mean and base (I never am, of course) but just responsive.

"No, I haven't," she answered and shrugged. "But I know Sochi is nicer."

Well, it *is* wonderful. Though it has a population of only 60,000, it appears much bigger. There are many, many luxurious-looking sanatoriums, surrounded by lovely gardens, occupying the fairly flat plateau atop the mountain ridge. There is the Sanatorium for the Members of the Soviet Army, where 500 a month come the year round and stay for at least twenty-eight days; the Sanatorium for Intellectual Workers, which can accommodate 325 professors, scientists, doctors of history and mathematics, and other learned people; the Sanatorium for Teachers of Secondary Schools; the Sanatorium for Agricultural Workers—oh, heavens, there are right here sanatoriums for practically every trade union in Russia. Like almost all the other public buildings in Sochi, they are built of whitestone, a material native to the area and quite beautiful. And most of them, mind you, just like the Sea Gull, have their own funiculars to take their guests down the slopes to the sea and bring them back.

Besides the innumerable sanatoriums, there is a famous hospital, the Matesta, where people come from all over the world to take the sulphur baths. According to the Intourist guide, 275 patients enter there every fifteen minutes from seven o'clock in the morning until two o'clock in the afternoon. They come for the treatment of rheumatism and arthritis and skin, heart and nervous diseases. After twelve treatments, which is the limit any one year because of the heavy concentration of sulphur in the water, the patient goes home and usually stays fit for the next twelve months. At least that is what the guide told me. She claimed that ninety per cent leave in good condition.

Going to see this phenomenal place, we entered a lobby as huge as the Pennsylvania Station waiting room, with marble-like columns and marble floors and with dozens of people lolling in big leather chairs, seeming half asleep or half dead. They had had their bath for the day and it had so debilitated them they must rest for three hours.

The head doctor, who is a man (the first male doctor I've seen in Russia, by the way, though I've already visited several hospitals), showed me through the Matesta and did his best to make me understand how the concentration of the sulphur in the water is regulated to the condition of the patient; but still I'd hate to try to explain it. Then we visited men with varicose veins, sitting with their feet in tubs of water; men with dandruff and other scalp problems bent beneath faucets of gushing water ("The hair grows very nicely after these treatments," said the doctor); men with sinus trouble, holding to their noses tubes that shoot water through their aching heads; and many other men with many other complaints.

There were women, too, but not nearly so many as men. I could see that in Russia, just as in the United States, women are definitely the stronger sex.

Leaving the hospital, we toured the town, where people walk and ride along streets shaded by heavenly-blue eucalyptus and yellow-green sycamores. We passed the open-air summer theater; the winter theater, surrounded on all four sides by thirty-two enormous Greek columns; the main public park, teeming with trees, of course, but also with five dance floors, two open-air auditoriums and four movie houses; the exciting coral-colored, white-trimmed Orthodox church, the only one now functioning; and a large calendar made entirely of growing flowers, in which, of course, some of the plants must be changed every day.

"Not to like this city is impossible," said the guide.

And though it was against my better feelings to agree with her, I had to do it.

7   *Evening*

THE TIME HAS COME FOR Nila, Jenna and me to leave beautiful Sochi. It is time for the Capitalist, Ruby, Mrs. Ratoff and her guide to leave, too; but as they are heading for Tiflis and we for Rostov on the Don, our paths must separate. However, in spite of its being the hour for the Capitalist and Ruby to leave, they will not go until tomorrow.

Ward, on learning some days ago that he and Mrs. Ratoff were scheduled to travel on the same train, became absolutely frantic that he would have to share a compartment with her and began to move heaven and earth to change his plans. First he asked Ruby to get him and, of course, her on a commercial plane. Then, finding that was impossible, he asked her to charter a private plane. This threw all the Russians, but especially Jenna, into a state of shock. Jenna had never heard of anybody being rich enough to charter his own plane. Her eyes went around and around in her amazed face. As it turned out, Intourist had never heard of it, either, which left the Capitalist only the train. For a while it looked as if he might shoot himself; but then surprisingly, considering the red tape in the Soviet Union, he succeeded in getting his reservations postponed for twenty-four hours.

We parted from him and Ruby in rather troubled spirits. While sunning on the beach today, Ruby confided to Nila that she is married (she had really gone to see her husband at Yalta) and is four and a half months pregnant and extremely apprehensive about the Capitalist's reactions when he learns the facts. Foolishly, she had told him when they first started out together that she was single. Nila urged her to make a clean breast of everything right away. There were tears in her eyes as she told us goodbye.

Then it looked as if we weren't going to leave after all. The office of the Sea Gull couldn't find Jenna's passport, which she turned over to them on arriving. She was wild, for she had to have it for identification to stay at any hotel or sanatorium. Her eyes staring, her hands curled into claws, she ran up and down. It was impossible for her to leave Sochi without it, yet, to keep our schedule, we must go. She was really beside herself and it became shockingly clear to me that the U.S.S.R. is still frighteningly strict about its citizens always having their passports for identification.

When Jenna was on the verge of collapse, Nila remembered that when she was waiting at the desk for her own passport she noticed a Russian passport, which is quite small, caught inside a bigger passport. Maybe that was what had happened to Jenna's.

Her long face lighting up, Jenna rushed back to the office, but she returned shortly even more wild than before. The clerk had gone carefully through all the foreigners' passports and hers was not in any of them. Then, rather idly, Nila reached in her bag and brought out her own passport and riffled through it and, lo and behold, there was Jenna's.

While Nila and Jenna were supervising the storing of our bags in the Intourist car, and I, still feeling a little ill, was sitting at the top of the Sea Gull's imposing cascade of steps, a nice-looking, red-cheeked woman in her thirties, maybe, stopped hesitantly by me and asked in halting English, "You want to leave Sochi?"

"Oh, no, but I must go," I answered. "I'm a tourist and my time is up here."

"You from England?"

"No, the United States. And you?"

"East Germany. I'm with a delegation."

"Oh."

She pushed her blond hair back from her forehead. "How many are in your group?"

"There are just two of us," I said, waving my hand toward Nila.

Her eyes, which are a gas-flame blue, widened in surprise. "Just you two, touring about Russia?"

"Yes."

"Moscow allows it?" Her voice was breathless with incredulity.

"Yes. We do have a young girl guide-interpreter with us on this trip to the Black Sea, but she spends most of her time on the beach and leaves us to do as we please."

Her shock at this news was written on every feature of her face.

Nila called that the car was ready and I stood up and held out my hand.

"Come and visit us, too, in Germany," the young woman said earnestly, clasping my hand.

"I'd like to very much," I said, "but I can go only to West Germany. I'm not permitted to travel in East Germany, you know."

"We are still one people." Her voice was low, urgent. "You must feel sorry for us. We're . . ." She searched for the right word, then pressed her spread hand down toward the ground.

The Sochi railroad station is staggering. Mammoth columns and arches surround a huge circular space paved in marble and open to the sky. This, believe it or not, is the waiting room, and from the rear of it a pair of broad, marble stairs wind up to the elevated train platform.

Women and boys were selling tight, tree-shaped bouquets of mixed flowers—dahlias, roses, zinnias, cosmos and goldenrod—and a man was selling purple-red coxcomb and gladioli by the stalk.

The train, called the International, swept in at the expected moment and left us, as Nila remarked, "swooning and wooning." It was long—at least eighteen very long cars long—and every car was a spotless spring-leaf green trimmed with narrow yellow lines running lengthwise, and on every platform, standing at attention, was a woman conductor, her little flag, rolled snugly about its pole, upright in front of her face.

Our de luxe car consists of two-berth compartments with dazzling washrooms, minus toilets. The seats are covered in spick-and-span white linen, as are the tables between the berths, each of which holds a bright-red glass lamp and an ash tray painted with the words "For Peace and Friendship."

These compartments compare favorably with compartments on one of our own trains, except there is no air conditioning and no possibility of ringing for a porter and getting a bowl of ice and some glasses and more coat hangers.

As the train was hot and would remain at Sochi for twenty-five minutes, Nila, Jenna and I got back off and walked up and down the platform. The tight bunches of flowers now graced the tables in all the compartments except ours. Also on the tables were bottles of yogurt, string bags of apples, nests of hard-boiled eggs and loaves of bread.

A woman walked along the cars, selling *pirochki* covered with sheets of cellophane. Nila brightened. "Never before have I seen such a hygiene," she said. "I'm just surprised."

Several groups of Georgians were swaggering along the platform, their faces dark and lean, their black mustaches bristling, their teeth gleaming, their eyes dancing. One was especially gay, talking with wagging head and waving hands. He was wearing what Nila called a Georgian or Stalin blouse of dark-gray natural wool, "soft as cashmere," and a tight, narrow, silver-encrusted belt. The blouse, plain in front but fully gathered in the back, was worn outside his pants. It is the same style blouse that all the militiamen wear.

"If you ask me to describe you a Georgian man, Willie," said Nila, "there he is. You can see him dancing with a dagger in his mouth or his teeth sunk in a wonderful shashlik."

The train under way, we went to the restaurant car for supper. After a thorough search of the small three-page menu (there is usually only one menu in a dining room, no matter whether the dining room is in a hotel or a train, and people move from table to table borrowing it) we chose boiled chicken and tomato salad. In due time the tomatoes came and we consumed them, then sat back and waited for the chicken. Ten minutes went by, fifteen, twenty. The director of the restaurant appeared, shook hands and inquired if we would just as soon have duck. The chicken was "too hard."

How long would it take to prepare the duck? we asked. Oh, no time at all. It was already cooking and would be ready in fifteen minutes. Okay, then, we'd have duck.

Again we waited. Nila showed us a trick with a mashed ball of bread that felt like two balls when rolled about with the tip of the finger. For some time we practiced this. Twenty minutes went by; twenty-five; thirty. Then the waitress sidled up and asked Jenna would she step into the kitchen.

Jenna, returning, reported she had found the director gnawing on a leg of duck and she proceeded to illustrate. Standing in the aisle, she held an imaginary leg to her mouth, bared her teeth and tugged away. Her eyes protruded, the muscles in her neck stood out, but she continued to tug. Eventually she managed to tear off an imaginary piece and this she chewed endlessly, rolling her jaws and eyes in the most exaggerated fashion. Nila and I were convulsed. At last she gave up, just as the director must have given up, and gasped that the duck was too tough to serve.

What would we have now? the director wanted to know. "Egg omelet," Nila and I said in unison.

The omelet consumed, we stood at a vestibule window and looked out at the Black Sea, along which we are traveling. The moon was high and the sea shimmered like a lady's metallic evening cape spread across a bed. Then suddenly, as if on a movie screen, a small group of men and women shoveling sand and rock into a cement mixer by the light of an acetylene torch flashed in front of our eyes—and was gone.

"To fulfill the plan," commented Jenna. Then, seeming to sense our continuing astonishment, she added, "They do it voluntarily. Nobody makes them."

VIII

The Don-Volga Canal

1   August 24

WHEN I OPENED MY eyes this morning the train was standing
in the station of Krylovskaya, which is evidently famous for
those round yellow melons that resemble our cantaloupes. Men
in pajamas and women in rumpled, soiled ginghams and babushkas rushed by my window empty-handed and, in a few
minutes, returned with arms piled high. One woman was carrying six melons; a man in a blue undershirt and pajama pants
had a string bag full of them and also several ears of corn, and
another man cuddled a watermelon in the crook of his arm
while he sucked on a fat dill pickle.

Nila sprang up, jumped into her clothes, raced out and came
back, cupping in each of her big hands a papa-sized melon.
"Willie, just look!" Her face was absolutely radiant. "A gentleman helped me to choose." She illustrated, holding one melon
to her ear and thumping it with her middle finger.

"Willie, I'm so sorry you didn't get off," she went on. "I
never saw such an abundance. Sausages, fried chicken, pickled
cucumbers—slightly salted and heavily salted—tomatoes, and
melons from this size—" she balanced the biggest of her pur-

chases in her hand—"to this size—" she made a circle with her thumbs and third fingers. "And, Willie, here they put chicken in a *white* paper. Such a civilization! Can imagine? When I lived in Russia they used to sell chicken in a piece of newspaper, but now—*white* paper."

The train began to move. "Look, Willie, Look! Look!" Nila hurried to the window, dragging me with her. "Hard-boiled eggs! Milk! Sour cream! Hot cutlets!" she sang out like a train dispatcher announcing stations. "This must be a very rich place. This is the Don region, where the Cossacks used to live—the Cossacks of the Don. They were very rich here. And, by God, judging from the market, they still are. Look, look, the flowers!"

A bed of loud zinnias broke the pavement of the platform, close by the pale-green station.

Nila went into the vestibule and I started to dress, but Nila, flinging open the door and crying, "Come quickly!" interrupted me. I threw on my dress and rushed out. "Look, Willie, pumpkins grow all along the railroad track. This gentleman—" she gestured toward a man at the next window—"explains me that the people who work on the railroad tracks plant the seed here, for the land doesn't belong to the collective farms and they can gather the pumpkins for theirselves and their animals."

For many miles, the cindery banks were festooned with the big-leafed vines splashed with large yellow blooms.

Proudly bearing the melons in front of her, Nila, followed by Jenna and me, went in to breakfast. She called peremptorily for a knife, cut the melons in large sections and distributed them among us.

Jenna's eyes stared. "You eat them now—first?" she asked.

"Certainly," answered Nila with a most superior air. "We always eat fruit first for breakfast in the United States."

Jenna slipped a knife between the juicy, golden meat and the rind, cut the meat into small pieces, then, holding the crescent to her mouth, bit off the pieces one by one.

We ate until we were uncomfortably full. "I'll die," mourned Nila, "but it will be a beautiful way to go."

Soon after breakfast, we arrived at the station of Bataisk. "It is a station just for trains," Jenna explained, "not for people." There were many, many tracks, and hundreds of flatcars loaded with tractors and airplane bodies and wings, and thousands of boxcars.

We slowed down to cross the Don and on the far banks we saw a widely spread mass of yellow and white stucco buildings, presided over by a towering cathedral crowned with huge, emerald-colored, onion-shaped domes. It is the city of Rostov, with a population of approximately 700,000 people.

At the station were more people clutching bunches of flowers. One yellow-haired little girl, waiting by a rolled-up mattress and two suitcases, held in each hand a bunch almost as big as she was.

The entrance and lobby of our hotel were shabbier than any other we've been in; however, the management is striving for better things. In Nila's and my room were printed sheets in French, German, English, Chinese and Russian, requesting the guests not to:

> Sing or play musical instruments between midnight and 10 A.M.
> Keep bulky belongings and inflammable materials in the rooms.
> Use any heating device.
> Bring animals or birds to the rooms.

Also there was a sheet on which the management pleaded for "suggestions to increase the quality and culture of the service."

Starting out to show us the sights, the local Intourist guide began: "Rostov on the Don is a comparatively young city. It was not built until 1748. It is the industrial, cultural, intellectual center of the Rostov region. There are six institutes, one university, one hundred and seven secondary schools and twenty-four parks and public gardens. In fact, there are eight parks on the main street alone."

We saw these parks, the university, and factories that manufacture self-propelled wheat combines, enamelware, shoes, champagne and many other products. The wheat combine plant employs 16,000 workers. The buildings are new, as the Germans bombed the old ones, but the machinery escaped because it was shipped to Tashkent in the middle of the U.S.S.R. at the beginning of the war.

There are many, many other new structures. The Germans occupied Rostov twice during the war and bombed hundreds of houses, public buildings and factories. They also killed a total of 113,000 people, including 20,000 Jews and 53,000 non-Jewish boys and girls.

After the tour, Nila and I rode on a children's railroad that circled for one hour about a large recreational park. The Ministry of Railways presented the train, including a shiny black diesel engine, to Rostov's young, and they run it completely. Railroad-minded boys and girls in the eighth, ninth and tenth classes of school take courses at Rostov's Pioneer Palace to learn their jobs as engineers, conductors, brakemen, stationmasters, switchmen and what have you. Only those who pass the course on diesel machines can be engineers, naturally the most coveted assignment. During the summer months as many as eight hundred work on this one railroad line. But this isn't the only one. There are three more, in Kharkov, Tiflis and Dnepropetrovsk.

Nila and I were escorted onto the train by the stationmaster himself, a small chap with glowing blue eyes. He was dressed for the part in a salmon-colored coat, white pants and black cap. Nila rode in one of the coaches and I rode in the engine, just behind the seventeen-year-old engineer.

The light signal ahead changed to green, the horn blew, the bell rang and we were off. A solemn-faced lad in a pink shirt, a red tie and white pants stood at attention beneath the signal.

People were gathered along the tracks to watch us go by. We stopped at several stations, put off and took on passengers, clanged our bell, tooted our horn, swished off steam and raced on.

When we returned to the hotel for dinner, we discovered that an Intourist party of twenty people or so had arrived to board the same ship as we for the trip through the Don-Volga Canal to Stalingrad. The group includes an Australian couple, two

Canadians, two or three Englishmen and a Swede. The rest are Americans, mostly young; several are Yale students and one is a sturdily built, handsome, ruddy-faced man in or around his fifties, from my own state of Kentucky.

Though Nila and I of course have nothing against any of these people personally, we were upset that they are traveling with us. The trip from Rostov to Stalingrad takes three nights and two full days and we had hoped to be closeted on the ship with only Russians. Having run into so few American tourists since leaving Leningrad, actually not more than seven or eight, we had stopped expecting to see them in large numbers. Yet here they were, all over the hotel.

The sight of them reminded Nila of a remark a woman made to her in St. Louis a year or more ago. The woman had just returned from a Russian tour and she said, "Russia is a very boring country." Naturally Nila was taken aback. The woman might have said Russia was frightening or depressing or uncomfortable and Nila wouldn't have been too shocked, but to say it was boring . . .

"How do you mean boring?" Nila asked.

"Everybody there is from St. Louis," the woman answered.

Nila and I didn't take up with any of these newcomers, but as soon as dinner was over we strolled on the main "drag." Hundreds of other people were strolling too, for, though we had forgotten it until that minute, it's Sunday. They looked as colorless and bedraggled as their fellow countrymen in Leningrad and Moscow.

Attracted by a group in front of two large plate-glass display windows at the edge of a park, Nila and I joined them. The windows are of two types frequently seen in Russia, Nila told me—the Window of Self-Criticism and the Window of Satire.

In the Window of Self-Criticism were printed sheets, similar to pages of a newspaper, with the banner, "In the Clean Water," across the top. "It means," Nila explained, "that they take people who have done something bad to clean water and wash them. For instance, Willie, when I played dominoes half the night instead of taking part in the ceremonies I had been sent to attend, a picture with my name under it and a story

224

about my behavior were put in one of these sheets for every-body to see."

Today in the paper "In The Clean Water" was the picture of a woman with a complicated hairdo and heavy make-up, wear-ing an extremely low-necked dress. Her real name, address and place of work were given, along with the comment that she is so busy beautifying herself she has no time for her social-welfare work.

Also, there was a picture of a student in a loud, flowered shirt with his name and address and an account of his offense. He wore this flowered shirt to class, the story said, and when he was asked why he did it he answered, "It's what they are wearing in Europe." Beneath his picture ran the reprimand, "Shame on you that you, a citizen of the U.S.S.R., should fol-low the bourgeois taste."

The Window of Satire, Nila told me, can carry stories and cartoons about internal Russian matters, too; but usually it is filled with international affairs. Unfortunately, the type beneath the cartoon today was very small and, as Nila didn't have her glasses, she couldn't read it to me.

Back once more at the hotel, Nila and I were stretched on our beds, resting, when Jenna burst into the room and cried, "Look out the window! Such a crowd as you never saw before is in front of the hotel."

We looked and saw the wide sidewalk and the grassy space between the sidewalk and the hotel packed with people. They had spotted an Intourist bus at the curb (the newcomers were not traveling in "Lux," but in second class), had learned that a goodly number of Americans would shortly board it and were waiting patiently to see them.

I stepped out on a nearby balcony to get a better look and immediately the people saw me and began to wave, smile and call out friendly greetings. I knew they were friendly from the warm tones of their voices. Feeling as if I were Queen Eliza-beth, I smiled and waved back.

They were mostly boys and girls in their teens and twenties, but there was a sprinkling of very old women whose brown wrinkled faces framed in white babushkas reminded me of baked apples, topped with whipped cream.

Finishing what little packing we had to do, Nila, Jenna and I hurried down the stairs to the front door. A hotel attendant was gesturing with a switch broom to the people to stand back. They withdrew a few feet, then stopped. Their faces were eager and expectant.

The time for the tourist party to board the bus for the sea station was at hand. As the first one appeared at the hotel door, the Russians voluntarily separated, leaving a foot-wide path for him to walk down. One by one, the others came. The crowd buzzed excitedly and those in the rear stood on tiptoe to see them and those in front fluttered their hands timidly.

Then it was my time to go. Smiling my broadest smile, I caught as many of the hands that were held out to me as I could and pressed them warmly. I regretted that I was not more rewarding to look at and that I had no Russian words to express my appreciation for their unmistakable hungry curiosity and interest.

2   August 25

THIS IS THE LIFE, sailing along the Don River. The sky is a brilliant blue and the sun hot, but our boat, moving at a fast clip, sweeps cool air against our faces.

The boat came as a shock last evening after the big boats on the Black Sea, for it is small. It has only two decks, with staterooms no bigger than bathrooms on both sides of a central hall. Nila's and my berths are permanently made up and the passage between is only wide enough for one of us to maneuver between them at a time. We have no closets and no drawers; but we do have one washbasin, with a mirror above it, a table beneath the window (which opens on the deck), and a very narrow shelf right above our berths. When we first walked in, we looked around aghast; then, unable to decide where we were supposed to put our clothes or even hang my hat, we turned right around and walked out on deck to see the people come aboard.

Jenna was already on deck and she was giggling mightily. She had been put in a stateroom for four and three of the four were young American males, who instead of being delighted at this stroke of luck were horribly upset and were pulling strings to move her out. In their defense, I must say that they had been in the U.S.S.R. only a few days and hadn't had time to adjust to its customs.

The passengers coming on board were a revealing study in classes in this supposedly classless land. Those Russians with cabin reservations on the upper deck, where we Intourist travelers were assigned, were dressed with some pretension of style and carried only suitcases, satchels and one or two packages; but those for the lower deck looked like peasants of the time of the czars. The babushka-covered women trudged, backs bent, up the gangplank, laden like donkeys with rolled mattresses and many big, loosely woven sacks (in the South we call them "crocus sacks") bulging with what seemed to be clothes and other soft materials, while the men, in sleazy shirts and slick pants, strode gaily on, swinging only stuffed string bags.

Shortly after we shoved off it was suppertime, and we of Intourist crowded into a dining room about an eighth the size of a basketball court and became immediately an informal, friendly, slightly crazy house party. For one thing, there was only one very pregnant, pretty blond waitress for twenty-five people and not nearly enough knives, glasses or cups. My fellow Kentuckian and another youngish man, perhaps in his forties, which is youngish to me, jumped up to help the waitress. In the small galley, this made matters even more confusing, though that hadn't seemed humanly possible the moment before. However, they did succeed in finding small bowls from which we could drink our tea.

Today, all is calm and bright. The land on both sides of the Don is flat and the fields where sunflowers grow are a tweed mixture of yellow, green and brown. Every few hours, the boat sidles into the river station of some small village and unloads passengers, wine, vodka and a few other items. Once it even put off a glossy blond-wood wardrobe.

The river stations are all similar and very picturesque. They look like the old paddle-wheeled show boats on the Ohio and Mississippi rivers, painted pale green and decorated with yards and yards of intricately cut out white wooden trim.

In the middle of the morning I attended a lecture on the Don-Volga Canal that a Russian guide delivered to his group of Russian tourists. Jenna interpreted for me.

The canal, as you without a doubt know, connects the Don and Volga rivers, which means in bigger terms that it joins the Black Sea, into which the Don flows, with the Caspian Sea, the outlet of the Volga. The canal was a dream of the czars for centuries, but it was Stalin who made the dream come true. It was started at the beginning of 1948 and was completed in four years. Twenty thousand people and 500 excavators (those giant dredges that move on legs) worked on it at a time.

The canal proper—that is, from the town of Kalach on the Don to Stalingrad on the Volga—is ninety-one miles long and has thirteen locks or sluices—four that take you up and nine that bring you down—three dams and many pumping stations and reservoirs.

However, before you even reach the canal itself you are lifted seventy-eight feet by two locks to reach what the Russians call an artificial "sea," the Sea of Tzemlanskaya, but what we in the United States would call a lake. The "sea" alone is 112 miles long and approximately twenty-two miles wide. Seventy-four thousand people were moved out of their homes and villages to make way for the dammed-up water.

The guide stressed the economic importance of the canal, first as a generator of power, second as a carrier for lumber and manufactured products, and third as a reservoir to irrigate the land.

"Originally, the land through which the canal flows was like a desert," he lectured. "Nothing would grow. Now hundreds of small canals extend from the main canal to bring water to farms and gardens."

At the village of Konstantinovka, Nila, who got off the

boat to look about, came unnervingly close to getting left. "Wait for *Amerikanka* tourist," Jenna shouted at the top of her big voice. "Wait for *Amerikanka* tourist!"

Nila came running, completely out of breath, one arm curled about a watermelon and one hand clutching the corners of her handkerchief, filled with sunflower seeds. "The man was coming with the melons," she said between pants, swaying to and fro, "and I just couldn't resist waiting for them."

One of the Yale students also leaped on at the last second with a watermelon. He was going to try an experiment, he announced. He would take a plug out of the watermelon and fill it with vodka.

The boat is so small that all the passengers on the upper deck, including the Russians, are cozily friendly. Nila, Jenna and I spent a lot of time with a group of young Russian women, all dressed in crepe-de-Chines. One is quite beautiful, a blonde with large gray eyes and a mole at the corner of her mouth. Her crepe-de-Chine is printed with large red and pink flowers and black leaves on a once white but now yellowed background.

Nila showed them copies of *Life, House and Garden* and *Better Homes and Gardens* that one of the new tourists had brought on board, and they got terribly excited. She pointed out to them the brightly painted bathrooms, the modern kitchens, gay linoleums, sunporches and swimming pools and the advertisements for automobiles, television sets, electric sweepers and waxers, hair rinses and face creams.

The pictures of the face creams inspired her to open a beauty parlor right in the ship's bow and go into what she calls her "beauty act." She draped towels about their shoulders, lectured them on the care of the skin and then massaged their faces with the best concoctions of Elizabeth Arden.

A goodly number of other Russians, hearing of the "act," crowded into the bow to watch. A short, fat woman with puffy cheeks and sprawled-out nose stood with the backs of her hands on her hips. When the beauty session was over, she pushed forward and, after a minute of talking about the face cream, announced with a proud toss of her head that she is a seventh-category cook—which, peculiarly enough, is the highest cate-

gory in Russia—that she can cook *entrecôte*, and beef Stroganov . . .

Abruptly, she broke off the list and eyed Nila sharply. "Do
you know what beef Stroganov means?"

Nila, repressing a smile, shook her head.

"The word 'beef,'" the woman explained, beaming, "is
French, but Stroganov—" she beat her ample bosom with both
fists—"is ours."

She works in a restaurant and gets 360 rubles a month for
cooking 40,000 items, which include dishes that can be made in
quantities, such as borsch, bouillon and salads. For each dish
over 40,000 she gets a bonus. Her best month she made 800
rubles.

"And I have all the food I can eat," she said boastfully.

"I can see that," Nila retorted, and she reached out and
patted the woman's protruding stomach.

"I'll not be like your women." Again the woman put her
hands, palms outward, on her hips. "When they walk, you can
hear them." She took a few mincing steps, her loose fleshy
bottom swinging.

"What do you mean, you can hear them?" Nila asked.

"Bones! Bones! Bones!" The woman's voice dripped with distaste. Then she returned to the subject of wages. "What do
cooks make in America?" she inquired.

"I don't know exactly," Nila answered, "but they are very
highly paid, especially cooks in restaurants."

Quickly, as if to catch her out, the woman shot her finger at
Nila and asked, "Can cooks have cars?"

"Of course, and their cars don't belong in the second-class
categories, either, but the new-car categories."

"All right, so the American cook has a car." The woman
nodded her head slowly, her lips pursed, "But how does she
feel working for a capitalist?"

"I don't think she minds. You see, in the United States
a cook works where she wants to and when she wants to. She
can either work in a public place or work in a private home.
Wouldn't you work in a private home?"

"Who? Me?" The woman's nose sniffed the air above her

head and one fist slammed her chest. "Me, a seventh-category cook in a private home!"

"Please excuse me," said Nila.

Then to change the subject and include more people in the conversation, Nila took off her "popover" beads and demonstrated how she can snap them apart and put them back together. The Russians watched in a daze, all except the big fat cook. "Sell them to me," she said.

Nila shook her head. "They're not for sale."

"I'll pay you anything you ask," the woman argued excitedly. "I'll give you 500 rubles."

"They are all I have and I need them."

"Why didn't you bring a whole suitcaseful?" The woman was impatient at Nila's shortsightedness. "You could have easily sold them all."

The boat drew into a river station at a primitive, sun-baked, wind-swept village. The few houses were doll-sized and unpainted and the roofs were thatched. No roads were in sight, just bare, hard ground stretching between the wharf and the rows of small dwellings.

The radio on the boat was playing, of all things, "Rock around the Clock."

Everybody began to stream off. The village, so the word went around, is famous for hand-woven shawls. The Russian passengers held the shawls against their cheeks and one of them purchased one for 474 rubles. (Imagine it—in her money, $118.75.)

As the boat pulled out, I watched the village women plodding up the pathless incline, their backs stooped beneath the sacks of unsold merchandise. Shortly we passed unpainted barns and some tractors and other farm machinery. It was evident that here was a collective farm and that the women were making their way to it.

On the banks of the river a few men sat fishing, and in the water small boys were swimming.

Late in the afternoon we steamed into the first lock; but it is not just a lock, it's a monument—in fact, two monuments. Mammoth squares of white blocks (marble, I presume) rise on each side of the waterway, supporting tremendous rearing bronze horses with bronze Cossacks in the saddles.

The water gushed in and lifted us thirty-nine feet, and we steamed to the next lock. More water gushed in and lifted us another thirty-nine feet, and we steamed out upon the broad, choppy surface of the Sea of Tzemlanskaya. Ahead of us, on the right, was the port of Tzemlanskaya and we turned toward it. A handful of nondescript new buildings spread over what appeared to be an island, but there could be a strip of land which I couldn't see connecting it to the mainland.

It was announced we would stay here for two hours and so everybody got off and fell to entertaining himself madly. We'd been on the boat only twenty-four hours, but we'd seen and heard so much it seemed much, much longer. I myself felt as if I'd come to the end of the earth.

The American college boys, the Kentuckian and the Australian couple swam off some boulders across the strip of land from where we were tied up; the Russian boys and girls formed a circle on the wharf and played a version of volleyball. Nila eyed them longingly, having been, as she says in her modest way, "very, very good" at volleyball when she was young. Most of us, however, sauntered to the bazaar and bought fat, luscious cucumbers that were not pickled and yet were salty and a wee bit sour, and dried, salted fish. One Russian woman carried her half-dozen fish, unwrapped of course, spread out like a fan.

Then, nibbling on the cucumbers, we walked down a dusty, unpaved road with a grain elevator on our left and the "sea" on our right. It was an exciting hour of the day. The sun, as reddish pink and round as a Christmas-tree ball, hung in a billowing mass of storm-blue clouds just above the horizon and threw off gold lights along the edges of other billowing clouds high above us, both storm-blue and creamy white.

On our return to the boat, the Yale boy who was trying the experiment with the vodkaed-up watermelon, invited a half-dozen of us to the sun deck to sample the results. For some minutes, like judges at a state fair, we stood about, solemnly biting off small hunks and savoring the flavor. An American woman said that one thing for certain the watermelon hadn't hurt the vodka, and the Kentuckian pronounced it quite good; but our Yale host was not so sure. "All I can say is," he said finally, with the air of a connoisseur, "it's better than watermelon and gin."

We arrived in the dining room for supper in the happiest of spirits; but we were scarcely seated when the fortyish man, who had been helping with the serving, rapped on the back of a chair to get attention and stated very, very quietly, really under-quietly, "One of our number, our very good friend from Kentucky, has just received a cablegram that his wife has died and he's now trying to make arrangements to leave the ship."

Then, at that very second, a bird flew through a window into the dining room and flung itself against the ceiling.

"It's the sign of death," exclaimed an elderly gentleman from Canada in sepulchral tones.

"Yes," agreed Jenna, her eyes and her long, thin face full of awe and fear, "it is the sign of death."

Nila gasped and clasped her hands beneath her chin.

"You believe this?" I asked her.

"Of course," she answered. "A bird in the house always means a death in the house."

For many minutes the bird fluttered wildly from one wall to the other. Several people jumped up to try to catch it before it hurt itself, but because the tables were so crowded together they couldn't move freely and it escaped again and again.

At last, however, the director of the dining room cornered it and handed it to the gentleman from Canada, who was nearest the doorway opening onto the deck.

The bird freed, the Canadian, white-faced and trembling, clutched a handkerchief to his index finger and sank into his chair. "It has left its blood upon me," he muttered in a hollow voice as if he would assuredly be the next to go.

Supper turned into an indifferent affair. Everybody seemed to be thinking, as I know I was, that disaster can reach out and find a person anywhere. Here we were, thousands of miles from home and in a most out-of-the-way spot, and yet tragic news caught up with us.

I was anxious to go to my fellow Kentuckian and say a few words of sympathy, but his friend who made the announcement advised against it. The captain of the ship and the interpreter-guide of his group were with him and they were very busy figuring out the best and fastest way to get him to the United States. Fortunately, we were still tied up at the port of Tzemlanskaya and so, if it could be arranged to get him out of there to Rostov, the nearest large city, he would be put ashore.

After what seemed an interminable time, the ship began to move and the interpreter-guide, a small, seemingly defenseless young woman with a long golden bob, no doubt dyed, came in and joined Nila, Jenna and me at our table. Her big, soft brown eyes were red from weeping, and her fingers, which she kept putting to her lips, shook terribly.

Our Kentuckian, she said, had been left in Tzemlanskaya, where not a soul speaks a word of English. He will spend the night in a private home there; then in the morning he will be driven to a town that has an airstrip, and there a Navy plane will pick him up and fly him to Rostov, and from Rostov he will fly to Moscow, and from Moscow home. The guide and the captain have sent a dozen cables to prepare the way.

As the little boat headed out into the "sea," the wind rose, shook the windows, banged the doors and howled unconsolably.

<u>3</u>   August 2

AFTER A TEMPEST-TOSSED NIGHT, we woke to another beautiful day. It really seemed too good to be true, considering the wildness of the storm we had been through. Indeed, toward midnight the wind rose so high and the little boat wallowed, groaned and creaked so continuously in its seeming determination to split asunder that the captain finally had to tie up for three hours at a rocking and rolling wharf.

I slept very little; however, I was up early and went to the stern to commune with my soul and make a few notes. But immediately I was joined by two sailors who were sweeping the deck with a large-sized whisk broom, and by a Chinese who, unabashed by my presence, exercised every muscle and bone in his body, even to his finger bones.

Then Nila and an elderly Russian man from Rostov in an unbleached linen suit, with no shirt so far as I could detect and, of course, no tie, joined me and soon we were involved in conversation like old friends. And in truth we felt like old friends. We'd passed each other many times on the narrow deck, smiled, bowed and murmured greetings.

Now it developed that the Russian has an especially warm spot in his heart for Americans, for during the war he received such a wonderfully good overcoat from Russian War Relief in the United States that he wore it for ten years and then had it made into a coat for his wife, which she's still wearing.

But he wasn't the only person in Rostov to receive clothes from Russian War Relief. Everybody got them. "At one time," he said excitedly, "so many people were wearing American clothes, Rostov looked like a foreign city. All a person had to do to look like a one hundred per cent foreigner was to put a folded handkerchief in his breast pocket."

His small, clear blue eyes beneath thick, reddish-blond eyebrows danced merrily and his mouthful of steel teeth flashed as brightly in the slanting rays of the sun as the now still surface of the sea.

Nila, grinning, told him that I had been Kentucky chairman of Russian War Relief, and instantly he was on his feet, reaching for my hand, bowing over it and kissing it fervently. His lean, clean-shaven, sensitive face and even his shiny bald head glowed with gratitude.

At last spent, he fell back upon the bench along the rail and confided that the Russians were amazed at receiving such good, clean clothes.

"Did you know at the time that they were from the American people?" I asked.

"Yes, everybody knew that," he answered.

Then we talked of many things. He and his wife both work; he is an engineer in a factory and makes 1,050 rubles a month, and she makes 850. They have two rooms plus kitchen and bath (which total six more meters of space than a couple is supposed to have) in a new apartment house, for which they pay 52 rubles a month, which is considered quite high.

Food, however, is their greatest expense. It costs them 500 rubles a month in spite of their cutting corners. They learned. about canning vegetables and fruits from the cans and jars of food we sent them during the war. They buy tomatoes, eggplant, cucumbers and even caviar when the markets have them in abundance and put them up for the long winter days when they are so scarce.

There are still queues for food and other items all over Russia, he said. Maybe fifteen or twenty queues a day. Some sausage will arrive from Moscow, or bread, or cheese, and then there will be queues of twenty-five people.

"But that's no queue," he exclaimed, throwing up his hands. "The queue is a hundred or two hundred people. That's the queue!"

"Do you and your wife shop in the government market or free markets?"

"The free markets and, though they cost usually five rubles more, it's worth it. When you go to a government market, you take a chance; the meat might be excellent and it might not; but in a free market you can make your choice."

Then I asked him about automobiles and he said that ten years ago he didn't know personally anyone who owned an automobile, but today he knows three persons. One is his sister-in-law and one is his close friend who works in the same plant in which he's working.

"How can they afford to own cars?" I asked.

"They are just saving and saving and saving."

"Do you buy many things from China?" Nila questioned him.

"No, in Rostov we have only fans and umbrellas from China. Recently I bought my wife an umbrella for a hundred rubles and a fan for twenty-five rubles." Suddenly his aesthetic face lighted up even more glowingly than before and he pressed his palms exuberantly together. "The fan is such a beautiful thing," he said, drawing in his breath. "We bought it not to fan with, but to smell." He chuckled elatedly. "It smells so wonderful because it's made of sandalwood."

Nila asked him to tell us how he and his wife spent the rest of their salaries and, without hesitating, he gave us a complete breakdown:

For books, magazines, newspapers and stamps	50 rubles
For telephone, water, gas and electricity	50 rubles
For clothes, entertainment, presents, miscellaneous	598 rubles
For soap, cleaning and other extras for housekeeping	50 rubles
Savings	300 rubles

"Do you save for your old age?" Nila inquired.

"No, no." He was shocked. "We have old-age pensions. We save for big things like trips and large clothes items, such as winter coats. My winter coat costs two thousand rubles and my wife's fifteen hundred rubles. When we buy coats we don't take long trips. However, this last winter, when we didn't have to buy a coat, we went to Czechoslovakia."

"How often do you entertain guests?" asked Nila.

"Until recently it was very hard to have guests because we didn't have enough chairs; but now in Rostov there is an agency where you rent anything for a party. You go there and say you are having fifteen people and they send a man to look at what you have." He talked with great liveliness and spread out his hands and swung them to suggest the man looking about. "Then they send tables, chairs, dishes and whatever else you may need." His sharp blue eyes began to twinkle and he added, "But you have to furnish and cook the dinner."

"That's tough," Nila and I murmured together.

He laughed appreciatively, then said, "Also, now in Rostov is a school where everybody can go and learn how to use the fork and knife correctly. Also, every month in some place there is a fashion show, which my wife adores. A ticket costs five rubles and she never misses one."

"This I understand," commented Nila. "The fashion show is completely virgin soil."

Then we talked what Nila calls the "sit-u-ation." We wanted to know if he thinks the morale of the people has changed in the last ten years.

"Yes," he said, "the people live more freely; they feel more quiet, more sure."

"Why?" Nila asked.

"The amnesty, of course," he said emphatically.

Then he reviewed the war history of the region through which we're traveling. Not too far away, he said, is the settlement that voluntarily joined Hitler, that even sent Hitler a white horse. Indeed, many, many people in this area went with Hitler. So, when the war was over and the Nazis were defeated, railroad cars and trucks came and took everybody, even the secretary of the Communist Party, into exile. But when Khrushchev came to power, he gave amnesty to all these people and they were returned to their homes.

He was quiet for a moment, his keen eyes beneath the reddish-blond brows studying the floor; then abruptly he looked up, smiled in a warm, pleased way and said, "So we are free of fear now. Fifteen, ten, five years ago I wouldn't have dared talk to you, but now I have no fear. I'm so sorry I didn't know you were in Rostov. I would have been very pleased to have had you at my apartment."

Nila and I thanked him, but he was still apologetic, especially to me, who he feels did so much for Russia through Russian War Relief. If he could only show his appreciation in some way. He knitted his brows. Then he remembered he had a small folder of post cards of Rostov that he was taking to a friend in Stalingrad. It was the only gift he had for his friend and it would show him how amazingly Rostov had been restored since the war; but, never mind, he would present it to me. The friend will certainly understand.

He fished in his inside breast pocket and brought out the small folder. Then once more he got to his feet, bowed, handed me the packet and then pressed his lips to my bony knuckles.

All during this conversation, which was much, much longer than I've recorded, we'd been steaming over the Sea with monotonous acres of bare, eroded land on our left. If the Russians are irrigating them from the dammed-up waters of the Sea and the canal, they have not yet benefited from them.

Around noon we tied up at Kalach, the port at the head— or rather the foot—of the actual canal. The two locks and the Sea up to now have been just the preliminaries. After a long stop at Kalach we entered the first of the thirteen locks at three o'clock in the afternoon, and twelve hours from then we'll steam out of the last one. Though I've never been through the Panama Canal (poor, underprivileged me) and so have nothing comparable to judge by, this Don-Volga construction impressed me as one terrific engineering achievement.

When we were through the first lock (we were still being lifted up, by the way) we tied up at a wharf where many old women in clean, brightly printed cotton dresses and babushkas were selling vegetables and fruit in a grove of lovely aspens.

The director of the dining room, a fishing pole over his shoulder, was the first one off. Swiftly he strode along the wharf, settled himself on the paved canal bank and tossed in his line. (Apparently we were going to be here for some little time.)

Then the Russian and American young dashed off, formed the volleyball ring and began to bat the ball about; then the other tourists flocked off, some to swim and some to shop in the bazaar, but Nila and I had a better idea. Leaving Jenna aboard (her head had been buried all day in Stephen Leacock's *Perfect Lover's Guide and Other Stories*) we struck out for the nearby town to visit in a home.

It is, of course, a new town—just six years old—built since the construction of the canal. The streets are wide and bordered with parks, and the public buildings are spacious and nice-looking; but the houses, which are all cottages, are fashioned of stucco that has already begun to crack and are painted in pink and blue "wash" that has already begun to streak and fade, and the fairly roomy grounds in which they sit are poorly kept.

Nila and I were timid about barging up to a front door and asking whoever answered to let us come in and look around, so we hurried along the main residential street until we saw a woman sitting beside a low baby carriage, one hand flung over the leather top and her head resting on her arm. Nila called to her that I, an American, would like to see her house, and slowly, languidly, she got up and, without glancing into the carriage, moved toward the door, beckoning us to follow.

The house was a mess, she apologized. Her son, who is in the Russian Army, and her daughter-in-law and infant grandchild left this morning for a three-year tour of duty in Germany and she hasn't had the heart to do anything all day. Nila and I glanced at each other. So, that baby carriage was empty. A sharp pain ran through me.

There are three good-sized rooms, a kitchen with an electric stove and even an electric iron, and a bathroom, but the woman was so right—they were a mess. The scuffed, bare, dirty floors were cluttered with rags; the cheap iron beds were soiled and unmade; flies crawled over the tables, which were spread with dingy cloth covers; and papers and pasteboard were stuffed in the empty squares of several broken-paned windows. The only bright spot in the whole house was a cluster of tomatoes on the blue kitchen table.

Nila and I dashed at top speed back to the wharf. I was almost panicky, for I was convinced the boat had left us; but when we reached the pier, completely winded, nothing had changed, except that a few more American young had joined the volleyball game. Regaining her breath, Nila got into the circle and, as the ball headed her way, swooped out to meet it and lifted it with both hands, then staggered back. The ball had been batted several times into the canal and was soggy and heavy as wet wash.

When the captain made up his mind to leave this happy playing ground, he was like a mother trying to get her large, unruly family to start home from a picnic. He blew the whistle, again and again; he rang the bell, again and again; then he did both together. Several Russian boys and girls were swimming almost in the path of the boat and were loath to come out. Only when the boat began to ease away from the wharf did they come running and leap across the widening water to the deck.

The minute we were on our way, Nila settled down in the stern with three Russians to play dominoes. One was a tall, handsome man, neither too young nor too old, whom Nila, in spite of the high wind, spent last evening dancing with to jazz records from the loud-speaker. And one was a short, wiry young fellow and the other a pretty, black-haired woman. They played intensely, shouting excitedly, clapping their hands and slamming the dominoes down with such force I expected them to crash through the table top. Many times I walked to the stern and leaned on the rail to watch them; but they never gave me a glance.

Nor did they give anybody or anything else a glance. We passed extremely long rafts of logs lashed together, with men and women and even dogs living on top of them, pieces of canvas their only protection; but Nila and the other players never looked up. Very peculiarly, so it seemed to me, these rafts were the only traffic we met on the canal the entire afternoon. On one raft a man had a wood fire going right on the logs— at least it looked so—and on other rafts women had strung their wash out to dry.

When it was completely dark and Nila and her friends could no longer make out the spots on the dominoes, they reluctantly pushed their chairs back. They were all excited, but Nila was the most so. Her gray eyes glinted and her brown cheeks bloomed with color.

Reaching the privacy of our cabin, Nila poured out the tale of her triumph. "Oh, Willie, if these people had only known about me!" she gloated, massaging her palms and chuckling her deep, wicked chuckle. "This man who I met on the dance floor last night asked me would I like to play dominoes with him and two others and I said I would if they would show me how the game is going. I made out I never played before, for I was afraid I had lost the touch. My dancing companion was my partner—I called him Comrade Peter—and the pretty woman played with the young man, who Comrade Peter said was the champion of dominoes.

"So we began and they explained me very carefully the technique of the game. At the beginning I played most delicately; I almost curled up my little finger; but then Peter and I won by such a big score, I forgot to be delicate. I slammed the bones down, z-z-zhip! like you're supposed to do to give the game an air. And then, as we continued to win I forgot everything, until once, when we finished the game before our opponents could take the breath, I slammed the bone and shouted the way the sailors shout, 'Count the fish!'

"Shocked, Comrade Peter looked at me and said, 'Bozhe moi, Comrade Nila, where you know this expression?' and I just laughed and said, 'I learn the game fast.'

"Willie, Comrade Peter and I won five games in a row. Can imagine that? Did you notice the champion who played against us? He was so nervous. I'm sure you saw it yourself."

Nila popped one fist exuberantly into the palm of her other hand. "God, we played for about four hours and everything came back to me; but I didn't tell 'em anything. I just let 'em think Americans are as quick as that."

She dragged her suitcase from under her berth and took out her fine red linen and every string of her "popover" beads. No one had been changing in the evening on this small boat, as it was almost impossible to move in the cabins, much less to unpack, and I asked, puzzled, "Nila, are you dressing for supper?"

"Certainly," she said, tossing her head. "I can't let my Russian friends down."

During supper she continued in gala fettle, but afterward her mood seemed to change abruptly. As we walked out on deck, I started back to the stern, where the loud-speaker was again playing dance records; but, impatiently, Nila stopped me. "I don't want to go back there and get involved," she said. "Let's go to our stateroom and pack. There'll be no time in the morning; as you know, we get to Stalingrad at five o'clock."

I was reluctant to go inside, for the night was exhilarating.

The wind again was high, and the moon, almost full, rolled a thin coat of shining yellow across the water. Besides, we were entering locks every hour now and dropping steadily to the level of the Volga, which I found fascinating. Nevertheless, I followed Nila to our cabin.

The wind, pouring through the window, almost swept us off our feet as we opened the door, but subsided as we closed it. I took off my clothes and put on a robe to be more comfortable, packed and then crawled into my berth to read.

Nila continued to pack for a few more minutes and then, without a word to me, she jerked open the door, creating such a draft the curtains stood straight out in the room, and with a swish of her skirts disappeared.

I tried to read but couldn't keep my mind on the words. I could imagine Nila dancing with that handsome, neither too young nor too old Russian, the moon streaming down upon them and the gleaming canal sliding past.

After an hour she whirled back in and I felt better. I mustn't have missed much, I reasoned; the dancing couldn't have been too gay for her to return this soon.

Humming some Russian song in her high voice, she peered at herself in the mirror, tucked a stray hair or two beneath her net, patted her beads into place and then, so help me, once more jerked open the door and whirled through it.

And I, before the door even slammed shut, was drenched to the skin in cold water. The draft-wafted curtains had knocked the big glass water bottle off the table, beneath the window, onto my chest. I was not only wet, I was bruised. And every stitch of cover was wet and even the sheet and thin mattress beneath me were wet.

I had to get up and take every layer off me and the bed. I had to turn the mattress and the pillows over and switch the sheets and blankets around so that the soaked areas were at my feet. I even had to prop my book against the light to dry out the pages. I was in such a rage I could have killed Nila. Why couldn't she either come in and stay or go out and stay? Why did she have to keep switching in and out when she knew very well that the draft blows everything in the cabin helter-skelter?

I squirmed back into the dampish bed and contemplated ways to get even with her. On the narrow shelf above her berth were a couple of small watermelons. I eyed them speculatively. Maybe one of them could roll off in the night and crack her skull—or, better still, squash open in her face. Neither one of them though, seemed to be in quite the right spot. I got up and eased one just above where I calculated her head would rest.

I realized there was slight chance of it rolling off; still the very fact that I had done something positive made me feel almost happy. Grinning, I squirmed quickly back into the bed.

IX

Stalingrad

<u>1</u>   August 27

SPEAKING OF URBAN RENEWAL, as we do in Louisville all the time, Stalingrad has accomplished it on the grand scale. She had to, I admit, but she didn't dawdle on the job. Completely razed in the war, she is now completely rebuilt. Beginning on February 2, 1943, she has steadily planned and built until now she is a spacious, green, modern city.

Before the war her population was 400,000. Now it is 600,000. The parks and squares right in the heart of the business section are well landscaped; the main streets are unusually wide and the many white stone buildings that line them are big, squarish and most substantial-looking.

The Volga river front is especially beautiful. Besides an enchanting river station, similar to those along the Don but much larger and more elaborate, and a round white building circled by columns in the fashion of a Greek temple, and grass-sodded embankments, there are extremely broad stairs, ornamented with statues and handsome light standards, sweeping up from the river to the plateau on which the city stands. And at the top of the stairs a parkway extends for six or seven blocks into the city's center.

Yet the local guides don't brag as much about the Stalingrad of today as they do about the heroic efforts of the Russians in withstanding the siege of the Germans. The first thing after our arrival, a young man guide took Nila (alas, the watermelon didn't roll off on her), Jenna, the Australian couple and me to a high hill overlooking the city and the valley of the Volga and described those terrific days.

"More than two thousand German airplanes bombed Stalingrad in the first few days," he recounted. "Whereas fifty thousand fire bombs dropped on London, a million dropped on Stalingrad. All was flames and smoke. There was no city left at all, no water supply, no lights, no heat."

Altogether 47,800 buildings were destroyed, he said. "The Nazis thought they would spread panic and the city would capitulate, but the Russian Army and the Stalingrad people fought on magnificently."

"Leave out the poetry," said Nila, walking about restlessly, kicking up stones with the toes of her shoes. (The fact that Stalingrad is the last stop before our return to Moscow, has, I believe, put her on edge.)

For a moment the guide hesitated; then, noticeably flustered, he hurried on: "One hundred and fifty thousand civilians and forty-seven thousand Russian officers and soldiers were killed; but the German casualties were much greater. Their number of dead totaled one hundred and forty-six thousand."

Nila, her head down, her face dour and her hands clasped behind her back, continued to roam about.

"There was fighting on every corner," the guide said. "Every street was a trench. Burning oil floated on the river."

"We don't need the poetry and the literature," snapped Nila, stopping her nervous pacing for a minute. "We'd rather read it in a book."

This did it. Blushing to the roots of his short black pompadour, the guide brought the lecture to an abrupt end and we moved on to other sights and experiences.

Among these was a documentary film on the Battle of Stalingrad, put together in 1957, and no longer was Nila restless. She got terribly excited because Zhukov is depicted as the hero he was at the time of the siege and she grew impatient with me because I didn't get excited, too.

"For somebody like Mark or Robert or Jimmy Pope (Jimmy Pope is executive editor of the Louisville *Courier Journal and Times*), who understand the situation," she said tartly, "it will be most significant."

So, having been put in my place, I listened carefully to her explanation.

"You see, Willie, despite the fact that Khrushchev, when he came to power, didn't agree with Zhukov and banished him, Zhukov is still shown in the picture as the great hero of the war at the time of the Stalingrad siege. This movie was made, remember, in 1957—after Zhukov was banished—and yet here are several war pictures of him in the midst of everything. For me it is very important.

"In the olden days, when Stalin criticized somebody, z-z-zhip! the human being just melted away and not only he melted, but everybody around him melted. It was the end. It would have been out of the question for a man criticized by Stalin ever to be heard of again. Yet here today we see an important film, which couldn't have possibly been made without the most careful attention to the party line, picturing Zhukov, whom Khrushchev banished. It means there is a new attitude. A new party line." Hunching her shoulders, Nila put out her hands in a gesture that asked eloquently, Isn't is perfectly apparent?

"Also General Rokossovsky, who disappeared under Stalin, was shown," she added. "Rokossovsky is not as significant, because he was banished under Stalin. But Zhukov . . . !" Again her shoulders hunched and her hands went out.

2   Later

AFTER SUPPER, Nila suggested that she and I set out on foot to explore Stalingrad's night life.

So, with an air of casualness, we left the hotel. (This, by the way, is the very finest, best-run hotel we've been in since arriving in the U.S.S.R. It is new, of course, and has screens at the dining-room windows and no paper napkins in blue vases; the Russian guests, who rarely unfold their cloth napkins, but carefully set them to one side, have to use them here whether they want to or not, and the food is excellent. For supper I had the most juicy, tender small steak "with blood" and ice-cold watermelon.)

Walking diagonally across a large, empty, paved square, we reached the far side, which borders a park, and saw the customary windows displaying the pictures of the city's leading citizens, topped by plaster bas-reliefs of Lenin and Stalin.

"You realize that we see no statues and few pictures of Khrushchev anywhere?" Nila asked me. "I've been wondering about this ever since we got to Russia but somehow never had the time to talk about it. You know, in Stalin's day statues and pictures of him were everywhere. He started to build himself up the hour that Lenin died and he built himself to the highest point. It was completely absurd. You come to the station and there is a picture of Stalin; you come to the place where they sell kvass—that's Russia's Coca-Cola—and there is a picture of Stalin. You sleep, eat, play, sing, do everything with Stalin. Only the public toilets not included. You can't imagine, Willie, what it does to the morale. Before, when you opened a paper, you see a huge picture of Stalin right there.

"But now you see no statues and pictures of Khrushchev." Nila creased her brow in thought. "Only one with Adlai Stevenson can I remember. There are plenty of new statues. Statues to Gorky, Mayakovsky, Alexander Nevsky and other famous people; but none to Khrushchev. The people must no longer have the feeling of being watched every minute. They must have the feeling they belong once more to themselves."

We turned from the square into the park and strolled along a wide, hard-packed dirt walk lined with trees and sturdy benches and those same tall, slender street lamps with white bulbs resembling snowdrops that we saw in Sochi.

Many other people were walking, too. Some were young women and girls in their teens, frequently walking two by two, though now and then alone, and some were boys and girls together and some were groups of boys. I tried not to think about it, for it made me feel disloyal, but the thought kept recurring how ironical it is that all these people, including Nila and me, could saunter in this park, as well as others, in the Soviet Union without fear of being molested, while people don't dare to go after dark into Central Park in New York or Rock Creek Park in Washington or other parks in other cities of the United States.

A goodly number of boys and girls were sitting on benches, but, to my amazement, I saw no love-making. And some of the males, mind you, were sailors and soldiers.

We came to a Park of Culture and Rest and heard music, and, following the sound of it, we found two large groups of dancers. One was in an enclosure surrounded by a high fence, and to get inside cost a ruble; the other was in a large, open paved space.

Nila and I stood on the outskirts of the open space. As in Leningrad, many girls were dancing together and so were many boys. Some of the girl couples were dressed alike and I thought at first they must be twins, then realized there couldn't possibly be so many twins in Stalingrad. A woman with a big voice and a shrill whistle was very busy organizing square dances, schottisches and other folk dances, but none was particularly Russian. In fact, we've seen no native dances outside of the ballet.

Then Nila and I moved over to the more exclusive dance that cost a ruble. A militia woman circled the middle of the floor to keep order, and she was so comical a figure she looked like a caricature. She must weigh at least three hundred pounds and, as Nila remarked, "she is as forward in the front as in the back." She had a short, fat neck and very short, fat legs. Her white tunic stretched tightly over her skirt and a small beret sat on the very back of her head.

"If she wasn't in such a solemn dancing place," said Nila, "I would think she was hired to add to the gaiety."

After a few minutes here, we roamed over other areas of the park and, lo and behold, if we didn't come upon another free dance floor; also, a movie house; a Room of Laughter (those crazy mirrors, you know); a shooting gallery; a latticed-in reading room where boys and girls in their teens sat about tables, poring over magazines, newspapers and books; one of those machines by which you test your strength by hitting a lever that sends a weight up a pole; and sixteen huge swings the like of which I've never seen before. They are in the shape of boats, and boys and girls stand in them and pump madly until the boats swing straight above the bars. Nila and I watched them for many breathless minutes. We were sure the boats were going all the way over and would spill the occupants upon the hard dirt. In one swing a girl pumped alone and her thin clothes stuck to her body as if they were sculptured on her.

It was ten-thirty when Nila and I left the park, but evidently this was much too early an hour to depart, for the young were still everywhere, walking, dancing, swinging, talking, reading. Everything except making love.

Crossing the big square to the hotel, I eyed the still high, round moon and thought with a pang how wasted he seemed here in Stalingrad.

🌱   🌱

🌱

3   *August 28*

WHILE HAVING BREAKFAST this morning in our room, Nila and I gazed out the window into the huge square on which this hotel faces and the streets leading into it. It was nine o'clock, but the square and the streets were empty, except for frequent buses and some people on foot. For at least ten minutes at a time not a car, not a truck, not a motorcycle, not even a bicycle went by. In such a modern-looking city of over a half-million people, it seemed absolutely eerie.

"No doubt the few rich, important people who own cars don't get up so early," Nila suggested. "Or maybe they're waiting for their chauffeurs to come. Nobody who owns a car would drive himself."

When our own car made its appearance, we hied with the other tourists who were with us on the Volga-Don trip to one of the biggest tractor factories in Russia and streamed through it. Knowing nothing more mechanical than how to change light bulbs, I appreciated only the excellent lighting, the good air and the leisurely pace at which the workers worked. They even had time to look us over carefully and to speak and smile.

Also, I was impressed—and surprised—at the slogans tacked everywhere. For instance, I had no idea workers in the U.S.S.R. could agitate for a shorter work day, yet one sign read: "Let's create the condition that will make it possible to transfer the people to a seven-hour work day." (Now it is eight.) Other slogans declared: "We must supply the cheapest tractor possible for the Soviet Union" and "There is no other way to happiness except the way of free labor." Then there were many posters with graphs showing the growth of industry under Soviet power and the accomplishment of the workers of this plant.

After the tramp through the factory we were herded into the very elegant auditorium of the plant's Palace of Culture and there the factory manager offered to answer questions. They flew from all of us, and we learned that the average wage of a worker is 930 rubles a month, men and women making the same wage for the same amount of labor, and that out of his wages a worker pays one half of one per cent to the trade union and from one to six per cent as income tax to the government.

Also, we learned that the State Planning Committee furnishes the plans for the tractors and the orders for their distribution; that the cost of producing a tractor is 14,300 rubles and that it is sold to the consumer for 16,200 rubles; and that part of the profit goes to the state and part to the Council of the People's Economy of Stalingrad.

With statistics running out of my ears, I very sweetly asked the factory manager, "How did the workers feel about Khrushchev's speech denouncing Stalin?"

"They discussed it and decided Khrushchev was right," he answered calmly.

"Were they surprised that Khrushchev waited so long to make the speech?" I then asked.

And quick as a flash, he answered, "Better late than never."

"After the regime changed did you notice an improvement in morale?" I asked next, and I felt quickly a change in the friendly atmosphere.

"What do you mean, 'regime'?" he asked the interpreter angrily.

"I'm just repeating what the *Amerikanka* asked," she retorted just as angrily.

He shrugged his shoulders as if the word was of no importance and answered, "The morale improved under both Stalin and Khrushchev. The workers have always been happy and content."

Our request to visit the factory's nursery for the children of working mothers was flatly denied. It was not on the planned tour, the manager said.

We had a spirited ride back to our hotel. Seeing a peace poster proclaiming, "Long live the Soviet Union, which is the bulwark of peace in the whole world," I asked the local male guide, didn't he and the other Russian people realize that we of the United States want peace just as fervently as the U.S.S.R., and he replied that of course they didn't realize it, for it wasn't so. If we of the United States stopped preparing for war, he went on with the air of an authority, nineteen million munition workers will be thrown out of work and we, with our already large number of unemployed, can't take that.

Naturally I argued angrily that we don't even have that many munition workers, but my cause was weakened because I haven't the slightest notion how many we do have.

As soon as Nila and I alighted at the hotel, we set out alone for the city's free market—that is, the market where the farmers bring the produce they raise on their own little plots of land and sell them for their own profit.

It was fabulous. Hills of watermelons, yellow melons, purple plums, white plums, green plums, peas, parsley, laurel leaves, which Nila told me the Russians use in everything they cook, fish—half dried and thoroughly dried—tomatoes, tomatoes, tomatoes, even long tomatoes like cucumbers, and, of course, cucumbers themselves; grapes, eggplants . . .

Our attention was drawn to a whitish root, looking something like a long turnip, and we approached the salesman behind the counter and Nila asked, "For what do you use it?" The salesman was what Nila described as "a typical old kulak," with the shrewdest little eyes, seeming to bore into us, and a small mustache and beard. For a minute or two he and Nila carried on a lively conversation and then she turned to me. "Willie, it is called Adam's Root and it is some kind of Geritol for tired blood. It's good for headaches, nerves, teethaches and weariness."

Then there were beautiful baskets of all sizes hand-woven from a long yellow grass that grows in water, called *mochalka*, and also loose hanks of it. "The Russians buy it loose," Nila explained, "when they go to the baths to scrub themselves."

Many customers already possessed these hand-woven baskets and they had them partly filled with unwrapped liver and other meats bleeding into unwrapped loaves of bread, vegetables and fruit.

The only queue in the market was in front of a window where a man was selling putty. Patiently, twenty-five women or more stood in line as the man weighed, cut and handed them the proper-sized lumps.

"Putty is quite a precious thing," Nila said. "Winter is coming and the people have to seal their windows."

A handful of gypsies with open satchels wandered from stall to stall, begging for withered and partly rotted produce. Among them was a swaggering, wiry, wrinkled old creature with a busted-open watermelon in her satchel.

Nila told the old crone that I'm an American and would like to have my fortune told.

Her black eyes narrowed to slits and she studied me excitedly; then, turning to Nila, she asked, "Is she actually an American? I've never seen an American, so I can't be sure, but if you're not telling me the truth, God will punish you."

Nila assured her that she was speaking only the truth and, finally convinced, she agreed to tell my fortune. "Put the money in the hand," she peremptorily ordered Nila. "Three rubles."

Then she led us out of the market, peering furtively about for a secluded place, for it's not permitted in the Soviet Union these days to tell fortunes. Finally she spied a narrow space between the backs of two booths and I held out my palm.

"I don't need it," she said, waving it aside. "I tell the fortune by the lines in the forehead." (Heaven knows in my case she had a richly plowed field in which to work.)

She told me I had a happy life and that tomorrow I will receive much mail with good news; but at the very second she started to reveal the nature of the good news, a militiaman in a spotlessly white, unwrinkled blouse and high shining boots appeared and silenced her.

"If I see you around here again," he said sternly, shaking his stick in her crinkled face, "I'll arrest you. I mean it, you hear? This is the very last time I'm warning you."

Nila swiftly poked her index finger into my shoulder and addressed herself to the militiaman. "My friend here is an American and she has never had her fortune told by a gypsy. Won't you please let her have this experience?"

"Stop making up such stories," the policeman answered curtly. "I have eyes and I can see your friend is one hundred per cent Russian."

Nila clasped her hands beneath her chin and looked at me with troubled eyes. "How can I make you more presentable?" she mourned. "God knows I work hard."

I had no answer to this and the militiaman had no change of heart. Wagging his stick, he sent the gypsies and us on our separate ways.

However, Nila and I stopped in the market long enough to purchase four squashy cucumber pickles and a big yellow melon. Then, as we paraded triumphantly with them in our arms through the streets, Nila gloated, "I've come into the Russian spirit. I've bought this melon to take with us to Moscow."

4   Evening

ALL LARGE CITIES IN Russia have permanent buildings for circus performances, and they are open almost nightly. I heard about the circuses in Moscow, Odessa and Sochi and wanted to go; but I've had my first opportunity here in Stalingrad.

Going to the same Park of Culture and Rest where we went

last night, Nila and I located the shabby, round wooden circus building, put down $1.50 each for tickets and were ushered to chairs in the front row, scarcely a foot away from the low wall, topped by a frail iron rail, that encloses the one big ring.

We deposited our raincoats—which we had worn for warmth only, for there was not a cloud in the moon-flooded sky— beneath our seats; but in a few minutes we were poked in the backs by newly arrived people who told us kindly that our raincoats were on the floor.

"Thank you," said Nila and, in order not to embarrass the people, we picked them up and deposited them in our laps. Shortly, however, they grew heavy and sticky and we decided to put them back on the floor; but before doing it, Nila explained to the people that we really had put our coats on the floor on purpose. "In America," she concluded, "we always do it."

Their faces mirrored their disapproval. "You can't do it," the oldest woman of the party argued excitedly. "They are such beautiful coats and the floor is so dirty. You simply mustn't do it."

Her concern was touching; nevertheless, Nila grabbed mine and hers and thrust them beneath the chairs.

Then a small-bodied, though big-bosomed, lively middle-aged woman took the seat beside me and, after a brief moment, spoke to me in Russian.

"*Amerikanka*," I answered.

"Ah-h-h," she said breathlessly, her eyes widening and lighting up in the most astonishing, flattering fashion. If I had had wings and had floated straight from heaven she couldn't have been more transported.

She told Nila, her words tumbling over one another, that she had never sat next to an American before, much less spoken to one; then she stared at me dotingly, worshipfully. I felt my cheeks burning with embarrassment. My looks were so inadequate. Oh, if I only did have wings and a diadem, whatever that might be.

And when the circus got under way, she studied my reactions to each act as if I were a rare specimen under glass. Fortunately, the first act of the circus was delightful, with the hardest-working, most comical clowns I've ever seen and it took no pretending on my part to satisfy her that I was having a wonderful time. In fact, I laughed as hilariously as the packed rows of Russians, who are like children in their enjoyment and exuberance. The only difference was I didn't put my hand in front of my mouth as the Russian women do when they laugh.

There was a half-hour intermission at the end of the first half and the woman eagerly invited Nila and me to stroll with her along the park paths. All the other members of the circus audience were strolling too, many of them eating ice-cream cones and drinking soft drinks.

The woman told us she is a master teacher of geometry in the Institute of Technology in Stalingrad. She sometimes lectures to as many as 100 students of higher education; but her "practical classes," as she calls them, are limited to fifteen. She's paid 1,300 rubles a month. This, of course, is good pay in Russia, but it is not exceptional among the teaching profession. Many professors, she said, make as much as 3,000 rubles a month, and medical professors usually get double that because they not only have to teach, but must demonstrate their lectures at clinics and hospitals.

She was graduated, after sixteen years of school, as an engineer of shipbuilding and spent fifteen years actually building ships. Her husband was an engineer, too. They had one baby and the three of them lived happily and comfortably. Then the war came and the husband went to the front, leaving her and the baby in Leningrad. The husband was killed, and during the siege of Leningrad the baby died. When the war was over, she couldn't stay in Leningrad "where there were so many memories" and so she accepted the invitation to teach at the Institute of Technology and moved to Stalingrad. She now lives with her mother in one room with a private kitchen and bathroom.

There was no bitterness in her voice as she told us her story; indeed, she said that she is very grateful to have "this complete apartment" and that she and her mother "live very well."

She was dressed as if they do. She had on a well-fitting

dark-brown skirt and a printed silk blouse that matched the skirt, and she carried one of those Chinese sandalwood fans which the old gentleman from Rostov told us cost $6.25.

The instant we returned to our seats, the chief usher came straight up to me and said, "Citizen, I'd like to warn you about the hippopotamus act. The hippopotamus might come very close to you, but don't be frightened. Just be careful of your dress, for he might sneeze on you."

As you can understand, this added not one whit to my peace of mind. Nor did the gauzy, but impenetrable, curtain that, during the intermission, had been suspended from the ceiling all the way around the ring. The hippopotamus could already be right on the other side of that curtain, waiting to spring. I clutched my hands in my lap.

The curtain went up and revealed a peaceful woodland scene with a pool surrounded by rocks and rushes in the middle of the ring, and a small man dressed in a gnome's costume, and long-legged, lightly stepping herons.

There was no hippopotamus in sight and for a few minutes I breathed more easily; but then I noticed a big square of gray cloth humped in front of me, just inside the low wall and the frail iron rail, and grew uneasy again. Could it be possible that the hippopotamus was under that cloth?

The small man, shedding his gnome's disguise, put the herons through their paces. They walked in circles and stretched out their beaks for food. Then he sauntered over to the big hump and called softly, "Malchik." ("It means little boy," Nila whispered.) And at that Malchik stirred—it was like a grassless golf tee stirring—struggled to his stumpy legs and lumbered over to the low wall.

I held my breath. Surely the trainer would not allow him to come any closer. Yet he did. That mammoth monster hoisted himself atop the wall, his head turned directly toward me.

With one swoop I retrieved my raincoat from under my chair and held it in front of me. Only my alarmed eyes peered above it.

The circus hall rocked with laughter—Russian laughter; I assure you it was none of mine.

Deliberately, Malchik wallowed forward on the wall until he was opposite me. Then he laid his head along the top of the threadlike rail and opened the two-foot-wide cavern of his mouth. Sharp tusks stood up from his lower jaw.

I was fit to faint. His wet breath moistened the exposed area of my face; his stale, urine smell stung my nostrils.

Then, bored with me (evidently he had seen an American before), he wobbled a few steps farther, once more rested his head on the rail and spread wide his jaws.

This circling of the wall was only the beginning of the hippopotamus act. The trainer and "Little Boy" did all sorts of intimate acts together. The trainer stuck his head deep into "Little Boy's" mouth; then the hippopotamus lay down beside the trainer and nestled his head on the trainer's breast, chewed on his ears, nuzzled him in the neck and slobbered all over him. The Russians were absolutely "hippopotamized."

Nila, however, was not so carried away. "As much as I'm impressed," she announced solemnly, "I'll never advise anybody to train a hippopotamus. It is physically most unpleasant."

After the performance, the teacher walked almost all the way to the hotel with us. When finally she did leave us to catch her bus, she gripped my hand and pumped it vigorously. "Good luck," she said, her eyes shining warmly. "Good, good luck!"

Strolling on, Nila commented with satisfaction on the evening. "The whole atmosphere was very gay and I felt strongly we were together with the people."

5   August 29

THOUGH WE USE MONEY solely for opera, ballet and circus tickets, cucumber pickles, melons and tipping, since we never have to settle hotel or food bills or pay taxi fares, our rubles have still dwindled dangerously low. So this morning Nila,

Jenna, the local guide and I walked a goodly number of blocks to a bank to cash one of my American Express checks.

We could have ridden, of course, but we see and learn more walking. For one thing, we saw a huge sign across the entire top of an apartment house, vowing, WE WILL FULFILL THE DECISIONS OF THE TWENTIETH CONGRESS OF THE COMMUNIST PARTY and I learned those decisions from Jenna.

Very competently, it seemed to me, she told about the decisions affecting industry and agriculture, with the purpose of increasing production. Then she added casually, "You see, the Twentieth Congress determined that the Soviet Union must catch up with the United States in production in proportion to its population. As you know, everybody in America has more food and much more wearing apparel than in the Soviet Union."

She also discussed Khrushchev's denunciation of Stalin, concluding with the amazing statement, "The Twentieth Congress decided we must have frank criticism in our country, as frank criticism is the foundation of our state."

I looked at her sharply and found her long face serene.

For another thing, we saw men and women holding umbrellas over their heads as they sold books and magazines at open stalls along the sidewalks, and, for another, many women bent double with the weight of huge cloth bundles on their backs.

Reaching the bank, I felt perfectly at home. Any American would have. It's a handsome stone building and the entrance lobby on the ground floor displays colorful posters urging everybody to open savings accounts and collect regular interest.

"Do you have a savings account?" I asked Jenna.

Circling her eyes around and grinning broadly, she shook her head.

"Do you know anybody who has a savings account?"

Yes, she said. She has a girl friend who has a savings account of 2,000 rubles. She's saving to buy a fur coat.

Then I turned to the local guide. "And you?"

He grinned, too. His savings account, what there is of it, is under the mattress. He and his young wife are moving shortly into a new apartment and he's saving to buy furniture.

"Is your kitchen already furnished with a refrigerator and an electric stove?"

He laughed elatedly, as if I'd told a good joke, and didn't even bother to answer me.

"I meant it seriously," I said when he quieted down. "Practically all new apartments in the cities of the United States are furnished with refrigerators and electric stoves."

Well, his isn't, he admitted. It's completely empty except for a two-burner gas stove.

From the ground-floor lobby we ascended wide marble stairs to another lobby as big as a tennis court, three stories high and completely surrounded by enormous white columns and fat marble balustrades.

To exchange my Express check for Russian money, we were directed to a locked door. After we had knocked on it for some little time, a woman appeared behind us, introduced herself as the assistant manager of the bank, unlocked the door and ushered us into a large room. In the center is a round table, covered in red velvet and holding an ornate desk set and an oversized marble ash tray in the shape of a lying-down dog with a hollow in his back. On one wall hangs an oil portrait of an important-looking official.

"Is he the president of the bank?" Nila asked of the assistant manager.

"Oh, no, that's Comrade Pervukhin."

"Who he is?"

"He's a member of the Soviet government."

"Why you choose him?" Nila persisted.

The assistant manager shrugged slightly. "It was for sale, so we bought it."

When I confided that I wanted to cash an American Express check, the assistant manager summoned a young woman and asked her to go for money. In a few minutes she returned, both arms straining to hold two stacks of Russian paper money that reached to her chin. With the help of the assistant manager she unloaded it onto the table.

"Now, how large a check would you like to cash?" asked the assistant manager in crisp, businesslike tones.

I wet my dry lips and swallowed uncomfortably. I could see that the figure I had in mind would be a terrible shock to her and I put off mentioning it as long as possible.

"Yes?" She prompted me.

"I planned to cash a . . . a . . . a check for twenty dollars."

There was a slight gasp; then the assistant manager got hold of herself. "Certainly, citizen, as you wish."

With an air of boredom—or was it disdain?—she reached out her hand and took a thin, thin 200-ruble layer from the stack of thousands.

          ❦   ❦   Later

For some reason (maybe it was because of the strain of the big financial deal of the morning) I developed shortly after dinner a severe crick in my right shoulder and, groaning, took to my couch. However, I wasn't there long, for Nila cured me with an old Russian remedy. She borrowed an iron from the hotel and ironed on me with all her strength just as if she were ironing heavy clothes. In fact, between ironing on me she did iron some clothes and never once changed her pace.

X

Moscow Revisited

AFTER A SMOOTH AND uneventful plane trip from Stalingrad we reached Moscow in the early evening. An Intourist representative met us and informed us that this visit we were to stay at the hotel of our choice—the Metropole.

We reached there too late to get our mail, but we found a note at the desk from our old Leningrad friend, Peter Gillingham, inviting us to his room for cocktails before dinner. Very shortly we put in our appearance and discovered the Capitalist, grinning impishly, sensing what a shock the sight of him would be, a glass of vodka in his hand. Also a slim, very youthful-looking lad from Yale and a big, handsome, light-colored Negro from Harvard.

I asked Ward about Ruby and he said she is in Moscow, but not at the Metropole, and is "pregnant as hell." He also said quite frankly and bitterly that he's been searching for a prostitute in every city he has been to and is convinced there isn't such a thing in all Russia. The Soviet government, he believes, has frightened every last one of them off the streets.

In a little while the Negro excused himself, explaining that he had a date with a Russian girl. Loud wails of envy from the other three males accompanied his departure. In a few minutes, though, he popped back to announce that his date had a girl friend and that the Yale man could come with him. Arms locked, they swaggered out, the sad eyes of the Capitalist and Peter following them until the door slammed shut.

<u>2</u>   *August 30*

Nila found no letter from her sister this morning, and so she decided she cannot hope any longer to locate her by her own efforts but must seek the help of someone in an official position. Nor did this move now seem dangerous. She has finally become convinced that the reins of the terrorizing secret police have loosened amazingly and that people aren't now being arrested on trumped-up charges.

So we went to the headquarters of Intourist in the National Hotel. I sat in the hall, opposite the open door, while Nila poured out her story to the chief of Intourist. I could see the pleading look on her pale face and the eloquence of her outstretched open hands as she leaned across the chief's desk, talking rapidly. And I could see the chief listening intently and making notes and, finally, picking up the telephone and speaking into it with an air of authority.

Nila's eyes were dry but glassy-bright when she rejoined me in the hall. She grabbed my arm and propelled me down the stairs to the street, where we could talk.

"He was more than considerate," she told me excitedly, "and he promised to do all he can, but he's worried that I haven't given him enough time. 'Why didn't you come to us when you first got to Russia?' he asked me, and I told him, 'I want to be absolutely frank with you. I didn't know when I came whether my sister and my mother, if she's still living, would want to see me; I didn't know whether they might be afraid that if they saw me it might be very dangerous for them. But now, after these weeks in the Soviet Union, I understand that if they are alive they will love to see me.'

"Then, Willie, I told him that when I got to Moscow I wrote my sister—to Penza, the last address I had—and asked her to write me in care of Intourist and, if she wanted to see me, to make plans to come to Moscow; but that when I got back here there was no letter, no message, no nothing, and so I'm sure she did not get my letter."

Nila, gripping my arm, walked as rapidly as she talked and I had to take little running steps to keep up with her.

"I then gave him the address of my sister and told him her age," she rushed on, "and also the name and age of my mama and of my niece to help him with the description. And then, Willie, he just picked up the receiver and called the Intourist bureau at the Metropole Hotel and told a woman there to send immediately two telegrams with paid replies; one was to the head of the Soviet Committee of Penza and one to the Penza Address Bureau, saying he wants to know if these people are still there and if not, where they are moved."

Nila was so keyed-up with her story and I was so involved listening that we bumped head on into a stocky woman shoveling fertilizer onto the circle of unpaved ground around a young tree.

Backing off with murmured apologies, Nila continued, "When he finished talking on the telephone, he stood up and gripped my hand hard and said if my family is still in Penza these people will find them and then I told him if they were there I would go and see them; but he said the easiest thing would be for them to come and visit me here at the hotel."

Reaching the Metropole, we went in the Intourist office and Nila found the woman with whom the head of Intourist had talked and watched her write out the two telegrams for Penza.

Then the woman said, "As this is Saturday, we can't expect a reply before Monday. But sometime Monday I'm sure we'll hear."

3   *Later*

As if her sister were already found, Nila was in the highest spirits at dinner and proposed that we go to the Department of Marriage Registration and try to see a Soviet wedding; then, turning to Peter and the Capitalist, who had joined us, she said, "You can go with us or drop dead."

Peter readily agreed to go, but Ward preferred to drop dead.

"I'm very anxious to see a Soviet wedding," Nila informed me hurriedly when Peter left to get his hat and camera, and Jenna, who had shown up after dinner, went to find out about a car, "for I hear they have changed since Robert's and my marriage twenty-one years ago. Ours is the saddest, grimmest memory. Willie, you remember, I told you we went to this dirty, dark room with the black, broken-to-pieces desk with only two windows there, one for deaths and births and one for marriages and divorces, and the man said, 'Passports,' and z-z-zhip he put the stamps on them and there we were, married. No witnesses needed. Nothing. We paid him three rubles and left. A wedding was the cheapest thing in Russia."

Nila had heard correctly about the changes. There are now two large rooms as pretty as a wedding cake. The walls look as if they're hung in pale-pink damask, though in truth they are stippled with a slightly raised design, paler than the background, to give a damask feeling. And all the pictures on the walls are of pastel-colored flowers—all, that is, except a large portrait of Lenin, but even Lenin has cheeks as blushingly rosy-red as any bride's.

Also, ferns in bright-pink paper holders flourish behind the big desk at the far end of the two rooms, curtains of natural-colored silk, gathered in soft folds, cover the windows, and a dozen champagne glasses of sparkling crystal are ready for the toasts on a round table covered with red velvet.

The judge in charge of the Department of Marriage Registration received us. She is a plumpish woman of forty or thereabouts with a kind, intelligent face. She is a member of the Communist Party and a graduate of the Party School.

She was expecting to perform seventeen weddings this afternoon, but as the first couple had not yet come she had a few minutes to talk to us about the present laws and customs of marriages and divorces in the Soviet Union. There is very little red tape about weddings, she said. The couple only have to register their intention to marry before the ceremony, but that doesn't mean they need to go through with it if, for some reason, they change their minds. If the bride and groom are eighteen, they don't need their parents' consent and they don't have to take blood tests, for every young Russian is registered at a clinic and has a health card. Usually there are between twenty-five and thirty marriages a day in all of Moscow, and ninety-four per cent of these are civil services.

"You mean only six per cent are married in church?" I asked, somewhat startled.

"Yes, of course," she answered emphatically. "What is to be gained by marrying in church?"

"It makes the ceremony more . . . more sacred," I stammered. "It brings home to the young that they are married in the sight of God."

She smiled, shrugged, and rolled her eyes ceilingward.

"I mean—" I tried again—"I mean a church ceremony is more impressive . . . more memorable . . ."

"We are trying all the time to make the civil service more memorable," she said. "Soon we will go to the Kremlin for our weddings."

"Do the bride and groom give each other rings?" asked Nila.

"Yes, very often they do."

"I thought, perhaps, since giving rings was such an old tradition," Nila explained, "the custom had been done away."

"But it's such a beautiful custom," the judge answered, smiling. "We don't urge it, you understand; we just leave it to the young people."

In comparison to the number who are married daily in Moscow, the judge went on, the number of divorces is gratifyingly small. Usually there are only three or four a day. "It is very, very rare when people with children get a divorce," she said. "Of course they can get them; but the court has to decide and it doesn't allow them without good cause. Also, divorces take time and they are very expensive. Generally a divorce costs two thousand rubles, but the exact amount depends on the salaries of those involved."

I wanted to know the chief causes of divorce in the Soviet Union.

266

"There are many causes," she answered. "Sometimes the husbands and wives get tired and bored or they don't love each other any more; but the main cause is that one member of the marriage goes ahead in his development and the other stands still. Many Russian men go to night schools and then technical institutes and become engineers, while their wives remain peasants. The Soviet government is trying very hard to get wives and husbands to move together to the same levels so as to eliminate this cause."

The first young couple, accompanied by four attendants of their own age, two male and two female, arrived. One of the males, who resembled Elvis Presley, with sideburns as long as his nose, had a camera and the judge said that he and Peter, too, could take pictures at any time during the ceremony.

The bride was wearing a thin purple dress, the skirt pleated, and around her neck was a string of pearl beads. She clutched a big bouquet of pink, red and white dahlias and pink button chrysanthemums in a cone of white paper. Her face was pretty in a young, fresh way. The groom was in a blue serge suit two sizes too large for him.

They approached the judge's desk, and, smiling warmly, she stood up and shook hands with them. Then they sat down, the bride and groom facing the desk. They handed the judge their passports and she asked their names, their ages (the boy is twenty-one, the girl twenty), their places of birth and their present addresses (they are both from a nearby collective farm).

The bride kept smiling nervously, showing steel teeth, and she waved continuously a folded navy-blue handkerchief in front of her flushed face, except during those moments when she knotted it up and mopped her upper lip.

The judge asked the bride by what name she wants to be known (Jenna whispered that a girl can keep her maiden name if she wishes) and she answered she wants to take her husband's name.

The Presley character teetered on a chair and snapped pictures.

With no vows exchanged and, of course, no prayers and scriptures, the judge pronounced simply, "Comrades, under

Soviet law you are now husband and wife." They then stood and the judge shook their hands and congratulated them. "Comrades, I congratulate you and I wish you a strong, long and happy marriage."

The groom at first shook hands with his bride, but after a moment he seemed to think better of it and put his arm around her and gave her a real kiss on the lips.

Then they went into the next room and the groom changed the low, sweet victrola record which had been playing during the ceremony for a quick dance number and turned to his new mate. She placed her flowers on the window sill and the two of them whirled away. Then the friends started to dance; then Peter and Jenna; then the judge and Nila; then the judge's assistant, who was a young woman, and I danced.

When the first record ended, the groom put on another and everybody changed partners. This time the judge chose me and she led vigorously and forcefully, as becomes a member of the Communist Party who has been graduated from the Party School.

I could have danced all night—or rather, all afternoon—but the next couple arrived and spoiled everything. The victrola was switched back to soft music; the judge took her place behind the big desk; the newlyweds disappeared to sign the marriage registry and Nila, Peter, Jenna and I went out into the mundane, unromantic street.

As the hour was still early, Nila had another idea. We must rush to the race track. When Nila lived in Moscow she went to the track frequently and she was enthusiastic at the prospect of seeing it again.

Jenna begged off and so we dropped her at the corner of the street where she lives. For some reason she didn't want us to know the exact place.

The entrance building to the track is new, huge and startling. It is really two buildings joined together, one in the style of Greek architecture and one in pure Soviet. Tremendous columns parade across the Greek façade, and a bronze replica of one of those famous man-and-horse statues that we saw on Anichkov Bridge in Leningrad rears on the roof.

Nila was taken aback by this new, terrifically lavish exterior; but when she got on the inside and saw the packed stands she was on familiar ground. Nothing has changed in the ten years she has been away.

"Absolutely nothing," she said in a flat voice. "The same dirty floors with the thrown-away no-money stubs. The same people with the red noses and unshaved faces and necks and all old. Old! Even those who are young look old. And all held together by the gambling fever."

She strode rapidly in front of the stands, her eyes darting swiftly over the people as if she was hoping to see some familiar faces, and Peter and I followed at her heels.

"This is the bottom of the life," she said, slowing down. "If you want to see the bottom of the life in Russia here it is. These people not stop for anything to get the money to gamble."

The crowd, which was nine-tenths male, was really tough. They could have come straight from New York's skid row. Their suits were green with age; their collars and cuffs were frayed and dingy; their shirts were tieless and they looked as if they had not washed in months. I saw one old woman in rags that seemed held together by grease, sitting on a box and studying her program through a monocle, a walking stick by her side.

We didn't go into the grandstand, but wandered among the knots of people in the wide space that stretches from the stands to the track, Nila's eyes always moving, always alert. It was between races when we arrived and the people were amazingly quiet. They are in deep study about their bets, I decided. But when the next race was run they were still quiet. Truly phlegmatic. They didn't shove and push to the rail; they didn't jump up and down and shout. Even those who won didn't shout.

I drew Nila's attention to this; but she didn't consider it interesting. "It's not the temperament of the people who play the races to shout," she said. "Just those who come casually to the races like your friends at Churchill Downs scream and yell and they do it because they're bored. Everybody who comes here plays the races. It's a business, not a holiday with shouting. To the Russians, betting is like a terrible disease. They lose themselves completely in it and, of course, lose all their money, too, which makes their families do without. I remember ten years ago when I was here a man lost all his cash; but he must go on playing. He took a government bond of fifty rubles, which was all he had left, and tried to sell it; but nobody would buy it for what it was worth. Then he tried to sell it for thirty rubles; then twenty. His hand was shaking like this—" Nila jerked her hand about as if she were having an epileptic fit. "Was he an example of Soviet ideology? Of course not!"

Nila was thoughtful for a few moments while the people milled about us; then she said "Just like ten years ago I couldn't understand why the government allows such gambling, I still can't understand it. They try to produce a new Soviet man who must not have the old bourgeois habits of life; yet gambling is one of the most widespread habits." She shook her head slowly. "The only explanation I can think of is the money the government makes. As you know, Peter and Willie, everything here is one hundred per cent run by the government—the horses, the betting windows, the jockeys. The government pays the jockeys' salaries and when they win a race they get a bonus. The bets are ten and twenty rubles and a man can buy as many bets as he wants. Just think of the terrific money the government gets."

This afternoon there were two kinds of racing—harness and flat racing. We watched one of each and, except for the drabness, stillness and quietness of the crowd, I could note little difference between them and those in Kentucky.

Then we bought hot *pirochki*, which a woman was selling from a basket, and, munching on them, returned to the hotel.

4   Evening

NILA AND I HAD PLANNED to go this evening to the Red Square and see the people dance as they do there every summer Saturday night; but Peter, the proud possessor of two tickets for the opening performance of the fall season at the Art Theater, invited Nila to go with him and she accepted. Chekhov's *The Three Sisters*—in Russian, of course—was the attraction.

She and Peter went early to the dining room for a quick snack and left me sulking in my tent (most unreasonably, I must say, for even if Peter had been able to get another ticket, which he tried valiantly to do, I wouldn't have been able to understand a word of the play). Then the telephone rang and Nila announced she had just run into the Capitalist in the lobby and he would be happy to have supper with me.

So the Capitalist and I ate together and danced once; then we parted for a span of time that at one crucial point appeared as if it would be forever.

The action opened, so to speak, when, at the end of this first dance, two young Russians whom I'd never seen before rushed over to our table, bowed from the waist and kissed my hand. For what I had no idea, unless they were congratulating me because, in spite of my gray hair, romping wrinkles and sagging jowls, I was able to follow the Capitalist's rather slinky, fancy steps. One was a blond with long, wavy hair brushed straight back to the rolled edge of the black turtle-neck sweater he wore beneath his coat; the other was small and neat in a tweed suit. Having finished pressing their lips to my hand, they bowed again and went back to their table.

Turning toward the Capitalist to ask what he made of this performance, I realized he hadn't even noticed it. He had spotted a very pretty Russian girl sitting with a well-dressed, much-above-the-ordinary-looking Russian man at a table near us, and he was completely lost in admiration. She had a shoulder-length bob of silky, wheat-colored hair and long, up-slanting dark eyes.

With the first note of the next piece, the young man in the turtle-neck sweater bounded over, murmured a few unintelligible words to the Capitalist and pulled me into his arms for the most athletic number I've worked through since the Highland-samba fling at Sochi. As if I were one of those little rubber balls attached by an elastic to a paddle, Turtle-neck tossed me vigorously away from him, then bent himself so far backward that he disappeared beneath the cloths of the tables edging the floor and then, when I'd about adjusted myself to the shock of seeing him no more, bobbed back, slithered forward and snatched me to him.

Most of the dance I was completely blacked out from lack of oxygen in my lungs; but once or twice I came to sufficiently to catch wavering glimpses of the Capitalist and to realize he was up to no good. He was dancing with the girl with the long golden hair, holding her tightly and whispering into her ear.

When the music ended, I dragged myself back to the table to rest. However, the intermission was frighteningly brief. Before I'd even got up my strength to pull my girdle down, the music started once more, and the Capitalist was off to get the girl with the long bob and I was off with the small, neat friend of the turtle-neck sweater.

The evening progressed in this fashion for some little time and then propriety raised its meddlesome head. An elderly Russian-American or an English-speaking Russian (in the excitement I never got him straight), with an intellectual face that marks him as a man of parts, had been watching the Capitalist take the long-bobbed blonde away from her companion for dance after dance and decided it was wrong and might lead to serious trouble, and so, as Ward started again for the table, he waylaid him and told him sternly to "lay off." He said Ward was taking advantage of the girl's companion's hospitality and friendliness for an American and he must stop it.

The Capitalist stood rigidly still for a moment, his big head thrust forward, and the man stood rigidly still, too, eying him, and his fists clenched and unclenched.

This was where I thought I'd lose Ward forever; but slowly he lifted his head, looked at the man, then turned and stalked back to our table.

He was furious, furious as only a man who is used to having his own way can be when he's thwarted. He slumped back in his chair and glowered. Then he roused himself and ordered vodka. Then more vodka. And then, alas, he began to sing in Japanese in full voice what he said was a Japanese love song.

I missed the end of it. After the first few lines, I fled to my room.

✤   ✤

TODAY BEING SUNDAY, there was no hope of hearing about Nila's sister. So we went on an excursion to the little town of Zagorsk, where the famous Troitske-Sergiyevskaya Monastery, built in the middle of the fourteenth century, is located.

It was a brilliant, cold day with a high, cutting wind and I had the feeling I should be getting out of Russia. I certainly didn't want to be caught like Napoleon.

Nila, Peter, Jenna and I made up the party. (Yesterday the Capitalist said he would like to go, but this morning he wasn't feeling up to it.)

Hoping to attend the eleven o'clock Mass in the cathedral of the monastery, we had an early breakfast, got a lunch packed and started out. Jenna was very gay. "I'll be glad to see those handsome monks," she commented wickedly.

For the first few miles we rolled along the broad, impressive Yaroslavl Highway. New apartment houses, business and office structures, including a giant printing plant, schools and college buildings, institutes and the entrance to the U.S.S.R. Agricultural and Industrial Exhibition line it on both sides.

Nila, Peter and I reviewed our last night's experiences, and among other interesting things Peter said that on the way to the theater he tried to buy me some flowers to make up for his and Nila's desertion of me, but he could find no fresh ones.

"That's right," broke in Nila. "They were all quilted."

Peter and I laughed and Nila, frowning, asked, "What's wrong? Is it only breasts that are quilted and not roses?"

Trucks, decorated with paper streamers and red flags and jammed with young people standing up, waving and shouting, passed us one after another. Jenna said they were on their way to celebrations in Moscow from the collective farms and villages, for this is the first day of the Holiday of Youth.

Leaving the wide highway at the outskirts of Moscow, we traveled a two-lane paved road that led through exceedingly picturesque country. Woods of tall, twinkling silver-and-green birches, carpeted with short bright-green grasses, and golden fields of stubble and of heaped-up stacks of hay checkered the land, rolling gently to the faraway horizon.

Now and then we came to a village that looked exactly like a Walt Disney movie set for a fairy tale. The houses were tiny and built of logs, the majority unpainted but weathered to a rich, dark brown, and on both sides of the doorways were square windows framed with fancy, intricately cut out wood painted the perfect shade of blue. Then to add to the fairy story appearance of the villages, the yards were fenced in and masses of golden glow nodded their yellow heads above the pickets.

I was in heaven until our chauffeur, driving at a terrific speed, passed a moving truck near the crest of a hill and scared the living daylights out of me.

"Tell him, please," I said to Jenna, who was sitting on the front seat, "not to do that again. A good driver doesn't pass trucks and cars near the top of a hill."

For some minutes Jenna hesitated to translate this admonition, but finally she did it. And was I sorry? Immediately the chauffeur slowed down to a snail's pace and passed nothing. Not even horse-drawn carts. I could easily have got out, if I had been of a mind to, and walked beside it.

Nila gave me a cold look. "You have hurt his pride," she told me. "He must be one of the best chauffeurs in Russia or he wouldn't be driving for Intourist, and you tell him how to drive!"

"But he could have killed us all," I protested.

Nila shrugged. "Nevertheless, you have insulted him, and now you will have to pay for it."

"But I didn't mean for him to go this slowly. Please, tell him to resume his speed, but just be careful."

"I'll tell him," Nila agreed, sighing deeply, "but it'll do no good. You'll see."

And I did see. We crept the rest of the way to Zagorsk. The hands of the clock arrived at the hour for Mass—and passed on. Everybody hated me and I hated myself.

However, when we came in sight of the monastery I, at least, forgot my irritation. Like a medieval fortress, great faded-red walls and towers, enclosing many dome-topped steeples, crown a low hill on the edge of Zagorsk. The domes, which are onion-shaped, are in clusters, some high and some low; some are the color of turquoise and are spattered with gold stars and hemmed with gold lines, and some are the bluish-green color of weathered bronze and some are bright gold.

We went through high, thick gates in the wall and found ourselves in an open court surrounded by the cathedral, which is huge, with a tall, beautiful bell tower and some ancient, very "foreign"-looking structures. The Troitske-Sergiyevskaya Monastery is the spiritual center of the Russian Orthodox Church. Besides the cathedral, it houses the Ecclesiastical Academy and the Ecclesiastical Seminary of the church.

Jenna sprinted away and returned in a few minutes, accompanied by a monk with a long, curly, reddish-brown beard, who led us through a side entrance into the cathedral. The floor space covers at least an acre and every foot of it was occupied by people clothed in black or some other somber color. There are no seats in Orthodox churches. The worshipers stand through the hour-long services. In this cathedral, however, near the front, there is a small platform with benches, reserved for foreign visitors. The monk ushered us toward it, but Nila refused to budge.

"Come on," I urged her.

She shook her head and set her face hard. "No."

"But the monk says for us to go there."

"I can't do it," she muttered.

"But why not? It's especially reserved for foreigners."

"I know, but I can't do it. Usually I love to be foreign and speak with the accent; but here in church I don't want to be separated from the Russian people."

So I left her standing shoulder to shoulder with the people, her arms folded under her breast and her face flushed and solemn.

A long-bearded and long-haired deacon dressed in magnificent robes of gold, a tiny black cap atop his head, was reading, or rather singing, in a big, deep voice a passage of Scripture, and a gloriously beautiful choir of both men and women, on the far side of the cathedral, was singing in response. At one point, the deacon removed his cap and, before putting it back on, smoothed down his flowing tresses with a gentle gesture.

Other deacons and priests, also dressed in gold, came and went, and finally two priests, one holding a bright-red towel and a vessel with bread soaked in wine, and the other a gold cross, came down from the pulpit into the congregation. Hurriedly many women pushed forward, carrying babies in their arms and tugging small children. I saw few teen-age children and not too many people in their twenties and thirties. The mothers and grandmothers held up the babies and small children as one priest marked their foreheads with the cross and the other spooned the wine-soaked bread into their mouths. One baby was asleep and one young child protested with angry screams, but the bread and wine went down just the same.

Leaving the mass, we huddled in the sharp wind while the monk with the curly reddish-brown beard briefed us on the history of the monastery. "It was founded by Sergiyevsky in 1340, six hundred and eighteen years ago," he said, "when all this part of Russia was a wild and dense forest. Then in 1422 the cathedral was built." His small gray eyes turned upon me and twinkled brightly. "That, young woman, was even before America was discovered."

He also told us that the cathedral has been open for services continuously ever since; but for a period of about twenty years after the Revolution, the monastery itself was closed. At present there are three hundred preparing to be priests.

The lecture over, we moved into the open space in front of the cathedral. A hundred or so pilgrims were sitting on the grass, eating hard-boiled eggs, tomatoes and bread, and another hundred were queued up to drink water from a well said to have been blessed by Sergiyevsky himself. Here, too, most of the people were old and in black.

We crossed the yard to a chapel—at least, I took it for a chapel—where the remains of Sergiyevsky lie in a glass-covered coffin. Pilgrims were lined up all the way from the entrance to bend above it and touch their lips to the glass just above his head.

It was now time for our picnic lunch and I suggested that we drive back toward Moscow and eat it in one of those lovely patches of birch; but Jenna, very excited, said absolutely no. It is not permitted to stop on the side of the road.

"You mean we can't stop anywhere between here and Moscow and have lunch?" I asked incredulously.

"Yes, that's exactly right. It's not permitted to stop along the roadside."

"Even if we drive up a little side road and park?"

"No, it is not permitted."

As Peter had brought along a bottle of vodka just in case somebody had a chill this unseasonable day, we felt it wasn't proper to eat inside the monastery walls and so went outside and found a grassy spot in a sheltered corner. Two brilliant gold domes, directly above us, glowed like twin suns against the intense blue sky and many pilgrims sprawled around us, having picnic lunches, too. Two old Russian women in seedy clothes, looking much beaten up by life, had a big, shiny thermos which brought from Nila the comment, "A most contrasting thing." They crossed themselves before they began to eat.

We spread a newspaper for a tablecloth; Peter poured the vodka clandestine-like from beneath his raincoat and we dined elegantly on ham, cheese, hard-boiled eggs, brown bread and, for dessert, the melon which we brought all the way from Stalingrad.

Driving back to Moscow at a good clip (the chauffeur forgave me after Nila took him some vodka and lunch and, no doubt, explained I was a crude American tourist) Nila recognized the name of a village that we passed through and startled Peter and me out of the drowsy lull into which we had sunk by remarking casually, "Here's where I taught the children to run under a slowly moving train."

"You did what?" cried Peter, sitting straight up.

"I taught children to run under a slowly moving train," she repeated calmly, "as an exercise in courage. I felt for them to be strong, Soviet citizens, they must learn to meet the hard moments of the life."

"Please, please start at the beginning," Peter begged.

"It happened one summer, when I was working at the tea factory in Moscow, I was chosen to come to this town of Perlovka—we just passed by it and I still saw the camp and the pole on which they raise the flag—and be a counselor for the children. I was about nineteen at the time. Well, I was the most favorite teacher. I was tremendously inventive with all sorts of games.

"So, one day, coming back from hiking, I saw this train slowly moving and it hit me on the head to check the children's courage. I understood they don't know the situation of the life; they don't realize that in the future all kinds of dangerous things can happen. I thought it just the practical thing to do to make them run under the train. I had already trained them to sit under water until they were blue and 'most drowned.

"The train had very high cars and I went first under it. Then, one by one, all the group went. It was perfectly fascinating." Nila stopped talking for a moment, evidently considering its fascination, then added smiling, "They were prepared for life, that group of children."

"I bet," murmured Peter.

"But the next Sunday when Papa and Mama came to visit the camp, I flew out like a feather. The children told Mama and Papa about the train and they just began to faint and I was sent quickly back to Moscow."

And so we, too, reliving in our minds this "exercise in courage" thirty-four years later, came quickly back to Moscow.

6   Afternoon

THE RUSSIANS ARE MAD about sports. In Moscow alone there are two thousand stadiums, ski centers, swimming pools, boating stations, tennis, volleyball and basketball courts, and other sport areas.

So, to be a part of this madness, Nila and I secured tickets and went to what I call a game of soccer but the Soviet citizens call football. A champion soccer team of Czechoslovakia was playing a champion team of Russia in a magnificent new stadium that has 130,000 seats but can accommodate several thousands more when the occasion demands.

This Sunday afternoon all the seats were taken and by much better-groomed and better-dressed people than were at the races. Nila and I were seated in the midst of the Czech delegation, which marred the occasion for Nila for about two minutes; but after that she soared continuously.

"Ah-ah-ah, isn't it lovely, Willie?" she asked, stroking her palms one against the other. "What a beautiful sun. . . . Ah . . . ah . . . ah." (The sun was shining directly in our faces.) "Willie, I feel wonderful. Of course, it would be better if two Russian teams were playing, but anyway you'll see excitement. I promise you that. The Russians are absolutely wild about football."

The teams marched in most sedately, headed by the referee, in dark blue, carrying the ball in front of him like a votive offering. The Russians were in red and white, the Czechs in blue and white. The game began and it looked more painful to me than football at home; the players frequently butt the ball with their heads. The crowd screamed lustily when they liked a play and whistled when they didn't.

Early in the game, a Czech hit the ball with his forehead into the wicket, scoring one, and all the members of the team kissed him. The Russians weren't able to score and the first half ended with the Czechs one, the Russians nothing.

The second half got really rough. The players ran into each other viciously; heads were cracked, noses bled, but nobody called time out. Then a Czech was knocked out cold. Two doctors ran out on the field and worked over him for about five minutes. Then two nurses ran out. The doctors started to take the injured player off the field, but at the last second he revived and returned to the game.

Nila was outraged. "He won five minutes of rest for his team," she stormed. "That's no good. I despise sissee playing. Nobody is supposed to take time out."

The game ended with the Czechs still one ahead and we got up to leave, but we realized quickly that nobody else was leaving and sat back down.

"Maybe, they're having a double-header," I suggested.

"No!" Nila said emphatically.

"Well, something is happening."

And for once I was right. There was a drawing for prizes of all kinds: a TV set, a radio, a patent-leather suitcase, a pair of ice skates with boots attached, a gold watch, a clock, a sport suit, a record player with records, a lady's bicycle, a tennis racket, an album of colored pictures of the stadium, a china tea set for twelve.

Nila and I pleasured ourselves wondering what we would do with a tea set for twelve if we won it.

After the entire stadium of spectators was given a chance at the main prizes, the four sections of the stadium, North, East, South and West, drew for the lesser prizes. "Now the numbers of North will be drawn for the next five prizes," the director of the lottery announced, and when they were drawn he called cheerfully, "That's all, North. You may make your way to the subway now and go home. I wish you a safe journey."

It seemed to me a clever way to empty a stadium gradually so that there would be no jams in the subway station.

Nila and I were in the West section and its numbers were the last to be called, but we waited happily. For no reason at all, we had a hunch we were going to get that tea set. And we did come very close to it. A man sitting in our very row, more shabbily dressed than his neighbors, won it. His deeply lined face was a study in perplexity as he hesitantly got up to make his way across the field to claim it. I was ready to swear he'd never seen a tea set for twelve before, much less owned one.

7   September 1

TODAY WAS PRACTICALLY a lost day. During the greater part of it Nila and I haunted the offices of Intourist, hoping for some word from Penza, but none ever came.

However, there were a few diverting incidents.

While we were having dinner in the early afternoon in the

street-level restaurant of the Metropole, the Capitalist came in and, in answer to my question, "Have you had a good morning?" said, "Wonderful! I went to five museums and they were all closed."

I wanted terribly to ask him, but never got up the nerve, about his Sunday evening activities, for when Nila and I returned from the football game he was hurrying through the lobby toward the elevator with the long-bobbed girl and then we saw him no more. The girl's companion of Saturday night ate in the hotel dining room with a couple of men; but the pretty blonde never showed up while Nila and I were present.

Also, Nila and I had an enlightening conversation with an operator in the Metropole beauty parlor. We went in to have our nails manicured, and instantly the operator, who was filing briskly away on a customer, recognized Nila.

"You used to come in here a lot in a leather jacket," she said in a flat, everyday voice, not missing a stroke with the file.

"Yes, that's right," Nila said.

The manicurist cocked her head a little to one side, a thoughtful frown on her face. "You had to leave Russia in a hurry, didn't you?"

"Yes."

"I remember you."

She is a most ordinary-looking woman with a pile of slightly askew hair, dyed russet, fat, loose jowls, and two gold teeth in the front of her mouth. Her white uniform is filthy and she smokes a cigarette while she manicures and, between puffs, balances it on the edge of her implement tray.

When it was my turn, she and I got on the subject of teeth and I asked her (it was rude, I admit) why she chose to have gold ones—why not white ones?

And quick as a flash, with no hint of umbrage, she answered, "I prefer gold ones because they don't break when I crack nuts."

Also, in our treks between the Intourist offices in the Metropole and the National, I noted the streets liberally sprinkled with children on their way to and from their first school day of the new year. Both the girls and the boys were in uniforms.

The girls had on dark-brown dresses with black aprons, and the boys suits which were big enough to swallow them, with white collars on the outside and bright orange-red ties.

"Each girl has one uniform and two aprons," Nila said. "One black apron and one white."

"They must have two uniforms," I suggested.

"Why?"

"They have to wash them."

"They wash them on Saturdays."

Also, we witnessed such a tumult, with five militiamen involved, at the front door of the Metropole that I thought surely someone had been murdered, but when we wormed closer we discovered that nothing had happened except a young woman had accidentally stepped on another young woman's heel, causing the strap about her ankle to break.

The woman who did the stepping apologized, but that didn't mollify the one stepped upon. "I can't put a new strap on your apology," she retorted angrily.

"That's right," yelled one of the many milling bystanders. "She must take the shoe and have it fixed for her."

"Absolutely," yelled another. "Everybody must watch his place where he goes and not count the birds."

"Make her pay for the damage," still another yelled. "She might do some more harm if she's not taught a lesson."

The girl with the broken strap finally went on down the street; but by then the culprit was so hurt and enraged with the crowd for siding against her that she railed at them until two of the militiamen, struggling to end the row, took her into the police station in a corner of the Metropole to quiet her down.

8 September 2

THIS MORNING THERE was still no news from Penza, but Nila decided we could accomplish nothing by hanging around the hotel and so suggested that we eat a hearty breakfast and go to the U.S.S.R. Agricultural and Industrial Exhibition, which, we hear, covers 511 acres.

While eating this hearty meal, I, who was facing the door of the restaurant, saw a big man walking toward us as if he had been on a horse for the last sixteen hours, and I thought to myself, Here comes a Texan, and so when he got abreast of our table I said, "Good morning, sir. What part of Texas are you from?"

And he, showing no surprise, drawled, "Lubbock."

Having a good friend, Charlie Guy, in Lubbock, I invited the Texan to sit down with us.

"I'll be delighted, ma'am." He laid his pale-cream ten-gallon felt hat on an empty chair, then pulled out one for himself. "Do either of you know how to speak this language? I just got here last night and can't find my way around yet."

A waitress walked by. "Honey," he called, beckoning to her, and a diamond, the size of a lump of sugar, on his finger caught the light and almost put out my eyes.

"Honey," with the help of Nila, took his order and while he waited for it to come he told us about himself, in answer to our questions. He is a lawyer and has just run over to Russia for three days because he has this time on his hands between his visit to Brussels and his next engagement in Germany. He wears shoes instead of cowboy boots and has never tied the laces in his life and has himself measured for ten suits at "one go-round."

I asked him how he feels about Alaska being our forty-ninth state and he said gruffly, "The rest of the country worries more about Texas than Texans do."

"We have to," I quipped, and felt rather pleased with myself.

By this time he was a friend and readily accepted our invitation to go with us to the Exhibition.

Now this Exhibition, which is a permanent, all-year affair, is really something. There are elaborate pavilions representing all the republics of the Soviet Union and many of the agricultural districts of these republics, and several of them are absolutely stunning. Also there are pavilions for cows, sheep, horses, bees, hotbeds and greenhouses, and for models of the sputniks and pictures of the sputnik dogs. In all, there are 307 pavilions and other structures, twenty-two miles of asphalt walks and twenty miles of gravel paths.

We entered the main gate in the shadow of the celebrated gigantic steel monument of the Worker and the Collective-Farm Woman by Mukhina and I was absolutely flabbergasted at the acres of red geraniums and cream-colored roses and the wide, spotless, roomy walks; but Nila and Jenna, who accompanied us, were carried away with the first Russian automat they have ever seen. It is a soft-drink machine with one glass beneath the spout. They dropped in fifteen kopeks and the glass was rinsed with water; but then nothing further happened. They decided they should put in two more kopeks. Then gas water with a faint fruit flavoring gushed out.

"Look! Look!" screamed Jenna, her eyes bulging.

Across the way from the "automat" is a huge billboard, framing the pictures of the fifteen members of the Central Committee of the Communist Party. Viewing it, the Texan said to Jenna, "Little girl, where is Eisenhower's buddy Zhukov?"

"We criticized him some time ago," she answered casually, "and now I don't know where he is."

Nila was fascinated by the picture of the only woman member of the Central Committee, Madame Furtseva, a handsome woman in a tailored white blouse, with her hair definitely coiffeured, if you know what I mean.

"Though Khrushchev is married, Madame Furtseva is his official hostess at every big reception at the Kremlin," Nila told us while Jenna listened with a most peculiar expression on her face. "She just went up and up. Many people say she's Khrushchev's mistress."

The Texan hopped nimbly on a bench, swept off his hat and posed beside Madame Furtseva's likeness for Jenna to snap a picture of him.

We went in and out of pavilions and saw many charts and banners boasting of Soviet production. One, stretching all the way across the side of a building, proclaimed: IN THE NEAR

FUTURE WE WILL CATCH UP WITH THE UNITED STATES IN THE
PRODUCTION OF MEAT, MILK AND BUTTER PER PERSON.

We also saw many audiences, mostly of boys and girls though
there were a few older people, listening avidly to lectures and
looking at documentary movies pertaining to agriculture.

"As I told you yesterday," Jenna reminded Nila and me,
"this is a holiday for youth from the collective farms and
villages and they come here to see and learn and to enjoy an
exchange of experiences."

However, it is not only during the Holiday for Youth that
the pavilions are packed with audiences. The chief purpose of
the Exhibition, to quote from the small guidebook *Moscow*, is
to "display and propagate all that is best and progressive in the
work of collective and state farms, machine and tractor stations
and of individuals engaged in agriculture. The Exhibition is
a school of progressive agricultural technique for hundreds of
thousands of visiting collective farmers, state-farm workers and
farm machinery operators."

We saw a lot, though, besides charts, banners and people.
In the handsome Siberian pavilion we saw beautiful displays of
all types of wood, minerals (Siberia is extremely rich in minerals), canned fish, wheat, pigskin, oats, millet, feeding grasses
and furs. Oh, such foxes and sables!

Standing spraddle-legged before a display of fur coats, the
Texan reared back and pronounced in his slow, draggy way,
"You sho' don't see many of the girls on the streets wearing
'em, I bet."

He also had something to say about the many blown-up
pictures of girls and boys with their prize-winning corn and
wheat and sheep and other products that hang on the walls.
"Maybe these old Bolsheviks have got the right idea showing
off the pictures of boys and girls with what they've raised. Our
boys back home are all working to make the football team."

He wagged his head knowingly from side to side and continued in this philosophical strain. "We're going to have to
learn to get along with these people whether we want to or
not. They're certainly on the way up. They're like a baseball

team that's been in the cellar—they can't go anywhere but up, and these Russians are sure climbing."

We then went through the exceedingly beautiful Uzbek pavilion with its exquisite mosaics of blue, green and gold and with its small, dark-complexioned citizens acting as hosts, in those little round caps embroidered in many colors; then the Ukrainian pavilion with all its products—apples, pears, peaches, flax, sugar beets, wheat, oats and linen—displayed in big, color-ful, hand-woven sacks; then the Georgian pavilion with full-grown orange and lemon trees, bamboo and other tropical plants growing jungle-thick beneath one glassed-in wing.

Then, barely able to drag our feet, we found the trolley line that runs through the grounds, boarded the car and headed for one of the Exhibition's restaurants. "Hi, kiddo," the Texan saluted the woman motorman, and evidently he made a hit, for when we alighted at our destination she waved and smiled until the car disappeared around a curve.

The restaurant faces a man-made lake, in which a huge, colorful fountain of gilded sheaves of wheat and cornucopias spilling colored glass fruit tosses up frothy geysers. The main dining room has carved cornices at least ten feet wide and glorious crystal chandeliers.

"Just like the Waldorf," commented the Texan, but I thought it was more like one of the Leningrad subway stations.

After an excellent lunch of borsch, steak and salad, the Lubbock citizen leisurely smoked a long black cigar. Then we wended our weary way back through the main avenue of the Exhibition to our Intourist car.

9   Afternoon

No TELEGRAM HAVING YET come from the authorities of Penza, and the day being only partly gone, Nila, Jenna and I set out again, this time for a fashion show of "original Soviet styles" in a barnlike place of three stories, called the House of Models. Here there are no ready-made clothes for sale; you can see only the models of dresses and buy the patterns from which they have been made.

We checked our coats in the basement (the Russians check coats everywhere) and walked up two flights of stairs to a big room with a runway between rows of chairs. Except for the absence of palms and music, we could be in a showroom in New York.

We were early and so had the choice of chairs in the center of the front row. While we waited for the show to begin, Nila told me that she used to have her clothes made at the House of Models in her last well-to-do years in Moscow.

"I remember once," she recalled, "the wife of Mikoyan was having a fitting the same time I was. Mikoyan was then the Commissar of Food and one of the most powerful men in the whole of Russia. In the midst of the fitting she excused herself and telephoned to her home and whoever answered must have asked what to eat, for she said impatiently, 'I told you to take two cutlets from the window.'"

Nila eyed me closely. "You see, Willie, that shows you how the window is the Russian icebox. You have noticed, I'm sure, that all the windows are double. Well, in winter the space between the two windows is the deep-freeze. Everything is put there."

Nila was quiet as two young women came in and took seats across the runway from us; then she continued: "This was the best atelier in Moscow and they made me the dress for Sir Stafford's dinner at the British Embassy. They knew it was for that occasion and they were very much impressed." Nila chuckled and rubbed her hands briskly. "Then they made me five or six other dresses and they asked me will I model these dresses for their customers. I just loved the idea. I swished and swished.

"Then, when I came back to Moscow from the United States after the war, I brought some interesting clothes and some hats and they again asked me to model. And my God, I knocked 'em dead! This time I had the shoes and gloves to match, and an umbrella. They invited only the people who were connected with them, but just the same the place was packed and they sat with dizzle-dazzle in their eyes."

More young women straggled in, looking more wretchedly dressed than usual, for, the day being chilly, they had put the coats of their winter suits on top of their thin summer dresses. They had notebooks and pencils and Nila surmised they are dressmakers.

When the chairs were half filled, the mistress of ceremonies, a stout blonde in a print summer suit, with two gold teeth right in the front of her mouth, came from behind velvet curtains and welcomed us. She explained that the styles we were about to see were first shown at a "Congress of Fashion Models of All the Democracies" in Warsaw during the summer and that the Soviet Union was awarded a citation "for elegance, practicality, simplicity and beauty of line for the Soviet woman."

Then three models, slim, long-legged and as beautiful as any on Fifth Avenue, and one plump one with, as Nila whispered, "the intention of getting plumper," came on, wearing clothes surprisingly good and therefore having no resemblance to the clothes of the drab creatures in the audience. The two could have been in different worlds.

However, there was nothing original about the models, nothing Russian. They looked like the clothes we saw before leaving home in the spring numbers of the fashion magazines. There were even many versions of the sack. "Look, the Soviet sack," snorted Nila, "just like the capitalist sack."

"The sport dress," announced the mistress of ceremonies at one point, and in walked a model in a long, loose, bright-blue sweater and pearl-gray slacks tied down into handsome, heavy boots, and over the sweater and slacks a short coat of some hairy cloth, lined in material matching the slacks.

"My God!" exclaimed Nila. "I expect something that fits the situation and look at that!"

The accessories, except for the shoes, were not as good as the clothes. With most of the costumes were shown innumerable strings of colored glass beads, gloves—some of suède, but the majority of that short, net variety—leather bags, and slim, very high-heeled, elegant shoes that Jenna said were Russian, but Nila seriously doubted it.

Altogether we saw fifty-six numbers, and when the last one went by Nila sighed and declared with fervor, "When everybody will be dressed like that I'll die of happiness. The details of the buttonholes—ah!" Her eyes roved heavenward.

Then the mistress of ceremonies asked if anybody would like to ask any questions. A young woman directly in front of us inquired about the price of a beige outfit, trimmed in braid, that had been shown.

Quickly a frown wiped off the smile on the face of the mistress of ceremonies and she answered brusquely: "We do not tell the price of the models. You can't buy them, you understand; they are not for sale; but you can write us which ones you like best."

The frown faded and the smile reappeared. "Any more questions?" The voice was quite animated, but nervous, too.

However, there was no reason for nervousness. There were no more questions.

❦ ❦   Later

RETURNING TO THE METROPOLE, we joined the Texan for a social hour before supper. "I have brought something with me I think you girls will be interested in," he had said in a very pleased-with-himself manner when we were parting after the Exhibition excursion. How about coming to my room around six?"

So, around six we came, full of high expectancy. He greeted us with exuberance. "Honeys, I've got a treat for you. A real honest-to-God treat. I might not have traveled as much as you two, but just the same I know what people should drink in Russia and I came prepared."

And with this boast, he strode across the room and took from his suitcase a bottle of American vodka!

As THERE WAS STILL no news from Penza when we went first thing this morning to the Intourist office, I suggested to Nila that she get on a bus and go there and see what she herself could find out; but she looked at me as if she thought I'd lost my mind, then burst out, "My God, Willie, won't you ever understand the sit-u-ation? There is no bus."

Her voice was impatient, sharp. She was, of course, under a strain, which I was liable to forget, for usually she put up a gay front.

The woman of the Metropole office who sent the first telegrams said she would send two more and insist on immediate answers, and so, somewhat encouraged, we went into breakfast and sat at a table next to our Texas friend. He spent part of yesterday seeing what he called "those boogers over there in that joint," meaning, I figured out after a few blank moments, the bodies of Lenin and Stalin in the mausoleum.

'Stalin looked mighty natural," he said, wagging his head in that knowledgeable way he has. "I believe that's him all right; but Lenin—I don't know. When I looked back one side of his face looked a little peculiar to me."

He had also visited the Lenin Museum and enjoyed it more than anything he had seen. "Lenin was real fond of the peasants," he told us as if he'd just discovered the fact. "He had a rough-go-round nature."

We saw, too, the Capitalist and Peter and, as they were leaving Moscow today for other parts of Europe, we regretfully told them goodbye. Though I've felt very close to both of them this month in Russia, I'm sure they'll now disappear completely from my life. That, I've found, is what always happens to people I've grown attached to, traveling.

To keep our minds occupied, as well as to learn all we can about the Soviet Union, Nila, Jenna and I sight-saw hard all day. First we drove to the outskirts of Moscow to Ostankino Palace; it is now called the Palace Museum, but by any name it is terrifically exciting and beautiful. Originally it was the estate of Count Peter Sheremetyev, a companion of Peter I, a field marshal and one of Russia's wealthiest noblemen.

The palace was built from 1792 to 1797 entirely by Count Sheremetyev's countless serfs; but among them were very talented carpenters, painters, carvers, sculptors and architects. The serf in charge of the construction was so exceptionally gifted that Count Sheremetyev gave him his freedom.

The painted ceilings, the carved woodwork, the chandeliers and the parquet floors are enough to make you lose your mind. For instance, in the round hall known as the Rotunda the parquet is composed of eleven different kinds of wood, with tin and mother-of-pearl incrustations. I wouldn't dare lay a foot upon it.

However, wonderful as all these things are, the palace is most famous for the big hall, connecting the two wings, in which the Count installed a complete theater, even to a stage that was raised and lowered by machinery. He was a lover of music and the theater. He had two hundred serfs who did nothing but act, play, sing and dance. The performances were for his own and his friends' enjoyment exclusively. Frequently he invited as many as two hundred guests to see a play. The sets were lavish and the slave actors and actresses wore the costliest robes and jewels.

"The actors and actresses weren't even known by names," Nila told me with a touch of bitterness. "The Count called them by nicknames. The girls stayed in a dormitory connected with the palace and the Count used to walk there with a large handkerchief in his hand and the girl in front of which he dropped the handkerchief, she was to be brought to his bed that night."

But suddenly the Count's life was completely changed. He fell deeply in love with a young slave girl. "He saw her on a road," Nila recounted with shining eyes. "She was only thirteen. She was walking with the cows with a whip in her hand, and this beautiful carriage, with two lackeys in back and two dogs in front, carrying the Count someplace, came by and the Count stopped and asked her from where she is. And she bowed low and said, 'Sir, I'm the serf of your honor.'

"At that the Count said, 'With your beauty you're not born to tend the cows.' And he took her to the palace and she went into the theater and became the company's most talented actress. Her name was Praskovya Kovalyova-Zhemchugova. Though she was the Count's mistress, she remained a slave until a son was born. Then he freed her, and finally, when she was in her thirties, he married her. Just one year later, though, after she became a countess, she died of consumption."

From the eighteen forties to 1917, the palace was occupied by Count Sheremetyev's descendants, who continued to be one of Russia's richest families; but came the Revolution, their wealth was confiscated, of course, and the palace was nationalized.

From the palace we went to an orphans' home in a wooded suburb. Seventy-five children, from three to eight years old, live there in what appeared to me an easy, relaxed, happy atmosphere. I'd like all mothers and grandmothers to see it. Bedrooms in which twenty-five children sleep and dining-play-rooms in which the same number eat and play are spotlessly clean and in perfect order. Not a pair of pants, not a sock, not a shoe, not a sweater, not a raisin, not a bottle is on the floor anywhere. And what's more, the children keep the rooms themselves. They even dress themselves, helping each other, and make the beds.

"This is part of the upbringing of a child for collective living," said the short, stout, motherly matron.

The rooms are light and airy, and pretty, too. The walls are painted pale pink or pale green, lace curtains hang at the windows and rubber plants sit on the sills. And in all the play-rooms are quantities of toys—trains, dolls, balls, tricycles, hobby-horses.

Some of the children had gone to the zoo for the day, but the six-year-olds were having classes in a pink room. The girls had pony tails with bows of ribbon at the crown of their heads and they were wearing bright-red and bright-blue dresses, smocked across the shoulders. The boys were in blue, garnet and dark-green suits. They were the best-dressed citizens I'd seen in Russia.

One little boy hopped up and offered me a chair.

The teacher called on a girl to recite a poem, and a boy, grinning, doubled over with amusement. Then they all piped out a song, smiling and cutting their bright eyes at me at every note.

The program over, the children crowded around my knees as impetuously as my own grandchildren, fingering my beads, my pocketbook, and staring at my fingernail polish. I could detect no sign of nervousness or fear from too strict discipline.

In fact, when I asked the matron did she have to resort to corporal punishment at times, she looked amazed and horrified. "No, indeed," she said emphatically. "Under the Soviet law any person working here who hits a child is punished and never allowed to work with children again."

"Then how do you punish them?" I asked.

"We sometimes deprive them of TV."

"No!" I gasped. "That's what we do in the United States."

The matron smiled. "We use it in Russia, too. The children love TV programs, and denying them TV is a very effective punishment. They also love to embroider and sometimes we say to them, 'You'll not embroider today.' We never deprive them of meals. Some children have no appetites and so it is no punishment to take food from them."

The children have singing, dancing, embroidery classes and many other extracurricular activities, according to the matron, and a few exceptional ones have piano instruction. Real schooling, however, is left to the schools, which the older children attend. "We try to teach here love for country and people," the matron said, "and that's all." There are twelve teachers and one doctor and one nurse on constant duty.

Some of the children here are not orphans; some have parents who are separated or divorced or parents who are unable to take care of them. But the matron insisted that none of them lacks love. The orphanage is "patronized" by a factory that supplies each parentless child with a patron, known as his godfather or godmother. These patrons come on Sundays and holidays when the real parents come, bring presents, take the children on outings and make them feel loved.

"The children who are orphans," said the matron, "aren't even conscious of the fact that they haven't families. They think they belong just like the children with mothers and fathers."

All houses for orphans—there are forty-six in Moscow alone —have these patrons.

There are also special houses for older orphans, and just recently—"very, very recently," the matron said—the Soviet government adopted a plan to open schools where children will go on Monday and stay until Saturday, spending only the weekends with their families.

"These are for children whose living quarters are not satisfactory," she explained, "or for children of parents who work such hours they cannot supervise their children in the afternoons. These schools will be very effective in keeping young boys and girls off the streets. Naturally, there is always some delinquency when children are on the streets. These schools will also be effective in relieving the crowded living conditions of many families. The children will be away six days, but still the family will not be broken up."

"Also," commented Nila, out of earshot of the matron, "putting the children in those schools will give the government complete control over their bodies and minds for six days out of seven. *Bozhe moi!*"

After the Orphan House we visited the Lenin Library, which the Russians used to claim was the biggest library in the world but now say modestly is only the biggest in the Soviet Union. It is eighteen stories high, has more than twenty million books in 160 languages and is visited by between five and six thousand readers a day.

With a library guide we marched and marched through its imposing marble halls, its many-windowed and high-ceilinged reading rooms, and even through its miles of musty stacks.

Then, just to be onerous, Nila asked to see a copy of John Gunther's *Inside Russia*, and, much to the guide's embarrassment, she couldn't find a card for it in the acres of catalogues.

"I'm sure we have it," the guide said finally, "but just haven't had the time to catalogue it yet."

🌲 🌲

11 🌲 September 4

WHEN NILA LEARNED THIS morning that there was still no answer to the telegrams, her face grew black with frustration. Trying to be helpful, I said, "Since there is no bus going to Penza, why don't you hire a car?"

"Just have mercy," she snapped angrily and moved away.

Unhappy for her, I stood against the wall, out of the main traffic of the tourists, waiting for her mood to change, but it didn't. Instead, she tackled the Intourist woman who had been sending the telegrams and pressed her to do more.

"How can I do more?" the woman answered impatiently. "I have sent wire after wire and no response." She threw out her hands. "What is to be accomplished by another wire? It's quite certain your sister is not there or we would have heard by now."

Then Nila suggested: "Then let me go there. I feel I must do all I can."

"It is impossible," the woman said flatly. "Intourist has no facilities for tourists there."

"I can fly there in an hour and fly back the same day," Nila argued, which surprised me, for it hadn't crossed my mind there was plane service to Penza.

"It cannot be done." The woman was extremely irritated. "It positively cannot be done."

Nila's face flushed, her eyes burned hot and she said imperiously, "I'll find that out for myself from some higher authority. I want to be absolutely sure before I take your word for it." She doubled her fist and beat the air in front of the woman's face.

"Very well!" The words sounded ominous with rage. "You can find out for yourself!"

The woman gave Nila an address, Kalpachnaya Street 9,

which is the headquarters of the militia that deals with foreigners' visas, special requests and other such matters. Nila recognized the address immediately; it was where she went with Robert in 1941 to renounce her Russian citizenship and give up her Russian passport.

Running her fingers nervously over her thumb, she rushed out of the hotel with Jenna and me at her heels (Jenna had been interpreting her conversation with the woman for me), jumped into an Intourist car and gave the address to the driver.

At the door of the building that houses the department of militia we were met by a grim-faced guard who reminded us that it was Thursday and Thursday is everybody's day off.

Blocked in this direction, Nila decided to talk once more with the head of Intourist at the National Hotel. Jenna went home for dinner, and I again sat in the hall and waited.

The head was cordial, Nila reported when she came out of his office, but he wasn't too encouraging. "He said thousands and thousands of mothers and children didn't find each other since the war," she told me, "and yet here I want to find my people in a few days. 'Yes,' I answered him, 'I understand how impossible after the war for people to find each other, but now it's long after the war and I had my sister's last address.' Then, Willie, I said to him, 'If there will be no answer today, I'd like to go tomorrow to Penza and look for her myself.'

"He said he was afraid that was impossible, but if I liked I could extend my visa for a few days and give myself more time to hear. Then I asked him point-blank, 'Will you have some information in a few days?' And he said, 'I can't guarantee that; but I'm sure it is almost impossible to find her in the short time you've given us. It will take at least from one to six months.'"

Nila's fingers moved rapidly over her thumb. "I was so nervous, Willie, I just can't tell you. Then he said for me to leave my United States address and when he finds out where they are he will inform me. Then he got up and shook my hand. He was really all to pieces, for he saw how I was distressed."

Back at the Metropole Hotel, we went first thing as usual into the Intourist office and immediately the woman jumped up from her desk, hurried to Nila and said she had a telegram for her.

Nila took it and read it and all the color drained from her face; then, slapping her hand to her forehead, she cried out, "My God, what's happened!"

"What, Nila?" I pleaded. "What does the telegram say?"

Her face closed up and she said curtly, "I can't talk about it now."

However, in a little while she discussed it without emotion. "Willie, the telegram reads: 'Shevko Safonova'—that's how my sister is called—'was not found living in Penza.' The first time I looked at it, I couldn't see anything. The room just went like this—" Nila tilted her hand back and forth. "Then the words came through and, after a few minutes, I had a great feeling of relief. At least the telegram didn't say she was dead, so I still have hope to find her."

We rested for a short time; then Nila suggested that she and I go on an errand.

Now, this errand was the culmination of a not-too-intensive search for the Magidoffs' cook, Lena, whom they had during their last years in Moscow. This week Nila asked two or three American correspondents who had lived in Moscow at the time, and who knew Lena, about her; but they said they didn't know where she is now. Then last night, while Nila was at a Russian movie, I had dinner with Roy Essoyan of the Moscow Bureau of the Associated Press and his wife and learned quite by accident that Lena cooks for the John Milkses and that she was right in the apartment the evening they entertained for us after the Puppet Theater show.

On my return to the hotel last night I excitedly broke the news to Nila, and she was thrilled and said we must see Lena before we leave. So now, finding we had a free hour before dinner, we went to the Milkses' apartment and, sure enough, there was Lena, giving the bedroom a thorough cleaning. She is a large middle-aged woman with an abundance of flaming red hair and high color in her cheekbones. She looks more like an Irish maid than a Russian one.

Nila embraced her and asked if she had seen her the first

time we came to the apartment. Yes, she said, she was sitting downstairs in the hallway when we took the elevator.

"Why didn't you speak to me?" Nila demanded.

"You looked right at me and didn't speak," Lena answered, somewhat haughtily, "and so I didn't speak. I have my pride, too."

Nila explained that she wasn't expecting to see her, so she didn't recognize her. "Were you surprised to see me, Lena?" she then asked.

"No. I've been expecting you and Mr. Magidoff to be back."

"But you know how we left, Lena."

"Huh!"

"What do you mean, 'Huh'?"

Lena shrugged her heavy shoulders. "Everything is changed now. Everybody is forgiven, and so already for the last two or three years I have asked Americans if you were coming back."

She and Nila sat down on the side of the bed and I left them together while I visited with Betty Essoyan, who lives directly across the hall; but I was scarcely settled in when Nila arrived, grinning triumphantly and clutching a piece of paper.

She has learned some information about her family, I thought immediately, and I was delighted for her. Maybe Lena knew a later address. Maybe Lena had seen her mother on the street. Maybe . . .

I knew better than to ask, though, in front of Betty Essoyan, so I acted as if I noticed nothing unusual until Nila, who remained standing, gestured with a tilt of her head toward the door. Then hurriedly I got up, said my adieus and followed her out.

On the way to the Metropole I died of curiosity, but I realized it still wasn't safe to ask anything. The Intourist driver might understand English and I knew Nila didn't want him even to know she had contacted a Russian former acquaintance. I may not have learned everything about the Soviet Union, but I've learned a lot.

Only when we reached the privacy of the bedroom did I open my mouth to speak—and then it was not necessary. Nila burst with her news. "Willie, I got the crab recipe all right!"

"The crab recipe?" I repeated, puzzled.

"Yes, the crab recipe." She chortled victoriously. "Ever since I left Russia I've always thought, If I ever put my hand on Lena again I'll get her crab recipe. And right in Canada when Robert was telling me goodbye, he said, 'If you see Lena, don't forget to get the crab recipe.' You see, Willie, my very first action when I moved to the United States was to buy these crab shells at an auction—"

I interrupted her. "And that's why you wanted to see Lena?"

Nila's face beamed. "Just wait, Willie, till you try the recipe!"

"Well, for heaven's sake, what is it?"

She put the paper close to her face and squinted at it. "You take two jars of crab meat, two tablespoons of flour, one tablespoon of butter, one cup of milk, some salt, pepper and grated cheese . . ."

"Yes?"

"You fry the flour in butter just a little bit, cool, then add the milk, salt and pepper. Then you take the shells, butter them and sprinkle them with the grated cheese; then fill up the shells with the crab meat and pour the sauce on top and add more grated cheese; then put in a 375-degree oven for twenty minutes. This will serve six."

I stared at her speechless for a second; then I gasped out once more, "And so that's why you wanted to see Lena!"

12   Afternoon

SHORTLY AFTER DINNER, Nila said in excitement, "Willie, we must prepare our bags to go to the public bath."

The suggestion did not surprise me. For days she has been saying we must go to a public bath, but we must wait until nearer the end of the week, for then the crowd is much bigger. Scarcely anyone washes on Monday, Tuesday and Wednesday, she told me; the vast majority wash on Saturday, but since we are leaving Moscow on Saturday we can't put it off until then.

"We must take washrags," she went on, "and towels and soap and clean underwear."

"Why clean underwear?" I asked. "I already have on clean underwear."

"Oh, all right if you don't want to, but all Russian women take everything clean to put on after the bath."

Nila then ordered me to remove my earrings and to change my best silk blouse for a button-down-the-front sweater and put on my "old beret."

"If you walk up to the bath window to buy a ticket looking like an American," she explained, "the ticket woman will quickly say, 'I'm sorry, but the bath is under repair.' "

There are innumerable public baths in Moscow to which Nila and I could go. The city is divided into twenty-eight districts and in each district there are at least four or five baths. Thousands of people bathe in these baths as a rule once a week, Nila says, but some go only once every two weeks. Nila and I chose the Center Baths, which are almost directly across the street from the Metropole. There is an entrance for women and one for men.

"You keep perfectly quiet, Willie, until we're inside the baths," Nila ordered me as we approached the entrance. "Then you can talk all you want to."

Going up the steps to the second floor of the building, we passed several very slick, shiny, red-faced, damp-haired women on their way down, carrying stuffed satchels.

"You ought to see the people in winter," Nila commented. "The bath is so hot that when they come out into the cold air they look like a steaming pipe."

"I should think the abrupt change into the cold air would give them pneumonia," I said.

"They are used to it, and anyway they pile and pile clothes on them like a cabbage."

On the second floor we entered a huge room, full of women in various stages of undressing and dressing among hexagonal-shaped tables. Through the middle of the tables run poles which support clusters of electric-light bulbs beneath enormous, silk-fringed orange lamp shades; the light fixtures also support rings with hooks on which coat hangers dangle. Around the tables, facing out, are straight chairs with numbers on their backs, and on the tables are flat plates for pins and such.

I couldn't bear the thought of undressing in the middle of the room, so Nila found two chairs against the rear wall and we began to take off our clothes. I took mine off most hesitantly, my body bent low above the chair, my back to the room.

"Can't I keep on anything?" I whispered to Nila.

"Certainly not."

"But I can wrap a towel around me, can't I?"

"Don't be a silly bum. The towel will get soaked."

"You mean I have to walk absolutely naked to the bathing room?"

"It's called the soap room and of course you walk to it naked. Nobody is going to pay any attention to you. Remember what Jenna said at Odessa: 'There's nothing new to see.' "

We hung our clothes on hangers against the wall and Nila was impressed. "I tell you, Willie, I never expected to see the clothes will be hanged like this. We used to wrap them in bundles; we wrapped and wrapped and then pinned them with a safety pin, so somebody couldn't take just one something but would have to take all and that would be too much."

Finally, standing only in my cringing skin and hunched over, a washrag and a bar of soap clutched to my bosom, I followed Nila to the door of the soap room. Women as naked as I, dripping wet, brushed unconcernedly by me.

Nila opened the door and in a huge room slightly fogged with steam I saw at least sixty women in the process of scrubbing themselves. Some stood with legs spraddled, washing what I had considered until this moment their private parts; some leaned far forward, washing their long hair that almost swept the floor; and some sat on stone slabs like the ones people are laid out on in morgues, their feet drawn up, washing most methodically between their toes.

With Nila leading the way, I walked gingerly about the edge of the room toward a somewhat secluded corner. The floor was completely covered with soapy water and only my agility from years of dancing kept me from losing my balance. Stone slabs extend around two sides of the room.

As soon as we found an unoccupied slab I crawled upon it and Nila went to a corner where big basins are stacked and filled one with water from two vigorously gushing spigots, one hot and one cold. Then she flung the water over the bench to clean it and returned for another basinful. This one she deposited by me. "For you to wash yourself, Willie."

Again she went to the corner, got another basin, filled it and put it on the floor at my feet. "It's the custom to stand in this while you wash your hair and other parts of your body."

So she had me all fixed up, but I was too near paralysis to start washing. I just sat stiffly on the edge of the bench, curled over, my arms and hands covering as much of me as possible.

Nila was now filling basins for herself. As casually as if she were fully clothed, she stalked from one side of the room to the other, carrying the big pans and filling them. "You see, Willie, I just melt into the situation with ease and experience," she remarked, depositing one more pan on the slab. "I went all my life to a bath like this. Not until I married Robert did I ever see a private bath."

My attention was riveted to the woman next to me. She was an elderly woman with breasts sagging below her navel like dripping bags of clabber or stewed fruit being strained for jelly, and when she sat down they sprawled on her knees. First she soaped her thin, very long black hair; then she began on the façade of her huge, flabby body. She held one breast out the length of her fully out-stretched arm and washed it with long strokes as one might clean a garment on an ironing board. She scrubbed it on top; then on the bottom. Her face was thoughtful.

"She thinks of her future and her past," remarked Nila.

Finally she took the basin of water, which was quite dirty by now, held it above her head and tilted it over her and the floor. Then she got a fresh basin and asked her neighbor on the other side, thank goodness, to scrub her back. With terrific vigor and a fistful of *mochalka*, that golden grass we saw in the market at Stalingrad, the neighbor scrubbed away for five or six minutes; then the woman said, "Thank you," and took the neighbor's hank of grass and scrubbed her back.

"How they don't take their skin away!" Nila remarked admiringly. "But what makes them really clean is they start to perspire and all the dirt and old skin rolls off."

Many of the women, I could tell, had been vacationing at the beach. Narrow strips of white skin appeared across the dead center of their bosoms and fair triangles over other areas.

A dainty, nice-looking woman waded by, a bottle of hair shampoo in one hand and a small cloth bag of bath accouterments in the other. Nila was outraged. "It's absolutely forbidden," she said, "for anybody to bring anything in glass inside the soap room."

The woman washed the slab with basin after basin of water; then she mixed the shampoo in a fresh basin until she got a good lather, and then at last she began to massage her head. It must be hard, I mused, for such a fastidious woman to have to bathe in such crude surroundings.

More women flapped in. The room, now very foggy with steam, became a forest of white, lumpy bodies and tossing limbs. "Not a one of 'em looks like Venus," remarked Nila. Then, shaking her head slowly, she added, "The crowd is just the same as when I used to come here twenty years ago. I don't see any difference."

After about an hour, when I was shriveled as an old grape, Nila consented to our leaving, though most women, she pointed out, spend two and three hours in the soap room.

Getting into my clothes, I noticed Nila's mood had changed. She must be remembering about the telegram from Penza, I thought; but in a minute or two I learned she was comparing the bath of today with the bath of yesteryear and the bath of today was coming off badly.

"In the old days there weren't these atrocious lights," she reminisced, "and it was much more cozy. Then all the women, after their baths, sat about, eating apples to restore their strength and drinking kvass, which is made from fermented black bread. Nothing gives such a pleasant belch as kvass. Everybody just sit here and belches happily and talk the sit-u-ation."

Today there were no apples and no kvass and as soon as the women were dressed they went out. That is, all of them did except those who were having pedicures in a beauty shop just off the dressing room. And, to my utter amazement, many were.

�   🌱

13   🌱   September 5

As THIS IS OUR last day in Russia, if nothing changes our plans, we have much unfinished business.

"Willie, put on your raincoat," Nila ordered me right after breakfast, "and hide all your hair under your old beret. You must look the drabbest drab. I want to take you to see Butirki Prison where I was for so many months—remember?—and you must not attract any attention."

We headed for a kiosk where information is sold for a few kopeks. "I must find out," Nila said, lowering her voice, "what trolley bus to take to the prison. I went there and left there in a Black Crow and didn't see the way. I won't mention the name of the prison of course; I'll just ask how to get to Butirki Street."

Nila put forty kopeks on the window ledge of the kiosk and the woman behind the grill wrote the number of the bus on a slip of paper.

Holding on to my arm, Nila propelled me hurriedly away from the kiosk and said, her voice still low, "My God, she ask me what number I want on Butirki Street and I have no idea, so I just say quickly, Number 'fifty-eight.' Now we will go ask the policeman where to catch this bus the woman wrote down. I will speak to the policeman not only in Russian, but I'll speak in pure Russian, even Muscovite, even a little bit singing in the Moscow drawl."

When she had performed this feat and had the needed information, she steered me to a nearby corner. "Now, Willie, don't speak one word on the bus. Keep absolutely quiet. I'll let you know when it's time to get off."

Unfortunately there weren't two seats together and I had to

sit near the front of the bus and Nila near the rear. Once I
looked furtively back at her, but she scowled and shook her
head. We rode for a long time. I kept my eyes peeled through
the front panes, hoping to see the prison in the distance and be
ready to spring up and off at the correct stop.

Finally, high, thick red brick walls, enclosing a conglomera-
tion of red brick buildings, loomed up on the left and I thought
this surely must be it and gave Nila a quick, inquiring glance
over my shoulder; but again she scowled and shook her head.

I settled back. Then, suddenly, I felt a light tap on my
shoulder and, looking up, saw Nila striding swiftly to the front
door of the bus. Instantly I was up and right behind her.

Outside, she gripped my elbow and we crossed the wide
street to the sidewalk. "When we passed those walls and buildings back there a few blocks," she said in a low, tense voice,
"I thought it was Butirki, but then there was no big gate like I
remembered. Now, Willie, you walk ahead like you're not with
me. I must ask somebody how to go."

Hurriedly I walked on and Nila dropped behind. Though I
couldn't understand what was dangerous about looking at
Butirki Prison from the outside, Nila's nervousness was beginning to infect me. Maybe Nila knew something I didn't. Maybe
the prison was not supposed to be recognized and stared at.

Nila slipped her hand beneath my arm and I jumped a foot.
"With my talent, Willie," she whispered, "I immediately invent a story and find out those walls and buildings we saw were
the prison. You see, there was this woman walking along and
I said to her, 'Excuse me, please, but I'm looking for an old
friend whose address I've lost; but I remember she lives right
across from Butirki Prison.' And so she directed me nicely how
to get there."

Nila and I retraced the bus's steps and shortly were beneath
the high, grim walls. Nila studied them intently and decided
there is now a building where the big gate once was and that
is why she didn't recognize the place. We walked the length of
the walls on Butirki Street, then turned and followed them
down a side street.

As if she were a college graduate visiting her alma mater,

Nila pointed out to me the window from which she tossed a pigeon with the sign, "Down with Stalin!" tied to its legs; then the narrow slit in the wall of the "punishment cell" of the Tower of Pugachov where she was "dragged" and imprisoned for running up and down the hall of Butirki, lifting the slots of the cell doors, calling, "Good morning! Good morning! Good morning!"

And as she pointed and talked, we stopped unconsciously in front of some gates that evidently Nila didn't remember or notice until, suddenly, there were creaking noises and they began to swing open and we saw, as high as the fence, in a little guardhouse, a militiaman with a gun.

Instantly I was terrified. I was absolutely positive the gates were swinging open for Nila and me. I could even feel the muzzle of the militiaman's gun between my shoulders.

Without having to be directed by Nila, I walked rapidly on until I reached a theater poster on the wall; then I stopped and began to study it as if the theater were my only interest in life. And almost immediately Nila joined me and studied it, too. She even gestured animatedly at the figures on it.

Slowly a big truck rolled out of the gates and then slowly, very slowly, the gates swung to.

After waiting a few minutes for our hearts to slow down and our knees to steady, Nila and I turned and walked rapidly to the bus stop. We'd both lost all interest in Butirki Prison.

Back in the heart of the city, we visited the big department store, GUM. I never before saw anything like it. It is really a three-storied city under clear glass domes. Streets at three different levels extend around the blocks of small, open-faced shops, and frequently, on the second and third floors, they span on iron bridges the wide canyons between the buildings. Stands erected on the sidewalks sell ice-cream cones, *pirochki* and other items of food.

More people were leaning on the iron rails of the second and third tiers, eating these delicacies and peering at the people below, than were inside the shops.

And the people on the first floor were really something to see. One whole street was completely taken up by a four-abreast line. I thought at first that the powers that be must have moved the bodies of Lenin and Stalin into GUM so that the comrades wouldn't have to wait out in the cold of Red Square; but when we bypassed the line and reached its head, I found these people were waiting their turn for blankets. Whether the supply on the shelves in the little hole-in-the-wall shop would last until all the would-be buyers were served seemed mighty doubtful.

There was another long queue for sheets, pillowcases and tablecloths, and on the second floor there was a mob in front of the stall selling winter cloth coats. I honestly don't understand how the women ever get their housework done.

Fortunately, Nila and I weren't buying any scarce goods. We were after a few hand-painted cigarette boxes, a few embroidered caps like the ones the Uzbeks wear, and some toys. All these were plentiful, especially the toys. If I didn't have to worry about my suitcases' weight, I could take home blocks to build a handsome reproduction of the walls and towers of the Kremlin, and even the red stars to top them.

Returning to the hotel for our last dinner, we decided to let ourselves go, since we still had plenty of food coupons. We began with a jar of caviar each; then we had *kulyebyaka*, a type of pie served with a clear bouillon and then cabbage deliciously pickled, peas, cucumbers and ham. We were as stuffed as prisoners about to die.

14	🌱	Afternoon

SINCE NILA FELT COMPELLED to make one last effort to locate her sister, she went straight from dinner to the Intourist Bureau and insisted that there must be something more that she could do.

"I pressed and pressed," she told me when I joined her a few minutes later, "and the woman finally said I might go to the Central Address Bureau."

With Jenna, who had come to tell us goodbye, we hurried to the bureau and found two sympathetic women. Their eyes and manner warm, they at first addressed Nila as "Comrade"; then, realizing their mistake, they changed to "Woman from America." After listening to her story, they gave her the name of a man who heads a bureau set up especially to help foreigners find their lost Russian relatives. Why no one had told us before of this bureau, Nila and I simply couldn't imagine. Jenna said she herself had never heard of it and she doubted if anyone in Intourist had.

On the way to the bureau Nila decided to tell the head of it that she is a close friend of Mrs. Roosevelt, for she believes this will impress him and encourage him to move more swiftly with the investigation. She has learned that Mrs. Roosevelt is expected to arrive in Moscow in the next day or two; the head of the bureau, Nila argued, will want to do everything possible to please her.

The man has an air of elegance and he received all three of us in his office with a rather courtly charm. Nila sat in the chair in front of his desk; Jenna and I sat on a bench along the wall. Jenna, her voice low, interpreted for me what the man and Nila said.

Nila began by telling him why she waited so long to ask for help. He listened intently, his eyes never leaving her face, and when she finished he said he will do all he can to find her sister.

"How long will it take?" Nila asked.

"With the best of luck, one or two months, but there is really no saying exactly."

"But everybody in Russia has to register."

"Yes, but sometimes a person leaves a city or town without checking out and, though she checks in when she reaches the place to which she's moving, it's difficult to find where she checks in. That takes time. Frequently a long time, especially if she's gone to a small village and if she's not working."

"But of course she's working," Nila said impatiently. "She has to be working. She supports a mother and a daughter."

The man leaned farther over the desk and spoke most deliberately. "But maybe she has remarried and is no longer known by her former name."

308

"I somehow don't feel she has." Nila ran her fingers over her thumb.

"Of course, you may be right."

"Look, I know her specialty. She's an engineer in the bread-baking business. That ought to help you."

"Yes, that should help us, but not everybody who works is registered in the Moscow area."

"You can telephone, can't you, to the Central Organization of the Bread-Baking Industry?"

The man shook his distinguished head. "There is no such organization."

Nila, apparently realizing she had come to the end of this tack, sighed and tried the tack about Mrs. Roosevelt. Moving a few inches closer to the man's desk and looking at him in the most appealing manner, she said, "My good friend—really, she's more than a good friend—Mrs. Roosevelt is coming here for the whole month of September and I'll appreciate it very much if you'll let her know when you locate my sister. I'll appreciate it and she'll appreciate it."

"The pleasure will be mine." He bowed his head and shoulders. Then, straightening up, he said, "I want you to write out all the details about your sister, your mother and your niece. I want all of them."

"I'm leaving tomorrow," Nila said, "but I'll write them before I go."

"Good." The man summoned his secretary and told her to be sure to take care of Nila's letter. "See that it's on my desk tomorrow," he ordered with an air of importance and urgency.

Then he stood up, shook Nila's hand and promised once more to do his best for her.

15   September 6

I WOKE AT FOUR-THIRTY in the morning to catch a Russian jet, which was scheduled to leave at seven o'clock for Copenhagen, where I change for a Scandinavian Airlines plane for

Frankfurt, Germany, where I will change once more for Pan American's nonstop flight to New York.

Nila insisted on accompanying me to the airport, though she had changed her mind about going on the same plane with me. She was now convinced it is safe for her to stay alone in Moscow until noon, when she will catch a plane for Zurich.

The streets were black and glistening, for it had been raining hard all night. Already women were cleaning them with long switch brooms.

We drove out the wide Lenin Prospekt, where so much terrific construction is under way. It appeared as if at least twenty-five huge apartment houses had gone up since I was last out this way and the land had been cleared for at least twenty-five more. Road scrapers, cranes and stacks of bricks and stones stretched for many miles into the country.

Peering at the apartment houses in the thinning dawn, Nila said, "Just think, Willie, what it will mean to the people of Moscow when they can move into these new apartments with running water and gas stoves and more room than they've ever known before. Oh, how I wish I could see their faces!"

When the new buildings and the freshly excavated ground ended, the real country began. Forests of small trees border the highway, and here and there big stone mushrooms mark the areas where mushrooms grow.

Nila sighed deeply. "Russian mushrooms, Willie, are the best in the world. I had hoped so to take you one day to the woods and hunt them and to have Lena along to cook them, so we could have a picnic, but, as you know, there was no time."

For this small favor of no time to hunt mushrooms I quietly thanked God.

We reached the airport at ten of six, even before the immigration and customs officers, who I thought never slept, were on duty, and so we rushed to the dining room to strengthen ourselves for the ordeal ahead. And it was well we did, for even with coffee and three *sirniki* with sour cream and strawberry jam inside me, I was a nervous wreck. I knew it was silly, but the old fear that possessed both Nila and me when we first arrived in Russia descended upon me now like a bone-chilling rain and I was certain that something would go wrong at the last moment.

And, sure enough, something did. When, under the cold eyes of the customs officer, I made out my declaration setting out among other things how many American Express checks I'd cashed and how much money I was taking out of the U.S.S.R., and he compared it with the declaration that I had made out when I entered the country, he drew down his brows in the most ferocious manner and barked at me in Russian.

I shook in my shoes and looked pleadingly at Nila for enlightenment.

"You silly bum," she said with forced gaiety, trying unsuccessfully to cover up her own nervousness, "you've declared you're taking out more money than you brought in."

"That's impossible." I said indignantly. "I cashed three Express checks, so I couldn't have more than I brought in."

"Of course, I know that. Nevertheless, that's what you've written on your declaration."

Nila turned to the customs officer and talked in her most winning manner. I don't know what she told him, but I can imagine. I'm just an ignorant American, she no doubt said, who has never learned to add and subtract. And if that's what she said, I can't deny it. I've never been able to tell from my checkbook when I'm overdrawn; but then why should I? The bank has people who always let me know.

The customs officer asked to see my money. With my hand trembling so that I could scarcely make connection with him, I gave him my books of checks. He flipped through them; then, seemingly satisfied that I'm a fool, he handed me back my last declaration to do over. Suffering sufficiently to bring on an ulcer, I finally managed to subtract $50 from $300 and was allowed to proceed.

Nila's and my parting was brief. "I'm terribly sorry we didn't find your sister, Nila dear," I said.

"I'm sorry, too, but, Willie, maybe they will find her while Mrs. Roosevelt is here or even after Mrs. Roosevelt has gone. The man said it would take time, you know."

"Yes. . . . And, Nila, if they do find her before the book I'm writing about our experiences is published, I'll certainly add a postscript."

Then hurriedly we kissed and I went into the waiting room for departing passengers.

I was given a seat number for the jet and when it took off two hours later I found myself on the inside seat of a two-seat bench, facing a young Englishman. Four rubber tubes connected to some metal sockets with bulbs on top dangled over the sides of the wide table between us. I didn't like the looks of the tubes; they reminded me of an operating room.

"What are they for?" I asked the Englishman.

"You see, when the jet is not properly pressurized, as sometimes happens, you have to put on masks and these tubes pump air into them."

"Ugh!" I ughed, not liking the sound of them any more than the looks of them.

Immediately after we were seated, the jet taxied out on the runway and the next second, with a long, loud, swooshing sound, we were up in the air. There was no bumping, no jolting, no contracting of the insides. And the next second we were in the clouds.

For a very brief span I could see between the clouds the green, green land of Russia, spotted with houses; then the land was completely blotted out. We were sailing as smoothly as a gull over what appeared to be plowed-up fields of deep snow.

The hostess passed around narrow cellophane bags for fountain pens, then placed large linen napkins in cellophane wrappers on the table. Gosh! Was I supposed to eat again? It was only nine-thirty, just three hours since I downed the three *sirniki* with jam and coffee. But if I must, I must. I've never skipped a meal yet.

The hostess put in front of me a tray laden with caviar, butter, slices of black bread, a white roll, four slices of roast beef, green peas, two slices of tomatoes, a stewed plum, a fresh apple, curls of cheese, fat cookies dotted with raisins, and hot tea.

Was this meant to be breakfast or dinner? But what difference did it really make? I've always been one to eat shrimp for breakfast when I could get them. I did away with everything. In fact, I even took the Englishman's stewed plum from him.

The tray cleared away, I studied the skyscape outside my porthole. The clouds had thinned and once again there beneath me was the U.S.S.R., still a bright, bright green, but even as I looked the blue Baltic flashed into view and Copenhagen was just ahead. It was hard to comprehend. We'd been in the air only two hours and had covered a thousand miles.

I peered hurriedly back at Russia before she dropped completely out of sight. Already she was blurring. I felt no sadness at leaving, but I was determined to return before too long a lapse of time and bring Mark with me. Indeed, I'd like to bring everybody in the United States with me. The Soviet Union has to be seen to be believed. So far, she's "under construction," but at the rate she's moving she'll someday be finished with construction, and then . . . ?

I'm sure I don't know; nevertheless, I don't feel easy in my mind. I'll simply have to go back. We must keep a sharp wary eye on her—and why not my eye, for one?

About the Author

WILLIE SNOW ETHRIDGE is a Southerner by birth, education and marriage. She was born in Savannah, Georgia, attended grammar school, high school and Wesleyan College in Macon, Georgia, and is married to Mark Ethridge, distinguished publisher of the Louisville Courier Journal and Times. They have four children, one of whom is Mark, Jr., publisher of five country weeklies in West Virginia. In addition to being a wife and mother, running a house and garden, and accompanying her husband on foreign missions for the government, Mrs. Ethridge has written nine other books and many newspaper and magazine articles. She also lectures under the auspices of a national lecture bureau.